"Sheldon Bull is not only the funniest brilliant when it comes to explaining how to be funny, and how to organize your creative ideas into the sitcom form. It is the clearest, best, and to my knowledge only how-to that tells writers, step by step, how to write for and break into the fabulous world of TV sitcom."

> — Blake Snyder, author, *Save the Cat! The Last Book on Screenwriting You'll Ever Need*

"Sheldon Bull has written a comprehensive, well thought-out guide for beginning writers. It would be a pleasure to read any spec script that used these guidelines. I only wish this had been around when I started!"

> — Susan Beavers, co-executive producer, *Two and a Half Men*

"Want a close-up look at what goes on inside a great comedy writer's head? Then you'll want to read *Elephant Bucks*. Sheldon Bull tells you everything he knows, and that's a lot!"

> — Ellen Sandler, co-executive producer, *Everybody Loves Raymond*; author, *The TV Writer's Workbook: A Creative Approach to Television Scripts*

"Comprehensive, breezily written, and on the money. If you're interested in the business of sitcom writing, this book will definitely help."

> — Earl Pomerantz, producer and writer, *The Cosby Show, Cheers, The Mary Tyler Moore Show, Taxi, Rhoda, The Bob Newhart Show*, winner of two Emmy Awards and the Humanitas Prize

"Sheldon Bull has gotten everything right! These are amazingly easy-to-follow instructions. Where was this book when I started writing?"

> — Arnold Margolin, Emmy-winning writer and producer, *Growing Pains, Love American Style, The Mary Tyler Moore Show*

"*Elephant Bucks* should be mandatory reading for every new writer wanting to try his or her luck in Hollywood. I just wish I'd had something this clear and concise to guide me when I was starting out."

> — Dan Berendsen, executive producer, *Sabrina, The Teenage Witch*

"*Elephant Bucks* gives you a great deal of sitcom experience, and you won't even have to eat dinner with an actor. Finally, a book by a successful sitcom writer and producer, rather than a teacher who never sold a sitcom and never sat in a room until three in the morning with seven other writers trying to think of a joke to end Act One. *Elephant Bucks* seems to be intended for the beginning sitcom writer, but I'll bet when no one's looking, veteran sitcom writers will buy it, too."

> — Lloyd Garver, writer and producer, *Home Improvement, Family Ties, Eight Rules for Dating My Teenage Daughter*

"The book is absolutely fantastic! It's the best writing book I've ever read — truly. It's the *only* one that gives a complete, hands-on, workable guide to writing sitcom. *And* it's not just for the novice — show runners could also benefit from following these formulas. It is, of course, *extremely* well written and informative — Sheldon Bull hasn't missed a thing. Now there is no excuse for anyone who has any talent to write a crummy spec!"

> — Zane Buzby, director and producer, *Blossom, Newhart, My Two Dads*

"It's about time a book like this was written for all those neophyte sitcom writers out in the world. Sheldon Bull does a phenomenal job of explaining the business of sitcom writing."
— Phil Klein, top Hollywood entertainment lawyer

"Now I understand what I've been trying to do for the last twenty years. Before you write another word, read this."
— Patric M. Verrone, president, Writers Guild of America, West
The Tonight Show, The Simpsons, Futurama

"Sitcoms are probably one of the hardest genres to write — but thank the heavenly muses of writing for Sheldon Bull, who has written a comprehensive, practical, knowledgeable, and most importantly, enjoyable resource on writing and selling for the sitcom marketplace. From selecting the right series to spec to what goes on the writers' room, this Hollywood vet lays it all out from beginning to end in an experienced, honest approach that makes this book a winner!"
— Kathie Fong Yoneda, author, *The Script-Selling Game*;
executive producer, *Beyond The Break*

"Sheldon Bull was there, in the trenches of some of TV's top sitcoms. He knows firsthand what it's like trying to come up with a clever line while fighting sleep in an all-night rewrite session after yet another dinner of delivered pizza."
— David Pollock, writer and producer, *Frasier, Cheers, MASH, Growing Pains*

"No matter what you want to do in television, you'll do it better if you understand how a script gets put together. Sheldon Bull offers insight and wisdom gleaned from years of putting the laughs on the page."
— Craig Wyrick-Solari, producer, *The Wayans Brothers, That's My Bush, American Body Shop*

"Elephant Bucks is a no-nonsense guide to writing scripts for the TV comedy sitcom industry. For the aspiring writer, this is an extremely useful compendium of how to write and improve your script, how to market yourself, sell your scripts, and find your big breaks. It's a must-have guide to navigating scripts, agents, pitch sessions, and success writing for the TV sitcom world!"
— Mark Sickle, managing editor, *Independent Rising Magazine*

"With a friendly, knowledgeable style, Sheldon Bull offers aspiring TV sitcom writers a roadmap to Hollywood. His step-by-step approach to the subject is accessible and informative, preparing readers as much as possible for the 'real world' of writing for television."
— Amy Andrews, *Absolutewrite.com*

"I was fortunate enough to have directed many scripts that I knew were wonderful, but I didn't always know why they were wonderful. After reading Sheldon's book, I now realize so much more about the techniques involved in telling a good story. This book taught me a lot about the art of comedy script writing. "
— Jay Sandrich, Emmy award–winning director, *The Cosby Show, The Mary Tyler Moore Show*

ELEPHANT
BUCKS

AN INSIDER'S GUIDE TO WRITING FOR TV SITCOMS

SHELDON BULL

Published by Michael Wiese Productions
3940 Laurel Canyon Blvd. #1111
Studio City, CA 91604
tel. 818.379.8799
fax 818.986.3408
mw@mwp.com
www.mwp.com

Cover Design: MWP
Book Layout: Gina Mansfield Design
Editor: Paul Norlen

Printed by McNaughton & Gunn, Inc., Saline, Michigan
Manufactured in the United States of America

Library of Congress Cataloging-in-Publication Data

Bull, Sheldon, 1952-
  Elephant bucks : an insider's guide to writing for TV sitcoms / Sheldon Bull.
    p. cm.
  Includes bibliographical references.
  ISBN 10: 1932907270
  ISBN 13: 9781932907278
  1. Television comedies--Authorship. I. Title.
  PN1992.8.C66B85 2007
  808.2'523--dc22

                              2006032907

TABLE OF CONTENTS

ACKNOWLEDGMENTS   ix

INTRODUCTION   xi
   Elephant Bucks   xi
   How Did I Get Elephant Bucks?   xi
   How Do *You* Get Elephant Bucks?   xii
   It Worked for Me!   xii
   Something You've Always Dreamed of Doing   xiii
   Breaking In   xiii
   Staying Successful   xiv
   How Do I Know That *You'll* Be Successful?   xiv
   What You Need Right Now!   xvi

Part One
MY STEP-BY-STEP GUIDE TO WRITING A SOLID SPEC SCRIPT   1

Chapter 1 — THOSE AMAZING SPEC SCRIPTS!   3
   What's a Spec Script, Anyway?   4
   The Shortest Route to Your Lucky Break!   4
   The Joy of Knowing What You're Doing!   6
   One-Trick Pony   7
   "What Else Have You Got?"   7
   Ready to Roll   8
   Calling Cards That Keep on Calling!   9
   A Portfolio of Solid Spec Scripts   10

Chapter 2 — PICKING THE RIGHT SERIES TO SPEC   13
   The Show That You Know and Love!   13
   "Hear It in Your Head"   15
   Beyond *Seinfeld*   17
   Scripts That Producers *Want* to Read   19
   Too Soon to "Hear It in Your Head"   20
   Planet MegaMall   21
   The Web   22

Chapter 3 — PICKING THE RIGHT STORY   25
   Story Is Everything   26
   The Right Story Is in Front of You   26
   Write to the Premise   27
   Write the Main Character   29

Write the Formula   32
The Paints Are Already in the Tray   35
Don't Reinvent   36
Don't Break New Ground   37
No New Characters   37
Use the Regular Sets   37
Test the Premise   38
Write It Real   40
See How Easy That Was?   42

Chapter 4 — STRUCTURING YOUR STORY   47
Seven Plot Elements   47
Using the Seven Plot Elements to Develop Your Story   48
Two-Act Framework   56
Six-Scene Template   58
How We Did It on *Coach*   62
Going to Work on Your Story   65
Turning Plot Elements into Scenes   66
Familiar Sets   68
"B" Story   69
Multiple Story Lines   73
Runners   74
Trust Your Instincts   75

Chapter 5 — OUTLINING YOUR STORY   81
Why Bother with an Outline?   81
The Whiteboard   83
How I Write an Outline   86

Chapter 6 — WRITING SCENES   109
Move the Story Forward   110
Much of the Work Is Already Done   111
A Different Way of Writing Scenes   111
Write It as a Drama First   113
Roughing Out a Scene as Drama First   114
Now for the Jokes   126
Making the Humor Easier to Find   139
Page Count   139

Part Two
GETTING OFF TO A GREAT START
AS A PROFESSIONAL SITCOM WRITER

145

Chapter 7 — YOUR FINISHED MASTERPIECE: NOW WHAT?   147
Now What?   147
"Who Cares What *You* Think?"   148
Someone Who Is Actually Going to Read It   149
"I Really Liked It Except for the Part Where…"   150
"There Is Truth in Even the Dumbest Note"   151
Three or Four People   152
"What Else Have You Got?"   153
May I Have the Address of That Show Biz Contact, Please?   155
Your Friend in Show Business   156
The Sitcom Universe   158
Where to Go in the Sitcom Universe   160
Fish Off the Company Pier   161
Farmer's Market   161

Chapter 8 — YOUR FIRST PITCH MEETING   165
Your Lucky Break Has Arrived   165
They're Doing *You* the Favor!   167
Preparing for the Meeting   167
Six Stories, Six Notions   168
How to Pitch a Story Idea   169
You Don't Need Perfect Pitch!   171
Pitch Meeting Supplies   172
Keep It in Perspective   173

Chapter 9 — YOUR FIRST ASSIGNMENT   177
The Story Meeting   177
Getting Home   183
Day Two   186
Day Three and Beyond   186
Notes on Your Outline   187
The Bad Story   188
Your First Draft   188
The Second Draft   189
Cut Off   191
They Rewrote Me!!   192
Go Ahead and Have the Party!   193
Getting That Second Assignment   194

Chapter 10 — **WORKING ON STAFF**   199
    The Sitcom Writing Staff   200
    The Production Season   202
    The Production Week   202
    Single Camera Series   215
    Your Primary Job as a Staff Writer   216
    The Other Writers   217
    Actors   218
    The Producer's Chair   219
    Creating Your Own Series   222
    Your Personal Life   222

Chapter 11 — **AGENTS & EXECUTIVES**   227
    Agents   227
    Picking an Agent   228
    A Business Relationship   229
    Never the Biggest Fish   231
    Grow at Your Own Pace   232
    Not a Parent   232
    Again, Trust Your Instincts   233
    Chinatown   234
    Executives   234
    Be Nice   236
    Everything Can Be Fixed   237
    The Kernel of Truth   238
    "We Have a Huge Problem in Act Two"   238
    "We Have Just One Tiny Little Note"   239
    Why Make Enemies When You Don't Have To?   241

Chapter 12 — **LEARN FROM THE BEST**   245
    Where to Look   246
    Websites   246
    Speaking of Museums   247
    What to Watch   247
    The Current Hits   259
    Conclusions   261
    I Wish All of This for You   263
    About the Author   266

ACKNOWLEDGMENTS

This first-time author benefited greatly from the talent, energy, encouragement and experience of a number of professionals who generously contributed to make this project a success. My deepest appreciation and thanks to Michael Wiese for his support and invaluable input, to Ken Lee for one extremely good idea after another, to copy editor Paul Norlen for judicious and respectful guidance, and to Gina Mansfield for creating such a wonderful look. Much heartfelt thanks as well to my wife, Annette, for endless support and love, and to every single one of the brilliant writers who taught me everything I know, especially Bill Idelson.

INTRODUCTION

ELEPHANT BUCKS

"Elephant Bucks" is what one colleague used to call the big money that we were paid to write and produce TV sitcoms.

And it *is* big money! The minimum fee for a half-hour TV script is now around $21,000. Those are pretty good wages for a couple of weeks' work. Then there are residuals — the additional money that writers (and actors and directors) are paid every time an episode of a TV series is rerun. Residuals are little unexpected Christmas presents in your mailbox all year long!

But the big, big dough in TV sitcom, the real Elephant Bucks, comes from working on writing staffs and from owning "back-end points" — a share in the syndication profits — on a TV series. Salaries for top sitcom writer/producers can run over a million dollars a year. Back-end points for the creators of hit series can be worth tens of millions, sometimes even hundreds of millions for mega-hits like *Friends* and *Seinfeld*. Now *those* are Elephant Bucks!

HOW DID I GET ELEPHANT BUCKS?

I learned how to consistently write solid, funny sitcom scripts so that I kept getting jobs as a staff writer and producer in Hollywood. With each new job, the little baby bucks grew up into great, big Elephant Bucks!

All of the money that I have earned over the past thirty years has come from writing and producing TV sitcoms (and from some screenplays).

I've worked on staff at eleven different prime time network TV sitcoms. I was a senior producer on *Newhart*, *Coach*, and *Sabrina, The Teenage Witch*. Google my name. Check me out at the Independent Movie Data Base (*imdb.com*) or in the directory of the Writers Guild of America.

I've been paid to write more than fifty sitcom scripts myself, and I've worked on over *three hundred* sitcom episodes. I've sold, written, consulted on and/or produced over a dozen TV pilots. I've been a Show Runner — the boss on a sitcom — more than once. I've freelanced for a number of series including M*A*S*H.

HOW DO *YOU* GET ELEPHANT BUCKS?

You get Elephant Bucks by becoming a successful sitcom writer and producer, *just as I did!*

How do you make *that* happen?

First, you learn to write a solid spec sitcom script. Then you write a bunch more. Then you use those spec scripts to make connections in Hollywood and break into the Sitcom Universe. Once inside, you keep your career going by consistently writing funny, delightful scripts and by making a big contribution on sitcom staffs.

Sound easy?

Look, nobody gets a million dollars for something that is a snap to accomplish. Writing for sitcoms may *look* easy. Critics or your neighbors may watch a sitcom and say, "Anyone could write this stuff." But you know and I know that it is hard, hard work! All writing is hard. It's hard to create compelling stories. It's hard to come up with interesting dialogue. That's why so few people make a living as a writer.

On the other hand, writing for sitcoms isn't impossible. And it isn't mysterious. You just have to know what you're doing and then *do it!*

The purpose of this book is to offer you an **effective, focused, proven plan** to launch and sustain a successful career as a TV sitcom writer — to earn Elephant Bucks.

I know what I'm talking about — because *I did it!*

IT WORKED FOR ME!

If you talked to ten veteran TV sitcom writers you'd get ten sets of advice on how to break into the Sitcom Universe. My guess is that all of the advice would be extremely valuable. Any pro is going to offer useful guidance.

There are other resources out there to help you learn to write for situation comedy and then break into the business. There are a few other books. There are magazine articles. There are writing classes. There are the sitcoms themselves in first-run on TV, in syndication, and on DVD. You should check out all of these. They will *all* help you.

I know that my advice works because *it worked for me*!

SOMETHING YOU'VE ALWAYS DREAMED OF DOING!

If you want desperately to be a sitcom writer, but it all looks daunting and impossible and quixotic or you aren't sure how to get started or whether you should even try, this book will answer your questions and allay your fears.

If you've written spec scripts already, but you didn't know what to do with them once you finished, or you got your spec scripts to some people in Hollywood, but all that came back was spirit-withering rejection, this book will help you improve your work so you can stop spinning your wheels and start making those Elephant Bucks!

But it isn't *all* about money. Come on. It isn't.

It's about making people laugh and having a wonderful time at what you do. It's about doing something that you've always *dreamed* of doing!

Oh, and by the way, writing for situation comedy should be *fun*, even at the beginning, even when you are nervously or naively writing your very first script. It should be fun, and it should be logical! And it is! That may be the most important piece of Inside Information that I can give you: It's fun! And it's logical! And I can show you how to do it!

BREAKING IN

I'll show you how to break into the Sitcom Universe by providing a detailed, Step-By-Step Guide on how to write a solid spec sitcom script that is better than the other guy's.

As I'm sure you already know, *the spec script is your calling card*, your way to show that you have the talent and the skill to write for situation comedy, and that you're better at it than the next person.

I will tell you how to pick the right sitcom to spec.

I will show you how to come up with the right story idea for your spec script.

I will show you, in detail, the right way to construct a story for a spec sitcom episode.

I will show you how to outline your script in a way that solves your story problems and frees up your imagination so you can concentrate on writing great jokes and funny scenes.

I will show you how to write those great jokes and funny scenes.

STAYING SUCCESSFUL

I will show you how get off to a great start and stay successful as a professional sitcom writer!

I will tell you how to make the connections that you'll need to get your spec scripts read by people in Hollywood who can hire you.

I will tell you how to shine at your first Hollywood pitch meeting.

I will tell you how to succeed with your first sitcom writing assignment.

I will give you the Inside Scoop on what it's like to work on a real sitcom staff.

I will impart the skinny on agents and executives.

I'll list some resources you can use to hone your skills.

HOW DO I KNOW THAT *YOU'LL* BE SUCCESSFUL?

Just as there's a path to the major leagues in baseball, there's a path to Elephant Bucks in situation comedy. Everyone has to go down that same path, whether they end up creating the next *Two and a Half Men* or come in once a week to pitch jokes on *My Name Is Earl*.

I can show you the path.

You're going to need three things to become a successful TV sitcom writer: **Talent**, **Determination**, and a **Lucky Break**.

Talent is a gift from a Higher Power or from funny Uncle Buzz. You can't will talent into being. I would love to pitch for the Los Angeles

Dodgers, but I don't bring high heat at 95 mph. Fortunately, I had some comedy chops to fall back on. Let's assume that you do, too.

Determination is something you *can* control. You can make a choice to learn the rules of situation comedy writing, and then write until your fingers bleed. In a ten-round bout between talent and determination, I'll put my money on determination every time. I've known extremely talented people, truly gifted people, who never did anything with their gifts because they had no determination. Maybe what held them back were jittery nerves, low self-esteem or ADD. Whatever the reasons, because they lacked determination their talent stayed locked in the guest room. It never got out and won an Emmy. On the other hand, I've known some very modestly talented people (*very* modestly talented) who worked their butts off — and probably kissed quite a few butts along the way — and ended up living in Beverly Hills. Determination, if you have it, will more than compensate for shortcomings in your talent.

If you're motivated enough to buy and read an entire book about sitcom writing, that's a sign of determination. I assume that you haven't gotten the bug to be a sitcom writer just because you enjoyed one episode of *Sex and the City*. You love sitcom, you've loved it for a long time, you've dreamed of seeing your name on the TV screen. You're ready to put in the time and energy necessary to make your dream come true, but you aren't sure what to do first.

You're in the same spot that I was in when I was starting out. You're no worse off, believe me. If you've got the determination to follow the advice in this book, and do the work that you need to do, then you have a real shot at making it the same way that I did!

This may sound crazy, but getting your **Lucky Break** is where I can help you the most. A book can't inject you with talent. Oh, that it could.... Imagine the money I'd make with this little tome if it could magically turn you into Larry David! A book can't fill you with determination either. The right guidance and encouragement might goose you along a little, but real day-to-day determination is an asset that you have to bring to the table yourself. But the advice in this book, along with your talent and your determination, can lead you to your Lucky Break!

There are specific steps that you can take to make your Lucky Break happen. You can be ready with the skill and the goods when Opportunity comes knocking. You can move yourself toward Opportunity by following my advice and doing the work that I tell you to do!

WHAT YOU NEED RIGHT NOW!

You don't need a history of situation comedy. You know all about *I Love Lucy*, *The Honeymooners* and *The Cosby Show*.

You don't need pages and pages of comedy theory, either. Yikes! Nothing ruins a joke like trying to analyze it.

What you need is a Step-By-Step Guide on how to get your career started and then keep it going!

That's just what you are holding in your hands *right now*!

Shall we get you started writing some solid spec sitcom scripts?

Shall we figure out how to get those scripts to people in Hollywood who can hire you? Shall we work together to launch you on a long and lucrative writing career?

Elephant Bucks, anyone?

PART ONE

MY STEP-BY-STEP GUIDE
TO WRITING A SOLID SPEC SCRIPT

CHAPTER 1

THOSE AMAZING SPEC SCRIPTS

My *first* Lucky Break happened because Larry Thor died. Larry was my favorite screenwriting professor at UCLA. I loved the man, but he passed away in the middle of my first year at grad school. I didn't even know who graded the screenplay that I turned in for Larry's class. When Spring Quarter started, I signed up for a writing course taught by a visiting Big-Shot Screenwriter. I figured, okay, maybe Larry's death is a blessing in disguise. Maybe I can finally make a Hollywood connection through the Big-Shot Screenwriter. On the first day of class, the Big-Shot Screenwriter informed his prospective students that he didn't teach comedy. "Didn't teach comedy??!!" He told us that he didn't respect comedy, knew nothing about it, and wouldn't accept any comedy scripts. This guy wrote heavy drama. I don't think he had ever actually smiled. He said he was going to make us tear open our guts and write something really dramatic, personal, and painful. I was twenty-three years old, trying to make it in show business, not succeeding, thinking I was tossing my entire future away on a foolish fantasy, and strongly considering law school. I was in enough pain already! So I left. Now I was way up the creek with nothing resembling a paddle. A graduate screenwriting course was eight units! That was two-thirds of my load! And I didn't have a writing class to go to! I took four hundred Tums and stopped by Bill Froug's class. Bill Froug was the most feared screenwriting teacher at UCLA, and I'd been judiciously avoiding him all year. He was imposing, smart, and blunt — even scarier than the comedy-hating Big-Shot Screenwriter. At first, Bill wasn't going to accept me into his class. He already had his students selected. But Bill turned out to be the teacher who had graded all of the screenplays for Larry Thor's class. Bill loved my script, "Mr. Perfect." I was suddenly *very* glad that I'd finished that screenplay and turned it in! Bill took me back to his office to discuss my future. I confessed that what I really wanted to write was sitcom, which in those days was heresy at the prestigious UCLA Film School, la dee dah. I hadn't realized it when I was hiding from Bill, but he was a working TV writer himself! He asked if I had any spec sitcom scripts to show him. Here was my *first* Lucky Break! I'd written about six spec sitcom scripts by then. I had a portfolio of spec scripts at the ready when Opportunity came knocking! Bill read and returned my scripts with brutal notes. Brutal. But I swallowed hard and rewrote. More notes. Just as brutal. More spec scripts. Finally, Bill liked a few of my spec scripts enough to show them around Hollywood. Six months went by. Nothing. I felt panic, despair, and the looming specter of law school. And then, one day in late October, the phone rang. It was Bill Idelson, a veteran TV writer. He was working on a new sitcom. Bill Froug had given him my spec scripts. Could I come over to his office at NBC right now? My *second* Lucky Break! All because of those amazing spec scripts!

WHAT'S A SPEC SCRIPT, ANYWAY?

Just for the record, a "spec script" means a script written on speculation. In other words, you're writing an episode of *Two and a Half Men*, but no one asked you to write it, and certainly no one is paying you. You're writing this script on your own, "on spec," to learn how to do it right, to avoid going to law school, and to hopefully use that spec script as a calling card, a sample of your ability that someone who is already working in television will read, and like, and because they like it, will decide to give you a job.

A spec script is like a spec house. A developer puts his time and money into building a new home, speculating that when the structure is completed someone will want to buy it, and he'll get back his investment plus turn a modest profit in the bargain. A spec script is the same idea. The only cost to you is your time and the paper the script is printed on. And if you write a wonderful spec sitcom script, your very modest investment could turn into an entire career as a sitcom writer. Pachyderm dollars!

THE SHORTEST ROUTE TO GETTING YOUR LUCKY BREAK!

Compiling a *portfolio of solid spec scripts* that you can show to people in Hollywood is *the* method that almost every aspiring writer uses to break into television or the movies.

Writing spec scripts is the shortest route to getting your Lucky Break!

When I was producing TV sitcoms, we hired new writers only after we had read their spec scripts. Most of the scripts were submitted by agencies like CAA, ICM and William Morris. (I'll talk about agents later. Let's concern ourselves with writing now.) A few scripts were "thrown over the transom." They were mailed in unsolicited by writers who didn't have representation. This is not a good idea because these scripts rarely get read. Other spec scripts were handed to us by someone we knew who believed in a promising new kid. (What Bill Froug did for me!)

There are all kinds of ways to get someone who can hire you to read your script. I'll give you advice on that later in the book.

But first you have to WRITE THE SCRIPT!

As I said, I started writing spec sitcom scripts in college, on my own time because UCLA wouldn't teach TV writing. I also joined a writers' group that met on Thursday nights. I think I was the only one in the group who was writing sitcoms. But I'd write my spec scripts and read them out loud to the group and get some laughs and some criticism. Getting positive and negative feedback from my peers and from my professors helped me correct my mistakes and build my confidence. I started to believe that I could really make it as a sitcom writer.

I think I wrote a dozen spec scripts for various shows. That's right, *twelve of them* at least. Those are the ones I finished. Who knows how many I threw away? Maybe I wasn't the world's fastest learner, but I kept at it because I very much wanted a career as a sitcom writer, and how else was I going to get my Lucky Break?

Today it's pretty easy to find a sitcom writing class. If there's a college in your area that offers film courses, there's a decent chance that someone is teaching TV writing. Depending on how far you are from Los Angeles or New York, you may not find a writing teacher who has actually written for TV, but that's okay. The important thing is to start writing. If someone fills your head with a lot of misinformation, you now have this book to set you straight.

If there's a TV writing course at your local community college or university extension, take it. What can it hurt? Maybe the teacher has never been any closer to Hollywood than you have, but if he or she knows anything at all about how to construct a story and write dialogue — and if someone is teaching a writing class, they better know all this stuff really well — he or she can probably help you cobble together a spec script. (You can help the teacher by giving him or her a copy of this book.)

If you find that you are by far the best writer in your writing class... In fact, if your teacher says that you are the most talented pupil he or she has ever taught... If your classmates are blown away by how good your stuff is... If peers keep taking you aside and saying, "Man, you ought to go for this. You're great!"... Then go for it! That's what I did!

Writing spec scripts is the best way to demonstrate to people in Hollywood that you have the talent and the skill they are looking for.

It's the shortest route to getting your Lucky Break!

THE JOY OF KNOWING WHAT YOU'RE DOING!

If you've already written for a sketch show like *Saturday Night Live*, or you've sold a screenplay, or your father is the president of CBS, you might get a job as a sitcom writer without ever writing a spec episode.
But then what?

Let's say that, based on your brilliant work as a sketch writer at *MAD TV*, or because of a very witty play you have running in the East Village, or because your mother's cousin runs Paramount Studios, you get hired to write a freelance episode of *Two and a Half Men* or you land a story editor job at *My Name Is Earl*. You've never written an episode of a sitcom in your life, but now you have to write one for real, and you have to write it today!

Are you going to be ready? Are you going to know what you're doing?

A friend of mine was plucked from a graduate playwriting program at a famous university and given a staff job on a sitcom in Los Angeles. TV producers or executives will do this occasionally. They want a fresh voice, so they'll hire a writer from a different medium and stick them on a sitcom. This award-winning playwright had never written a sitcom script in his life. I remember his first few weeks in the business. He didn't say much in the writers' room because he didn't have any experience with sitcom. The Show Runner got impatient with him. It wasn't his fault! The guy was a playwright, for Heaven's sake! Now, this person is very smart and very talented, and eventually had a successful career as a TV writer and producer. But he got off to a rocky start!

These days nobody can afford to get off to a rocky start. There are too many writers and not enough shows. You have to hit the ground running.

Sitcom staffs are not training grounds. No producer has time to teach you how to write for sitcom. He or she is too busy trying to keep the show on the air. So whether you have some professional experience or not, writing some spec sitcom scripts is worth your time. It provides you with the joy of knowing what you're doing!

ONE-TRICK PONY

When I was producing *Coach* for ABC, we hired two young neophytes based on a stupendous spec *Cheers* that they had written. Well, we found out later that they had been rewriting that *Cheers* for two years! We gave them two *weeks* to write their episode of *Coach*. The *Coach* script that they delivered was something less than stupendous. These guys were one-trick ponies. All they had in them was that one great *Cheers*. They never got another shot with us.

Writing a number of spec scripts for different sitcoms gives you the confidence and experience you'll need when your Lucky Break arrives. You won't be branded as a one-trick pony!

"WHAT ELSE HAVE YOU GOT?"

Let's say, just for argument, that you have written a fantastic spec episode of *According to Jim*. Let's also say that you already have an agent, Lance Lexus, at ICM. Let's say that Lance is so full of confidence in you that he places a call to the producer of the brand new NBC sitcom, *Fly Me to the Moon*. Lance sells his brains out hawking you to this producer. The producer says, "Okay. Send me over something to read." And Lance says,

"Great! She's got this fall-down-on-the-floor hilarious *According to Jim* that everyone here at ICM is just blowing their minds about and…" The producer cuts Lance off right there and says, "Nah. Don't send me a '*Jim*.' It's a good show, but I never watch it," or "I've read a million of those already. *What else have you got?*"

If Lance gulps and says, "Well… um… nothing," then the call is over and your opportunity is lost. Your Lucky Break is blown!

Many producers will want to read more than one spec script before they hire you. They don't want to get burned by a one-trick pony. Producers have different likes and dislikes. You never know which spec script is going to thrill them. The more choices you offer to a producer, the greater your chances of having your stuff read. Having your stuff read is the key to getting your Lucky Break!

When they ask, "What else have you got?" you say, "These five other great scripts right here!"

READY TO ROLL!

Compiling a portfolio of solid spec scripts *gets you ready to roll!* You've gathered experience and gained confidence from writing spec scripts for different types of sitcoms, and you have choices to offer when a producer asks, "What else have you got?"

My spec scripts got me my initial job in Hollywood. The first producer who hired me read more than one of my spec scripts before he gave me the job. My solid spec sitcom scripts also gave me a strong foundation of writing experience so that I could start contributing on the first day. I avoided a rocky start AND I knew what I was doing when it came time to write my first professional script. But guess what? Landing my first job wasn't the end of my spec scripts. My solid spec scripts also got me my second job, my *third* job, and my FOURTH job!

You know why?

CALLING CARDS THAT KEEP ON CALLING!

My first job as a sitcom writer was on a series that got cancelled very quickly. I was literally only there for a few weeks. Like most new sitcoms, this series didn't quite work. When we went on the air, the initial ratings were lousy, and the network pulled the plug after only eight episodes. In fact, this series got cancelled while we were actually shooting a show. I'd been in the business for less than three months, and already I was out of work!

I wrote only one script for that series. I was very lucky to get that one script. But was I going to be able to use that one script to get my second job? As it turned out, I wasn't. I was to discover that my very first professional script was worthless in terms of advancing my embryonic career. Producers on other shows weren't interested in reading it because the series had been cancelled so quickly. So to get me my second job, my newly acquired agent sent out my college spec scripts, the same ones that I used to get the first job.

It was those same solid spec scripts that got me my second job!

Then guess what?

The second job didn't last very long either. The producer who hired me for my second job had a huge fight with the executive producer and quit on my first day at work. I'm not kidding! I was working with this producer on a story idea on my first morning there. The producer walked into the executive producer's office to ask a question. The producer and the executive producer got into a huge argument that I could hear through the walls. After about ten minutes of yelling, the producer came back, cleaned out his desk and left. The now *former* producer was the guy who believed in me, and he was walking out the door before anyone had even given me an office or a desk. The production company shut the show down for a few days and brought in new producers. The new producers didn't know me. They hadn't hired me. They were under the gun because the series was now way behind schedule. The new producers hunkered down in their offices and wrote most of the episodes themselves. After a few weeks I was gone. I was out of work for the second time, and I hadn't even been in the business for six months!

To get me my third job, my agent once again sent out those same spec scripts, the ones I had written while I was at UCLA.

I got my THIRD job from my original portfolio of solid spec scripts!

Then guess what? (See about comedy writing? The joke is often in the repetition.)

The third series that I worked on also got cancelled right away!

So what did my agent do to keep me working? Right! He sent out that same portfolio of spec scripts. And guess what? I got my FOURTH job off of those spec scripts, just as I'd gotten the other three!

A PORTFOLIO OF SOLID SPEC SCRIPTS

Whether you're a new writer trying to break in, or an experienced writer making the transition to situation comedy, *a portfolio of solid spec scripts* is the best way to hasten your Lucky Break and avoid a rocky start. One of your solid spec scripts will get you your first job as a sitcom writer. The experience that you gain from assembling your *portfolio of solid spec scripts* will prepare you for success with your first professional assignment and with your first job on a writing staff. Your *portfolio of solid spec scripts* may also help you to get additional jobs after your first assignment.

CHAPTER RECAP — THE ELEPHANT REMEMBERS

It's hard enough to write one spec script, and here I am telling you to write four or ten! I know. It sounds like a ton of work. Well, it *is*.

It helps if you're a little obsessed, so I hope you are.

Writing a whole stack of spec scripts is going to pay off for you in the long run, though. Honest.

A good spec script is going to get you your first job as a sitcom writer.

A stack of spec scripts gives producers more ways to love you.

You may need those spec scripts to land your second job and your third one, so the more you've got in the drawer the better.

Making it in show biz is all about being able to deliver the goods when Opportunity knocks. If you spend time writing spec scripts now, you will gain the skill and confidence you'll badly need on your first day of real show business.

I had big fun writing most of my spec scripts. I was able to write my favorite characters. I was able to create my fantasy episode of my favorite show. Think of writing spec scripts as TV Sitcom Fantasy Camp! And you don't have to pay to get in!

YOUR "TO DO" LIST

Get and read as many professional sitcom scripts as you can find:

1) If you've got some extra cash, I'd send away to Planet MegaMall for some sample scripts of your favorite shows.

2) If you're at a college, you may be able to get your hands on some sitcom scripts for free.

3) Don't worry yet about making any notes. Just read scripts for pleasure. Get a feel for how a sitcom script sounds in your head. It's different to read a script than to watch an episode. Reading puts you one step closer to writing.

4) Look beyond the jokes on the page. See how professional writers handle stage directions. Think about the stories that are being told.

5) Pay special attention to the Act Break — the cliffhanger moment at the end of Act One. Notice how everything in Act One builds toward this moment. Notice how everything in Act Two is a reaction to this moment.

CHAPTER 2

 # PICKING THE RIGHT SERIES TO SPEC

My agent called and said, "They want to meet with you at M*A*S*H." At the time, M*A*S*H was one of the most respected series on TV. It was at the top of the ratings. It had won a million awards. And I was the greenest, most obscure, and worst dressed sitcom writer in Hollywood. They wanted to meet with me?! How did my agent do it? How did he get them interested? "I sent them that spec M*A*S*H script that you wrote." "You took a gamble like that with *my* career?!" Even I knew that you NEVER send the producers of a sitcom a spec episode of their own show! They're going to hate it, no matter how good it is! "They liked it. They want you to come in and pitch some story ideas." I only wrote that spec script because I loved the show. And I knew it really well. And I had an idea for a story that I thought was kind of cool. I never dreamed that anyone who worked on M*A*S*H would actually read it. And they liked it?? "They loved it! So get over there and blow their socks off," my agent told me. "Now *my* career is on the line!"

THE SHOW THAT YOU KNOW AND LOVE!

Aspiring writers have asked me over the years, "Which show should I spec?" I always ask, "Which show do you like? Which one do you watch every week?" If they come back with, "Well, I guess the one I like the most is *Two and a Half Men*, but I heard from a friend that it's smarter to write something *cool* and *hip* like *Entourage*." I take a deep breath and ask, "But do you *love Entourage*? Have you seen every episode or almost every episode?" And if they say, "Actually, I don't have HBO, so I've only seen it once or twice, but I want to write the *smart* show! I want to write the one that's *trendy* and *hot*!" I draw in a deeper cleansing breath and calmly reply,

"But the one you watch and the one you love is *Two and a Half Men*!

"Yeah, but my friend said…"

As you're trying to pick the right series to spec, please don't listen to your friends. Don't listen to the people in your writing class. Don't be swayed by something you read on the Web.

Write the show that you know and love!

Why?

What's the purpose of writing a spec script in the first place? To show off your talent, right? To prove to some producer somewhere who is in a position to give you a job that you have the chops to write his show. What gives you the best shot at impressing this producer? Doing a passable job on a hip, trendy show that unfortunately you don't really know very well, or doing a *great* job on a show that you love because you already know that show inside and out?

It does you no good to try to write a show that you don't like or don't know extremely well. You'll do a lousy job. You will! And you won't have any fun while you do it. No one is paying you to write a spec script, so if you're going to put in a lot of time and energy for no money, you might as well enjoy yourself. You'll do much better work if you're happy.

If you've read something on a "break into show business" website that says that the hot spec in Hollywood right now is *Entourage* or *Everybody Hates Chris*, but you don't love either of those shows, or you don't watch either of them all the time, why are you twisting yourself into a pretzel to write them?

If, later on, *after* your Lucky Break, someone is suddenly *paying* you to write a show that you don't know very well, *then* you can twist yourself into a pretzel. But why do it now when you're trying to show off your talents in the best possible light?

Write a show that you love, even if it isn't "hot," or even if you're going against the advice of your friends.

If you love a show, you already understand that show better than any other show. If you love a show then you watch it every week (or every day if it's already in syndication). You know the characters, you know the tone, and you know what kinds of stories they like to do. You know what stories they have already done. Knowing what stories they have already done is another great reason to spec a series that you love. If you've seen every episode, you reduce your chances of telling a story that they've already told. We'll get into what specific story you should tell in the next chapter, but for now, let's agree that in your spec episode you want to find a story that hasn't yet been explored on your favorite series. You can check the Web and get story synopses for all the past episodes, but if you actually watch the series all the time you'll have a better chance of coming up with a story area that the writers of that series haven't yet touched on. And you'll know what stories to avoid.

Go with what you know!

Even if your friend's cousin who works in the mailroom at CAA says to write *Entourage*, if you love *Two and a Half Men*, if that's the show you know, then that's the one to spec! You'll do a better job! If you love *Entourage* and you watch it every week, write that one.

"HEAR IT IN YOUR HEAD"

When you're writing for TV, you are writing someone else's characters. You're speaking with someone else's voice. Don't you want to be as familiar with those characters and that voice as possible? How do you get to know someone else's voice? By listening to it all the time!

If you're like me, you've watched every episode of *Seinfeld* seventy times. Even while *Seinfeld* was still on the air, I could hear that series in my head. If I think about *Seinfeld* right now, I can hear Jerry and Elaine and George and Kramer. I "do" Kramer for my wife all the time. She'll ask, "Are you sure you're ready for that meeting?" I'll strike a Kramer pose, point my index finger, and say in my hipster Kramer voice, "Oh... I'm ready." I can hear *Seinfeld* in my head because I've seen it so many times.

Writing for sitcom is like being an impressionist. A comic who does a great George Bush impression learns to do it by watching and listening to Bush over and over and over again. If there's a series that you've watched over and over and over again, like *Seinfeld*, you're going to do a better *impression* of that series than of some other series that you don't know. Your spec script is your impression of a particular series. Why not try an impression that you already know how to do?

When I got hired to write my first episode of M*A*S*H, I was writing characters that had been created by the guy who wrote the book, adapted by the people who made the movie, and then refined even more by Larry Gelbart and the people who wrote the TV series. I didn't get to decide who Hawkeye was. Hawkeye was very well established as a character. Hawkeye had a distinctive way of speaking. He had specific attitudes. He had his own moral code. I didn't get to alter any of that.

My job was to use everything that I already knew about Hawkeye in a way that the writers of M*A*S*H hadn't yet explored. "Here's a situation we haven't tried yet on M*A*S*H. Now, based on everything we already know about Hawkeye, how is he going to act in this new situation?" That was my job as a freelance writer coming in on assignment. I had to keep Hawkeye "Hawkeye." How was I able to do that?

I could write Hawkeye because I'd been watching M*A*S*H for years. I loved and respected it. I knew the kinds of things Hawkeye was going to say, and the kinds of reactions he was going to have, because I'd been listening to him for a long time. I could hear Hawkeye in my head.

It's the same as when you know what your girlfriend is going to do or say before she does or says it. You've been with her for a while. You know her quirks and her likes and dislikes. So when a neighbor calls and tells you that she is giving your girlfriend a surprise birthday party, you know how your girlfriend is going to react long before anyone yells "Surprise!" She's either going to be really happy or really pissed. But you can write that scene mentally before it happens because you know your girlfriend. You can "hear her in your head."

Writing for TV is the same principle: You write what is already there, based on what you already know. You "hear it in your head." So you want to pick a series to spec that you "hear in your head" already.

I'm not sure how I learned to "hear it in my head." I guess like a lot of kids, I'd been doing impressions for a long time. I did impressions of my friends and my family and the teacher and John Wayne and Nixon. I was able to do impressions because I paid attention to behavior, attitudes, mannerisms and styles of speech, as all writers do, and because some part of my brain was able to recreate them. I wasn't great at impressions, but I was passable enough to get a few laughs now and then. If you have any experience "doing" people — observing them, recreating them, predicting their behavior — then you're well on the way to "hearing it in your head."

Not all professional sitcom writers are able to "hear it in their head." I've worked with a lot of "Joke Men" over the years. Joke Men are almost always guys who are hired on staff at a sitcom to relentlessly pitch jokes. They aren't really writers. They're gag machines. These guys never hear it in their heads. They never have any real understanding of the personalities of the characters or the premise of the series. Ninety percent of the jokes they pitch don't get used because the jokes are generic. They don't fit the characters. Why? Because Joke Men can't "hear it in their heads."

Joke Men can never write the "moments." If you've got a scene in the Second Act of an episode of *The King of Queens* where Doug needs to pour his heart out to Carrie, the Joke Man isn't going to be able to write that scene. He can't write it because he can't hear it in his head. He doesn't hear the voices of the characters. He has never learned what makes them tick.

Joke Men can earn big money on a sitcom writing staff, but they always impressed me as the most frustrated writers of all. All they had were the jokes. They never had the characters or the tone or the soul of the series because they couldn't hear it in their heads.

If there's a particular sitcom that you really love, and you can hear that series in your head… If you understand the characters, can predict how they'd react to things, know how they speak, empathize with how they feel… THAT is the series to spec!

BEYOND *SEINFELD*

I know this will sound ridiculously obvious, but let's cover it for a minute so you can't say I never told you: *Don't write a spec script for a sitcom that is out of production!*

If the series that you want to spec isn't on the prime time schedule of one of the major networks anymore, then that series is over. They're done. You can find reruns of *Seinfeld* and *Friends* someplace every day. But both those series are out of production. They don't make new episodes anymore. The sets are torn down and the actors have gone home. Don't write a spec script for *Seinfeld* or *Friends*.

No one in Hollywood who can give you a job is going to read a spec script for a series that is out of production. They're also going to think that you're a dope for not knowing that.

You might ask, "What difference does it make? Why can't I write a *Seinfeld*? It's still a sitcom. They haven't reinvented the genre since *Seinfeld* went off the air." You're right. And if you can write a cracker-jack episode of *Seinfeld*, then you may very well have the chops to write any show. But you still can't spec a *Seinfeld* now because *Seinfeld* is over.

I've heard producers argue that anybody could write a good *Friends* or a funny *Seinfeld* because those series were on the air for so long. They're fool proof, goes the argument, so if you write a funny *Seinfeld* you aren't really proving anything.

I don't buy that reasoning. I've read spec episodes of *Friends* and of *Seinfeld* that weren't very good at all because the person writing the spec script couldn't hear that series in their head. You have to understand a series thoroughly in order to bring those characters to life, and to properly exploit the premise and the Formula. I think that if you can write a fresh and clever episode of *Friends* now, after all those episodes and all those Ross and Rachel fights, it proves something significant about your talent. But I'm not the one who is going to be reading your spec script and considering you for a job. You have to *write* what's current in order to *be* current. So just take my word for it and save yourself a lot of grief. Go beyond *Seinfeld*. Spec a series that is in production now.

If you're still thinking: "But I love *Seinfeld*. You said to write a show that I love. I'm busy. I really don't watch that much TV. The only show I know well is *Seinfeld*." What I'd say to you is: "Then you aren't ready to spec a sitcom." If you're working nights or going to school in the evenings, or you don't have TiVo or a VCR that you know how to program, now is not the time to be specing a TV script.

There are a million people out there writing spec scripts. I mean, really, a million. All of them have time to sit home night after night, week after week, and watch *My Name Is Earl* and *How I Met Your Mother*. All of the spec scripts that are being read right now in Hollywood — by agents and managers and story editors and producers and network executives and by the kid who picks up Indian food for the writers of *The Simpsons* — are episodes of series that are currently in production.

If you don't have time right now to be familiar with most of the sitcoms that are currently in production, not only at the broadcast networks like CBS, NBC, ABC, Fox, but also what's on all the cable outlets like HBO and Showtime and F/X and Comedy Central, then now is not the time for you to be trying to make it as a sitcom writer. If you have never sampled *Reba* or *Reno 911*, I promise you that your competitors have, and they are way ahead of you.

Write what you love, but write what is current.

THE SCRIPT THAT PRODUCERS *WANT* TO READ

Doesn't it make sense to spec the hottest sitcom on TV if that one also happens to be your favorite show? Well, if the hottest sitcom on TV is also your favorite sitcom, and that's the series you feel most comfortable writing, then, yes, on your *very first* spec sitcom script, go for it.

But as I just said a couple of paragraphs ago, there are thousands of other aspiring writers who are, at this very moment, already specing the hottest sitcom on TV. There are thousands of aspiring writers who are, at this very moment, specing *every* sitcom on TV. You can be absolutely certain that there is a burgeoning, billowing glut of spec scripts for the hottest shows. Producers and agents are being inundated right now with spec episodes of the most popular sitcoms. Everyone is *already* tired of reading them.

During the '80's and early '90's, no producer or staff writer anywhere wanted to read another spec *Cheers*. We'd already read fourteen million of them. We couldn't read any more. If the cast of *Cheers* could've been kept young by artificial means, or reproduced digitally, *Cheers* could have run for six hundred more seasons just on spec scripts alone. Those of us producing other series at the time could not bear to slog through still another spec *Cheers*. It was too much Cliff and Norm already. We were sick of it.

When *Seinfeld* was king, you could have built a stairway to heaven with the spec *Seinfeld* scripts pouring out of laser printers all over L.A. The same was true of *Friends*. I'll bet you that more paper has been used to print spec episodes of *Seinfeld* and *Friends* than was used to publish all of the novels in the world during all of recorded history.

Producers want to read a spec script that is as fresh as possible.

Producers are much more likely to open a spec script if they're just a tiny bit intrigued. I always was. If my first thought when I picked up a spec script was, "Hey, I haven't seen too many of these," or "This writer's got some guts," then I was much more likely to actually open the script and read it!

Yes, I want you to spec the series that you know and love, but if you can find a way to know and love a series that *isn't* the hottest one on TV — the same series that absolutely everyone else is specing already — then I think you have a slightly better chance of getting your spec script read. As a producer, I would rather read my first or second spec *Reba* than read my ten-millionth spec *Will and Grace*.

TOO SOON TO "HEAR IT IN YOUR HEAD"

Sometimes a new series will come on the air with all kinds of hype, not just from the network that is trying to sell it to you, but also from the press. Magazines and newspapers and blogs will publish or post a million articles about this hot new sitcom, and you'll think, "This is the show to spec! This is the scorching new sitcom that will be my ticket to wealth and fame!"

But if it's brand new, you won't be able to hear it in your head! How can you? It just premiered! Even the writers who are working on the series can't hear it in their heads yet! How can you?

You want to write the best spec script possible. You can only do that if you're intimately familiar with the series you have chosen. No one can be intimately familiar with a series that has only been on the schedule for three weeks!

And what if this hot new sitcom gets cancelled while you're still writing? It happens. Remember *Emily's Reasons Why Not*? It premiered on ABC in 2006 to all kinds of hoopla. It starred Heather Graham. It was going to be a big hit. And what happened? It was cancelled after one episode! One!

If a new sitcom comes on the air, and you instantly fall in love with it, by all means watch it every week. Make notes. Come up with story ideas. But don't start on a spec script until it gets picked up for a second season.

PLANET MEGAMALL

Let's say you've taken your first step toward writing your spec sitcom script. You've picked which series that you want to spec. You've picked that series because you love it. You watch it all the time. You don't care what your friends say. You know the characters so well that you can hear them in your head. You know the stories that have already been told. The series you have picked is still in production, and it isn't the hottest sitcom on TV at the moment.

Your next step, if you haven't taken this one already, is to get on the Web, go to Planet MegaMall, and order at least one sample script from your chosen series. It's going to cost you ten bucks, plus shipping. But you're going to do it anyway, even if you have to borrow the money from your parents.

Why?

Because once you have that sample script, there is no more doubt for you about the format of the series you have chosen to spec. You will look at the sample script from Planet MegaMall and know how to adjust your script-writing software. You may not have to adjust your software at all. If you write with Final Draft or one of the other script writing programs, you can click "Sitcom 1" or "Sitcom 2" and have the right margins instantly. But holding a printed copy of an actual episode of your favorite series in your hands is just too good a resource to ignore. You'll see how the real writers of that series do their stage directions. You'll be sure you're spelling all the characters' names correctly. You'll see the jokes on paper in front of you.

I think that a wannabe writer who doesn't use this resource is crazy. If I could have sent away for scripts from the series that I was specing back when I was trying to break in, I would have saved myself all manner of doubt and guesswork. You don't have time for guesswork. You are in competition with a million other wannabes who are all making use of this same resource. Don't be cheap now. Go to Planet MegaMall and order your sample script!

THE WEB

You have an enormous advantage that I didn't have when I was writing spec scripts. You have the Web. Your favorite sitcom has its own website, plus ten other unofficial websites. You can go to these websites and browse through all of the stories they've ever done. You can often pick up detailed information on the characters. You can fill in all the blanks! Lucky you. I was guessing. You don't have to guess!

CHAPTER RECAP — THE ELEPHANT REMEMBERS

Isn't it your dream to write an episode of your favorite sitcom? That was my dream.

Well, that's exactly what I'm advising you to do! Write an episode of your favorite show! Write the show that you love, even if you're afraid to admit that this is your favorite. Write it in secret. I don't care. Don't worry about the "cool" show or the "hip" show. Which one do you look forward to watching every week?

I wrote some spec scripts for some pretty forgettable shows, but I sure had a good time doing it! This should be fun! And while you're enjoying yourself, you're learning!

It's much easier to learn and to make yourself work when you're doing something that you enjoy. Keep that in mind, will you?

I'll bet that you can already hear your favorite sitcoms in your head. I'll bet you can make up entire scenes from those shows in your mind. I'll bet the voices of the characters are so real that it sounds like someone is playing a recording of the show in your brain. That's how well you know your favorite sitcoms!

Guess what? If you can hear it in your head, you're well on your way to being a sitcom writer! You've already passed the first test!

YOUR "TO DO" LIST

1) Make a list of every single sitcom that is on the air right now. Check off how many of those shows you know pretty well already. I'll bet you know most of them.

2) Of the sitcoms that you know, list them in order of which ones you know best.

3) Think about your top five favorite current sitcoms. Are they relatively new series or have they been on the air for a while? Are some of them coming to the end of their run? Have you read articles about this being "the last season"? Are any of them in their first season? Of your top five favorites, which ones are in their third or fourth year? Take special note of these. These are the prime candidates for your first spec script.

4) Think about the current sitcoms that you don't know very well. Isn't it time to start sampling them, just so you know what's out there?

CHAPTER 3

PICKING THE RIGHT STORY

Bob Ellison had been one of the top writers for *The Mary Tyler Moore Show*. Now he was going to run a brand new sitcom for MTM, the highly respected independent studio that had produced *The Mary Tyler Moore Show*, *The Bob Newhart Show*, *Rhoda*, *Phyllis*, *WKRP in Cincinnati* and a bunch of other hits. I was nervously sitting with him in his office on the MTM lot in Studio City. He was wearing a beautiful cashmere sweater. I'm in a T-shirt. Bob was at the zenith of his career. I drove over there in a broken down Volkswagen. He was looking over a spec *Mary* script that I wrote. "What made you pick this story?" he asked me, kind of bemused, maybe even a little disgusted. I kept thinking, "Any minute now he's going to toss me out of this very swanky office." So I stammered and said, "I wanted to test the premise of the series." He looked at the spec script again and then back at me: "So you gave Mary a pimple on her…" (I'd written a script in which the Mary Richards character developed a medical problem that might prevent her from having children.) I shrugged and squirmed in my seat. I was sweating a river into my shorts. Maybe it *was* a poor choice for a story idea. Maybe it *was* offensive. I was just trying to get somebody's attention so I could get a job. Mr. Ellison said that even though he NEVER would have written a script with a story like mine, and even though what I had written was entirely inappropriate for *The Mary Tyler Moore Show*, and was even in questionable taste, he was nonetheless impressed by how skillfully I told the story. He read the whole script because he was dying to know how the story came out. He hired me to work on his new show.

STORY IS EVERYTHING

Whether you're writing a novel or a play or a comic book or a spec episode of a sitcom, the STORY is what holds the reader's attention. It isn't the jokes or the snappy banter between characters. It's the STORY! The story is what keeps them reading. If the reader is dying to know what happens next in your story, he's going to continue turning the pages. If he's bored by the story, he's going to drop your script in the nearest blue bin.

I want you to have fun writing your script! Writers create their best work when they are enjoying themselves. Forget suffering for your art! Writing sitcoms should be fun! If you can't wait to get to the computer every day, you'll feel more confident, and you'll end up with a much better spec script. A good story is ALWAYS the difference between a script that is fun to write and one that is a chore.

Too many of the writers with whom I have worked have not understood the importance of story. Too many have thought they could fake their way through a script with jokes and sight gags. This never works. Without the right story, you always end up stuck. Your scenes aren't funny. The writing process becomes laborious. You avoid working on your script or give up altogether. *With* the right story, your spec script is going to be easy and fun to write.

THE RIGHT STORY IS IN FRONT OF YOU!

Think about the series you've chosen to spec. You've seen it a million times. You know it inside and out. But so far, you may have only watched the series as entertainment. There was never any reason to analyze it. Now you need to start picking this series apart. Your analysis will lead you to the right story.

Your goal is to write an episode that sounds like the series you have chosen to spec.

If your spec script sounds like the actual series, this suggests to people in Hollywood that you have the skills to write for TV. Writing for TV involves taking someone else's premise and someone else's characters and reproducing that premise and those characters in the same way that the series' creator would. If you're writing *Seinfeld*, you have to write like Larry David. Now, no one can do this perfectly. Only Larry David can write like Larry David. But you can learn how to get really close. Close enough to start working on sitcoms!

The right story is the key ingredient to making your spec script sound like the series. If your story is consistent with the series, then the characters will be able to speak and behave as they do on the real show. Everything about your script will fall magically into place. It will. I've been doing this for thirty years, and I can tell you without fear of contradiction that the story is the linchpin of any good sitcom episode.

So with all this build up, which story should you tell?

Don't worry. The right story is there in front of you. I promise.

WRITE TO THE PREMISE

Every situation comedy has a premise, a framework within which the characters were created and the stories are told. The premise, this framework, is also known as the *situation*. Thus the term *situation* comedy. It's a comedy about a situation. Well, what's the situation? What's the premise? What's the framework? Understanding the premise will help guide you to the right story.

What was the premise of *Everybody Loves Raymond*?

Raymond was about a married guy who lived across the street from his meddling mother. On *Everybody Loves Raymond*, they wrote a lot of "meddling mother" stories. That was the premise that the series was set up to explore.

Look at the title: *Everybody Loves Raymond*. Was that a joke or did they mean it? As I watched this series over the years, I decided that everyone *did* love Raymond. Ray was a nice guy. Ray lived across the street from his parents because they loved him, and he loved them. Ray's wife, Debra, loved him. Even Ray's brother, Robert, loved him.

So where did the comedy come from? Ray's mother, Marie, meddled in his marriage, which angered Ray's wife, Debra. Ray got caught in the middle of conflict between his mother and his wife. That was part of the premise, too. Ray was also a bit of a mama's boy. His mother, Marie, doted on Ray, and Ray liked it. But Marie's doting made Ray's brother, Robert, jealous. Ray often ended up in the middle of conflict between his mother and Robert. Ray's father was cantankerous and his parents bickered. Ray often ended up in the middle of conflict between his mother and father.

So the premise of *Everybody Loves Raymond* might be more thoroughly stated as: "The not always successful efforts of a somewhat immature but well-intentioned man to live in peace with his formidable wife, his doting but meddling mother, his jealous and insecure brother, and his cantankerous father."

If I was writing a spec episode of *Everybody Loves Raymond*, and I wanted to demonstrate with my script that I understood the series and the characters, then I would *write to the premise*. I would write to the heart of the series. I'd come up with a story for my spec episode that involved a family conflict — a problem — which exploited all of the well-known traits of the regular characters. I'd make sure that Marie meddled somehow in Raymond's life. I'd make sure that Debra got upset over Marie's meddling. I'd make sure that Robert got jealous of Ray. I'd make sure that Frank was cantankerous. And I'd stick Raymond in the middle of all of it.

What's the premise of the series you have chosen to spec?

Think about it for a while and then jot down the premise as I did for *Raymond*. Try to be as specific as you can in describing what the series is really about. This will lead you to the right story for your spec script.

Was *Seinfeld* really a "show about nothing"? Of course not. *Seinfeld* was about a very likeable but immature, anal, selfish, single, stand-up comedian named Jerry and his three equally likeable, immature, selfish, single friends. *Seinfeld* was about adult children (Jerry and Elaine were slightly more functional than George or Kramer) avoiding the emotional toll of a mature life — real relationships, real careers, real responsibilities — through childish goals, petty disagreements, adolescent competitions and obsessing about minutiae.

When you really lay out the premise of *Seinfeld* it's obviously a show about *something*, and that something is pretty easy to see. To write to the premise of *Seinfeld*, you'd want to explore the immaturity, selfishness and dysfunction of the characters through some minor and commonplace issue like chipping in for a wedding gift or waiting for a table at a Chinese restaurant.

Once you completely understand the premise of the series that you have chosen to spec, start thinking about a story area that exploits the premise.

WRITE THE MAIN CHARACTER

A spec script for a situation comedy should always be about the Main Character of the series.

Why?

Because writing about the Main Character is the best way for you to demonstrate that you understand the entire series.

Most of the stories on any sitcom evolve from the premise of the series and from the personality of the Main Character.

If I were writing a spec episode of *Everybody Loves Raymond*, I would write a story about Ray's meddling mother, his formidable wife, his jealous brother and his cantankerous father, but I would make the focus of the story about *Ray*. Ray has to solve some personal problem or family conflict that involves all or most of the other characters. Ray solves the problem in a way that is consistent with his established personality on the series.

It's rare to find a series that does not have a Main Character. The only one I can think of recently was *Friends*. But *Friends* is over now, so you won't be specing that series anyway. Even if the series you have chosen is an ensemble like *Scrubs*, you should create a story that is centered on the Main Character, J.D.

Writing a story about the Main Character on a sitcom reassures someone who is reading your spec script that you understand the series you have chosen. If you demonstrate a clear understanding of the series you have chosen, it suggests that you will likely understand another series just as well.

I caution you against creating a story about a supporting character on the series you have chosen. The best spec script is one that demonstrates your strong grasp of the entire series. You'll best demonstrate your grasp of the entire series by writing a story about the Main Character. Let the supporting characters play a supporting role in your story.

Since your story is going to be about your Main Character, take a minute to think about what kind of person your Main Character is. This will give you another important clue about what story to tell.

The right story will spring from an aspect of the Main Character's personality.

Lucy was an eccentric character, wasn't she? She was bigger than life. Lucy created problems for herself and for the people around her. She was a schemer and a plotter. If you were writing a spec episode of *I Love Lucy*, you'd have Lucy plotting and scheming to get something she wants, wouldn't you? Your story would likely spring from that powerful aspect of Lucy's character.

I remember seeing an ad for an episode of *The King of Queens*. The blurb read: "Doug discovers that Carrie is buying his clothes from the Big and Tall Shop." Embarrassed about his weight, Doug goes on a diet.

Here's an actual story from a hit series that springs directly from an aspect of the Main Character's personality. Doug was an overweight guy. His wife was trying to buy him clothes that would fit and be comfortable, but she didn't want to hurt his feelings by telling him that the clothes came from the Big and Tall Shop. This struck me as an organic story for *The King of Queens* and an excellent example of how to use aspects of the Main Character's personality as a source of stories.

For your spec sitcom episode, think about who your Main Character is. You've been watching the series for a while. You know it very well. Try to think of a story that exploits the series premise and springs from some interesting aspect of the Main Character's personality.

If you have an ACTIVE Main Character like Lucy, you'd think about a goal for Lucy. You'd think of something that Lucy would want based on her personality. Then you'd create an obstacle keeping Lucy from obtaining her goal. If Lucy wanted a new hat, you'd give her a good reason for feeling that she needed a new hat. Maybe Lucy's rival, Caroline Appleby, just got a new hat, and was flaunting it in front of Lucy, making Lucy jealous. Now Lucy feels that she must have a new hat to keep up with Caroline Appleby. The obstacle to getting a new hat might be money. Lucy spent her allowance, and Ricky won't give her any more money. Because of her scheming personality, Lucy concocts a plot to get the money for the hat. The plot somehow backfires, getting Lucy into even more trouble.

An Active Main Character usually wants something that improves his or her status: a new car or a better job or a starring role in the community play. Active Main Characters will then move heaven and earth to achieve their goal, inevitably getting themselves into even more trouble.

Examples of Active Main Characters are Christine on *The New Adventures of Old Christine*, Michael Scott on *The Office*, and Earl Hickey on *My Name Is Earl*.

If you have a REACTIVE Main Character like Ray Barone, you'll want to put your Main Character in a troublesome dilemma or an embarrassing situation.

If Lucy was the quintessential Active Main Character, Bob Newhart may have been the classic Reactive Main Character. The persona that Bob Newhart created for himself as a comedian was that of an ordinary, self-conscious man stuck in an eccentric world. Most Reactive Main Characters, like Ray Barone, have similar personalities. Reactive Main Characters are often the voice of reason as chaos swirls around them.

Katherine Greene wrote a wonderful episode of *Newhart* in which Bob's character, Dick Loudon, discovers that there is a body buried in the basement of his Vermont inn. It was an embarrassing situation for Dick, who had to figure out what to do about the corpse before his guests found out. The problem wasn't Dick's fault, but he had to solve it in order to stay in business.

This story sprang organically from the personality of the Main Character. Dick was a responsible guy. What can we do to make the eccentric outside world intrude on Dick's orderly existence and embarrass him?

We'll put a body in his basement.

A Reactive Main Character is a problem solver. Reactive Main Characters usually have to fix a problem or resolve a conflict. Reactive Main Characters are well-meaning, but their attempts at making things better usually make things even worse.

Examples of Reactive Main Characters are Ted on *How I Met Your Mother*, Charlie Harper on *Two and a Half Men*, and Chris on *Everybody Hates Chris*.

Decide whether the Main Character on the series you have chosen to spec is an Active or a Reactive Main Character. Write down as many aspects of the Main Character's personality as you can think of. In your mind, go through as many episodes as you can. Write down a synopsis of each story. Use the series' website to help you remember. Think about how aspects of the Main Character's personality have already combined with the premise of the series to create stories for actual episodes, like the "Big and Tall" episode of *The King of Queens*. Think about which aspect of your Main Character's personality you might like to explore in a story.

See how logical this all is?

We're already narrowing down the possible story areas for your spec episode. You're going to create a story that exploits the premise of the series and centers on the Main Character. You're going to use an interesting aspect of your Main Character's personality as a springboard for your story.

WRITE THE FORMULA

The next step in developing your story is to think about the episodes you've watched on the series you have chosen to spec and identify the FORMULA.

All sitcoms have a formula. The episodes are about basically the same issues every week. This isn't because the writers are lazy or unimaginative. It's because after you produce a few episodes of a new series, you discover what works and what doesn't. You go with what works.

On *Gilligan's Island* the formula was the castaways' repeated failed attempts at getting rescued. One only has to watch one or two episodes of *Gilligan's Island* to understand that simple formula. Each week, the castaways have some chance of getting rescued. They work hard to achieve their goal. Then Gilligan's bumbling thwarts all their efforts.

Many episodes of *Frasier* revolved around Frasier's snobbery and social climbing. Frasier was always trying to improve his status by chasing after some elusive goal. The producers of *Frasier* also loved to do farce. They would often build to a climax that found the characters frantically running in and out of doors.

When I was producing *Coach*, we realized fairly quickly that our series worked best when we followed the formula of classic series like *The Honeymooners* and *All in the Family*. Hayden Fox was an Active Main Character similar in personality to Ralph Cramden of *The Honeymooners* and to Archie Bunker of *All in the Family*. Hayden was a schemer like Ralph, who frequently concocted elaborate plots to achieve a particular goal. Hayden also got himself into trouble because of his pride and prejudice, much like Archie Bunker.

Barry Kemp's premise for *Coach* initially revolved around the ethical compromises that a football coach makes in order to win.

Our Main Character, Hayden Fox, was an ambitious, competitive man trying to succeed at an undistinguished school. Hayden suffered from moral lapses all the time in his attempts to achieve success.

The formula for *Coach* evolved from the way in which the premise of the series combined with the personality of the Main Character to produce stories. Hayden was often chasing after some goal to improve his football program. He'd try to recruit a star player or curry favor with the college administration.

Here's an example of an episode of *Coach* that followed the formula: Hayden Fox learns in the first scene that Minnesota State's biggest booster, Earl Rizendough, has just died. Hayden exhibits some genuine grief for a few seconds, then reminds his assistant coaches, Luther and Dauber, that Earl

Title card from hit series, *Coach*.

promised to leave millions of dollars to the athletic program when he died. With that money, the school can now build a state-of-the-art sports center which will improve the football program. Hayden can hardly wait to collect the money.

In the next scene, Hayden brings in drawings of the new sports center, counting his chickens before they hatch. He then learns that the rich booster's widow wants to give the money to medical research. Instead of graciously respecting the widow's wishes, Hayden feels cheated. He's furious. He's a competitive guy who wants to win, but he coaches at an obscure school. A new sports center will help him recruit better players. Giving in to his ego, pride, and ambition, Hayden decides he'll go see the rich widow and "recruit" her into giving him the money he was promised.

The widow turns out to be a tough nut. She doesn't like Hayden. She doesn't like football. His clumsy attempts at sympathy for her situation fail to hide his greed. He suggests that her grief is clouding her thinking. Hayden's insensitive presumption alienates the widow even further. She tells Hayden that he has no idea how it feels to lose a loved one. Hayden, desperate by now for the money that he feels is rightfully his, lies and tells the widow that his wife died. He lies more and claims that he has been raising his daughter all alone for many years. (Hayden is actually divorced and was an absent father for most of his daughter's childhood. The audience knows this. They're in on the joke.) The widow softens when she believes that Hayden is a selfless widower. It looks like Hayden will get his money. The widow invites Hayden to come for dinner and bring his daughter. She'll give him the money then.

In Act Two, Hayden has to talk to his daughter, Kelly. He doesn't want to lose Kelly's respect and look like a jerk, but he has to ask her to lie for him. She is furious with him when she hears the fib that he told. "You killed Mom?!" But he pleads with her. He admits that he's done a questionable thing. But coaching is so hard. He needs this money to build the sports center. He was supposed to have it. It isn't fair. Can't she just help him out? Out of sympathy for her father, Kelly agrees to go through with the charade.

As father and daughter are about to leave for the dinner, Hayden suddenly has a change of heart. He can't ask his daughter to go through with the lie.

Hayden shows up for the dinner alone and confesses his lie. The widow is appalled. He tries to get her to understand, but she can't. He loses the money and the sports center. But at least he did the right thing and kept the respect of his daughter.

Everything that *Coach* was about as a series was contained in that one episode. The story sprang from Barry Kemp's original premise about the ethical compromises that a coach must make, and from the personality of the Active Main Character. The premise and the personality of the Main Character combined to produce the series formula.

Carefully watch the series you have chosen for your spec script. Identify the formula for the stories. The formula is the particular way in which stories evolve from the premise of the series and from the personality of the Main Character. You'll want to use that same formula to develop your story. This isn't cheating. It isn't you being lazy or unoriginal. It isn't you prostituting yourself to a bunch of hackneyed clichés. *Everybody Loves Raymond* had a formula. So did *Cheers* and *Seinfeld* and *Friends* and *Sex and the City*.

THE PAINTS ARE ALREADY IN THE TRAY

In using the *premise*, the *personality of the Main Character*, and the *formula* as guidelines for constructing your story, you are using the paints that are already in the tray. You are demonstrating that you understand this series, and therefore are capable of understanding other series.

Remember, you want to write an episode that sounds like the series you have chosen to spec. The best way to do that is to figure out what the writers of that series are already up to, and play by their rules.

You now have the most important guidelines that I can give you for constructing the right story for your spec sitcom episode. It's all logical:

Define the premise of the series you have chosen to spec.

Define the personality of the Main Character. Is he or she an Active or Reactive Main Character?

What aspect of the Main Character's personality would you like to explore in a story?

How can the personality of the Main Character and the premise of the series combine to produce a story idea?

While you're thinking about all of that, let me give you a few more tips on developing the right story for your spec sitcom episode. These tips are based on my experience writing a number of spec sitcom scripts and from reading literally hundreds of them over the course of my career.

DON'T REINVENT

As the producer of a TV series, you get all kinds of crazy spec scripts in which Jerry Seinfeld goes to medical school or Ross becomes a woman. Stories like that change the series into another series. Don't write stuff like that. Spec scripts that are that loopy probably won't get past the gate keepers anyway, but if a script like that does somehow make it to the production offices of a sitcom, do you know what happens? Someone, probably a writers' assistant, eventually reads it. The script then gets circulated around the office as a joke. It is laughed at by everyone, and then the pages are tossed in the recycle bin.

Say you were writing a spec *Friends*. You wouldn't write an episode in which Chandler flies on the Space Shuttle. Why not? Because Chandler wasn't an astronaut! If you make Chandler into an astronaut, even for one episode, you are reinventing the series. You may not be sure what Chandler's job actually was, but we all know that he didn't work for NASA.

You might say at this point, "But I want my spec script to be special and memorable. I *want* Chandler to fly in the Space Shuttle. I have it all planned out where Chandler accidentally substitutes for his friend who is an astronaut, and he's floating inside the Space Shuttle, and Phoebe is talking to him on the radio from Houston, and it's really, really, really funny. I think the producers of *Friends* would much rather read a script that shows some originality!"

Originality is great! But altering the reality of the series is not being original. It's just ignoring the premise, the personality of the Main Character, and the formula. You want your spec script to demonstrate how well you understand the series as it is, not how far you carry it away from its roots.

DON'T BREAK NEW GROUND

Don't marry J.D. to Elliot in a spec script. Don't have Alan Harper move out of Charlie's Malibu beach house, even if it's just temporary. Don't take the characters to places they have never been or where the series would never go in an effort to be unusual. If the series is going to break new ground, the producers will handle it. They don't want gigantic new ideas coming in from outside.

NO NEW CHARACTERS

Don't add important new characters that have never been in the series before.

If you were writing a spec *Two and a Half Men*, you wouldn't add Charlie and Alan's mystery sister who has been in the Army but was never mentioned until now. You could certainly give Charlie and Alan a new neighbor or even a temporary girlfriend, but not some new family member. Adding a major new character like that changes the whole balance of the series. The producers would think long and hard before they took a step that large. It's not your place to do that. Your job is to prove how well you can write the characters that already exist.

Use the paints that are already in the tray. Demonstrate your creativity, your writing skill and your knowledge of the series by utilizing the familiar elements of that series in a new and interesting way.

USE THE REGULAR SETS

Don't send the cast of *How I Met Your Mother* to Las Vegas. Not in a spec script. The producers of that series may someday decide to write a Las

Vegas episode, or one that takes place in Hawaii, but those episodes are special. They are usually "sweeps" episodes designed for extra promotional value at certain times of the season. Again, your job with a spec script is to show how well you understand the series as it is. Your job is to tell a story within the parameters of the series, and that includes the regular sets.

TEST THE PREMISE

I wrote a spec M*A*S*H episode that got me a freelance assignment to write an actual M*A*S*H episode. To make my spec episode special, I decided to "test the premise."

I wanted to make my spec M*A*S*H stand out, so I asked myself, "What is M*A*S*H really about every week?" I was defining the premise for my spec script as I've asked you to do for your spec script. I decided that the premise of M*A*S*H had at least something to do with the irony of saving lives in the middle of a war. All the regular characters were doctors and nurses. They were in a war trying to sew together soldiers who had been maimed in that war. That was the premise from which the series worked. Then I asked myself about the personality of the Main Character. Hawkeye Pierce was an Active Main Character. He could be a plotter and a schemer. He was rebellious. He didn't want to be there. He was a great surgeon, and he saved a lot of lives. Hawkeye was so skilled and dedicated that his commanding officer put up with a lot of insubordination. Hawkeye was appalled by the war. He was a healer and a life-saver, not a soldier or a killer.

How could I combine the premise of the series with the personality of the Main Character and come up with an original story that M*A*S*H had never told? I thought about it for a while, and then I asked myself, What if I "test the premise"? I wasn't going to reinvent the series. I was going to use the paints that were already in the tray, but I was going to push the envelope.

To test the premise, I established in the opening scenes that Hawkeye had just pulled a horrendous shift, twenty-four hours in the O.R. without a break, one wounded soldier after another. When he finally is relieved,

Hawkeye is exhausted. He staggers from the O.R., trying to get to his cot across the compound. It's the middle of the night. No one is around. Suddenly, a gun shot rings out. Hawkeye dives for cover. He's exhausted and scared to death, as anyone would be. More shots are heard. Hawkeye is joined by Col. Flagg. Flagg was a gung-ho CIA guy who hated Hawkeye. Flagg was the opposite of Hawkeye. Flagg loved the war. Flagg tells Hawkeye there's a sniper in the compound, probably some rogue North Korean soldier. Flagg shoves a pistol into Hawkeye's hand. Hawkeye refuses, but Flagg won't take the gun back. Flagg tells Hawkeye to keep low. Flagg runs off to try to catch the sniper. Hawkeye wants no part of this gun, but suddenly bullets are striking all around him. It's as if the sniper has seen Hawkeye and made him the target. The sniper is closing in. Hawkeye tries to escape, but the sniper has found him. Now Hawkeye is joined by a nurse. She is scared to death, too. The shots are raining down on Hawkeye and the nurse. Hawkeye and the nurse are going to die! It's up to Hawkeye to save them. In a moment of exhaustion, survival instinct and pure panic, Hawkeye points the gun blindly into the dark and fires. The shot miraculously finds its mark. Hawkeye hits the sniper. In later scenes, Hawkeye insists on operating on the sniper that he shot. He tries to save the sniper's life, but he can't. The sniper dies. Hawkeye is devastated.

Funny, huh?

This was an unusually dramatic episode, but the story tested the premise of *M*A*S*H*. Hawkeye, the healer, takes a life in order to save his own and that of a nurse. He defends himself in an attack, thus abandoning, for a moment, his pacifist beliefs. He gets a taste of what soldiers go through, and maybe now he'll be a little less judgmental and self-righteous.

The producers of *M*A*S*H* didn't buy my spec script. That almost never happens. Don't think for a moment that you will ever sell your spec *Two and a Half Men* to the producers of that show. You won't. But by testing the premise with my spec *M*A*S*H* about the sniper, I got the attention of the producers of *M*A*S*H*.

I didn't reinvent the series. I used the premise, the personality of the Main Character and the formula. I didn't introduce any important new characters. I used the regular sets. I used the paints that were already in the tray. I didn't go exploring outside the boundaries of the series, but I did push the envelope.

That spec script got me a job writing an actual episode of *M*A*S*H*.

WRITE IT REAL

A story works best when it's believable, even on a sitcom... *especially* on a sitcom! You know why? You're trying to be funny. Comedy works best when it's grounded in reality. Characters are funniest and most compelling when they behave as real human beings.

Once you feel the inkling of a story for your spec sitcom script, I think it's worth a minute of your time to stop and give this question some thought: IS IT REAL?

Am I telling a story that sounds plausible, not only for this particular sitcom, but plausible in terms of human behavior?

Does Chandler going up in the Space Shuttle really sound very convincing? Whether *Friends* would have done an episode like this or not (and they wouldn't), is it believable that anybody who isn't an astronaut would end up on the Space Shuttle? I don't think so. You buy yourself a lot of problems later on when you stray too far from what is believable just for the sake of some jokes. Jokes will never sustain you when reality has been tossed out the window.

Sitcoms can be pretty silly. How many times have you watched an episode of a sitcom and thought, "Man, this is pretty dumb," or "No one I know would ever act like that"?

I don't know about you, but the comedy series that I admired most were the ones that seemed the most real. I respected *The Dick Van Dyke Show*, *The Mary Tyler Moore Show*, *All in the Family*, *Barney Miller* and *Cheers*. I aspired to write as well as those series were written.

I also loved *The Munsters*. Here was a domestic comedy in which all of the regular characters except one were monsters. Main Character Herman Munster was Frankenstein. His wife, Lily, was Vampira. His father-in-law, Grandpa, was Count Dracula and his son, Eddie, was a mini wolf man. I think *The Munsters* was one of the funniest series ever. I think that within the boundaries of the universe in which *The Munsters* operated, the series was real. You can be outlandish, even silly, even broad and slapstick, and still be real.

What is "real"?

I remember an episode of *The Munsters* in which Herman's old army unit was getting together for a reunion. Herman tried on his uniform, and it no longer fit. Sounds pretty believable, doesn't it? Sounds like that episode of *The King of Queens*. Herman wanted to drop a few pounds before the reunion. Thousands of people have found themselves in the same predicament. You've got a wedding coming up or a high school or college reunion, and suddenly you're calling Jenny Craig. Herman went on a diet. There was just one complication, one obstacle standing in the way of Herman achieving his goal. The reunion was scheduled for right after Thanksgiving. That meant no Thanksgiving feast for Herman. Herman first tried to use will power, but he couldn't control his appetite. Sounds like a very real and believable story, doesn't it? Taking this very normal-sounding story into the universe of *The Munsters*, Grandpa strapped Herman down on a table in the dungeon while the family went out to a restaurant for Thanksgiving dinner. Herman, crazed with hunger, broke out of his restraints and staggered through the neighborhood, just like Frankenstein's monster, looking for a meal. It was silly, it was broad, it was slapstick, but it was *real*!

Chandler going up on the Space Shuttle isn't real, because something like that would never happen within the universe of *Friends*. Herman Munster breaking his chains and roaming crazed through the neighborhood looking for turkey was well within the universe of *The Munsters*. A story about a man dieting because of vanity is grounded in reality. A story about a yuppie Manhattanite ending up on the Space Shuttle isn't. See what I mean?

When characters stop acting like real people, you take the audience right out of your story. Even when you're writing a sitcom, your audience has to care. They have to feel that what is happening is believable. They must be concerned that things are going to turn out right for the Main Character. This is called ROOTING INTEREST, and you must keep it alive in every scene. It's just like in baseball. The crowd has to be rooting for the home team or no one is going to stick around for the ninth inning. Whether your Main Character is Jerry Seinfeld or Frasier Crane or Herman Munster, if the audience stops caring about what happens to him, you've lost them. Audiences stop caring when they stop believing. Audiences stop believing when the action isn't real.

Herman Munster on a diet is believable. Chandler on the Space Shuttle isn't believable.

After you've decided on an area for your story, stop and ask yourself, "Is this real?" If you aren't sure, ask someone else. Ask your roommate or your girlfriend or boyfriend or your writing teacher. If you pitch them your story and they scrunch up their face, you may need to rethink your idea.

SEE HOW EASY THAT WAS?

You now have some logical guidelines to help you pick the right story for your spec episode. If you look back over the chapter, you have really narrowed it down. You don't have to pluck a story from thin air. You will have to come up with the actual idea that you are going to develop for your spec sitcom episode on your own, but you have your knowledge of the premise of the series to help you. You have your knowledge of the personality of the Main Character. You have your knowledge of the series formula. Your combined knowledge of all these important elements gives you a solid foundation for developing the right story for your spec script.

CHAPTER RECAP — THE ELEPHANT REMEMBERS

The right story for your spec sitcom script is in front of you!

A simple roadmap already exists to lead you to the right story.

Define for yourself as completely as possible the premise of the series you have chosen to spec. What's it really about every week? What common themes seem to recur in every episode? Is your series about how proud, chauvinistic Dad needs to learn a lesson in cooperation every week, as on *The Bernie Mac Show*? Or is your series about an immature and neurotic divorced woman trying desperately to prove that she can manage her own life, as on *The New Adventures of Old Christine*? The more clearly you can define the premise of *your* series, the easier it will be for you to *write to the premise* in your spec sitcom script.

You'll want to do some serious thinking about the Main Character. Who is this guy or gal really? Does your series have an Active or a Reactive Main Character? What are the aspects of the Main Character's personality that makes him or her fun to watch? Why do you like this person? What makes you root for the Main Character to succeed?

You'll want to do some work figuring out the formula of the series you have chosen. Review episodes of the series and notice how the personality of the Main Character combines with the premise of the series to create stories. Is your Main Character an eccentric nut who constantly gets himself or herself into jams pursuing some elusive goal? *The New Adventures of Old Christine*.

Or is your Main Character a pretty stable person who seems to get stuck solving problems for his or her eccentric family and friends? *Everybody Loves Raymond*.

In developing your story, use the paints that are already in the tray. Leave the series the way it is and work with what you've already got.

Try testing the premise. See if you can come up with a story that really goes to the heart of what the series is about.

You already know and love the series you have chosen to spec. What story would you most like to tell using these characters and this premise? I'll bet you have a special insight into your favorite series. Can you share that insight in a story?

YOUR "TO DO" LIST

1) *Clearly and completely define the premise of the series you have chosen.* The premise of any series is the central problem that the characters are trying to work out. The *Friends* pursued careers and love in an attempt to find their place in the adult world. On *The Brady Bunch*, Carol Ann and Michael Brady were trying to successfully blend their two families. On *The Office*, the characters endure the stifling boredom and petty rivalries of the work place. On *My Name Is Earl*, a former loser is trying to right all the wrongs he has committed in his life. (This is one of the simplest and clearest premises ever for a sitcom, and therefore runs the risk of becoming tiresome.) What is the central problem that the characters on your series are trying to work out? Your spec story should involve the characters in addressing that central problem.

2) *Clearly and completely define your Main Character.* Is it hard to tell if your Main Character is Active or Reactive? Sometimes it is. The best way I've found to answer that question is to rephrase it: Is your Main Character creating the hubbub in this week's episode or trying to fix it? Try to list as many aspects of your Main Character's personality as you can remember. These are the springboards to your story. What aspects of your Main Character's personality get him or her into trouble every week? Is he or she jealous, competitive, selfish, immature, controlling, lazy, neurotic, naïve, outspoken, dumb, horny? In which situations have you most enjoyed watching your Main Character? When he or she is in a jam? When he or she is pulling off a scam? When he or she is knocked down a peg? When he or she is an underdog?

3) *Clearly and completely define the formula of the series you have chosen.* How does the premise of the series combine with the personality of the Main Character to generate stories? Ray Barone's easy-going nature came into constant conflict with his meddling mother and his formidable wife. Bernie Mac's "I'm the king of my castle" attitude was regularly challenged and derailed by the needs and demands of his wife and

children. Michael Scott's immaturity, selfishness and irresponsibility create endless new problems for everyone at *The Office*. The right story for your spec episode will evolve from the unique way in which you combine the premise of the series with the personality of your Main Character.

4) As you zero in on the story you want to tell, ask yourself, "Is it real?"

CHAPTER 4

STRUCTURING
YOUR STORY

Early in my career, I drove over to Paramount Studios for a
meeting with Lowell Ganz. (He'd go on to write a bunch of
hit movies, including *Splash*, *City Slickers*, *Robots* and *Fever Pitch*.) At the time,
Lowell was the Head Writer of *Laverne and Shirley*, which was a big hit series
at the time. Number one in the ratings week after week. Lowell explained to
me and a group of other young freelance writers how to structure a story for
Laverne and Shirley. Lowell's advice to us went something like this: "First, we
think, 'Wouldn't it be funny if Shirley's head got stuck in a cake?' Then we
construct a story that *gets* Shirley's head stuck in a cake."

SEVEN PLOT ELEMENTS

When you're trying to develop a TV sitcom story, and you haven't done it
before — or you haven't been able to do it successfully — I've found that
it helps to break the story down into *Seven Plot Elements*. Sometimes this
process can oversimplify the structure, and certainly there are exceptions
to the rule, but if you're just starting out and trying to get a handle on how
to cobble a sitcom story together, I'm confident that these Seven Plot
Elements will help you.

First Goal (Active Main Character) or **First Problem** (Reactive Main
Character)
The Main Character discovers something that he or she wants or is con-
fronted with a problem that he or she must solve.
Obstacle
Something or someone gets in the way of the Main Character achieving the
goal or solving the problem.

First Action (*unwise decision*)

The Main Character must take some action to overcome the Obstacle and achieve the goal or solve the problem. In sitcom, this action almost always involves the Main Character making an *unwise decision*.

Act Break

The First Action backfires, and the Main Character finds himself even further from the goal or with an even bigger problem to solve.

Second Goal

The Main Character devises a desperate Plan B to solve the new problems created by the First Action and get back on track toward achieving the First Goal or solving the First Problem.

Second Action

The Main Character puts Plan B to work. Things get even worse.

Resolution

The goal is achieved or the problem is solved. Sitcom Resolutions often involve an ironic twist. An Active Main Character may discover that he or she has been pursuing a false or superficial goal. A Reactive Main Character may discover that the problem could have been solved more easily with a "wise decision" rather than with the *unwise decision* that the character chose.

USING THE SEVEN PLOT ELEMENTS TO DEVELOP YOUR STORY

To get you familiar with how to use these Seven Plot Elements in developing your spec sitcom story, let's develop a story for a spec episode of *Frasier*.

I chose *Frasier* instead of, say, *Seinfeld* or *Everybody Loves Raymond*, or even a current series like *My Name Is Earl*, for a number of good reasons:

1) I say "learn from the best." So let's learn from one of the best sitcoms ever.

2) Strong central stories. *Seinfeld* followed all the rules that I'm about to lay out for you, but I want a series that had a strong central story in each episode. *Seinfeld* used complex multiple story lines that are more difficult to master if you're just starting out.

3) Active Main Character. An Active Main Character like Frasier is a better learning tool than a Reactive Main Character when you are just starting out because it's easier to see how the Main Character drives the story. If you can learn to write an Active Main Character like Frasier, you can easily adapt those skills to a Reactive Main Character like Ray Barone.

4) Familiarity. Almost everyone has seen *Frasier*, so I don't have to spend time getting you familiar with the premise or the characters. When I teach classes, I find that I save myself a lot of time and save the students a lot of confusion if I talk about series that almost everyone already knows. If perchance you've been living in Uzbekistan for the last two decades and haven't seen *Frasier*, it is running somewhere in syndication every day. At the time of this writing, *Frasier* reruns could be seen daily on Lifetime. *Frasier* episodes are also available for rent on DVD from NetFlix.

5) Avoiding temptation. If I used *Two and a Half Men* or another well-written current series as an example, some unscrupulous reader might be tempted to borrow from what is discussed in this book. *Frasier* is out of production now, so you won't be writing a spec episode of that series.

6) The vagaries of fate and television scheduling. Even if I decided to flaunt temptation and show you how to write a spec episode of some current hit, how can we be sure that current hit would still be on the air once you read this book? Remember *Eight Rules for Dating My Teenage Daughter*? I bet a lot of aspiring writers wrote spec episodes of that series. Why not? It was a good show and a big hit. And then John Ritter, the star, tragically died.

The strong yet simple premise of *Frasier*, and the unusually well-developed characters, make it the best tool that I could find for explaining how to use the Seven Plot Elements to structure a sitcom story.

So here we go: To create a story for *Frasier*, we'll use the premise of the series about Dr. Frasier Crane, the intellectual and neurotic psychiatrist from *Cheers* who was spun off as the host of a Seattle call-in radio show produced by the randy Roz Doyle. Frasier shares a luxurious apartment with his father, Martin, a down-to-earth retired cop, and Martin's quirky physical therapist, Daphne Moon. Frasier is frequently involved in one-upmanship with his equally snobby brother, Dr. Niles Crane.

Frasier's pomposity, his insecurity, his desire to prove himself was central to his character on *Cheers*, and became the driving force behind his character on *Frasier*.

We know from the series formula that in nearly every episode Frasier's ego and his insecurity are going to get him in some kind of trouble with his family, his co-workers, his neighbors, or with the high-society world in which he circulates. We'll let our premise and the personality of our Main Character work together to generate a story.

If your series has an Active Main Character like Frasier, your story needs a **First Goal** for that character that springs organically from the character's established personality. Remember how Lucy wanted a new hat because Caroline Appleby had one? What kind of similar goal can we create for Frasier? As regular viewers of *Frasier*, we know that Frasier is always trying to improve his social status. He's a snob. He's competitive. He's highly sophisticated and equally childish. So as a **First Goal**, let's say that:

1) Frasier wants to be president of his opera club. He happily begins his campaign, confident of victory.

Our story now needs an **Obstacle** for Frasier, something or someone who will get in the way of Frasier achieving his goal. Because we want our script to demonstrate that we understand the series we have chosen to spec, the Obstacle should also be organic to the series. As our **Obstacle**, let's say that:

2) Frasier discovers to his horror that Niles is running against him for president of the opera club.

Frasier would be very upset to find his brother as his opponent, wouldn't he? This would create conflict between Frasier and Niles. Now we're starting to have some fun. Already we're eager to know how this is going to turn out.

Having decided on a **First Goal** for Frasier and having planted an

Obstacle preventing Frasier from achieving his goal, the Main Character must now take a **First Action** to overcome the Obstacle and achieve his First Goal. At this moment in a situation comedy, the Main Character will almost always make an *unwise decision*. There is no comedy without an *unwise decision*. If Frasier acted wisely either by withdrawing from the race for president of the opera club, or deciding to be mature and face his brother in a clean campaign, the story wouldn't be very interesting to watch, would it?

The fun of a situation comedy is watching the characters give in to the same human frailties that plague us all. Situation comedy usually exaggerates the degree to which the characters surrender to their shortcomings, but that's the fun. As viewers, we get to watch our favorite characters behave in a very human way, but we also get to feel superior to them because we probably wouldn't behave as foolishly as they are behaving. (Or at least we can let ourselves *think* that we wouldn't.)

In order to achieve his First Goal of becoming president of the opera club, Frasier must now take a First Action to overcome the Obstacle of Niles running against him. Frasier's First Action will involve an *unwise decision*. The *unwise decision* must spring organically from Frasier's established personality. So based on what we already know about Frasier from watching him over the years, what First Action do you think he would take? What *unwise decision* will Frasier make to overcome the Obstacle of Niles?

Let's say that as his First Action:

3) Frasier tries to discredit Niles.

By making this *unwise decision*, the Main Character is upping the stakes of the story. His *unwise decision* is going to make matters worse. This happens to all of us from time to time, doesn't it? In order to get what we want, we make an *unwise decision* and take action that only increases our troubles. This is normal human behavior. This is real. When our *unwise decision* unwittingly makes matters worse, the Obstacle we were trying to overcome just gets bigger, and we end up further away from our First Goal than when we started. Our plan backfires on us. This has happened to everyone.

This is precisely what ought to happen to Frasier now. His First Action should backfire and make everything worse. His attempt to discredit Niles should put Frasier further away from his goal than when he started.

Why?

In part, because that's what seems to happen in real life. But practically speaking, and for the purpose of a sitcom episode, Frasier's First Action has to backfire right now and make everything worse because we are already approaching the middle of our story. We are about to stop the story and go away for a commercial. So we want to leave Frasier in a real mess that our viewers or reader will be eager to see resolved. We want the viewer or reader to feel a rooting interest in Frasier somehow resolving his problem or achieving his goal.

As the writer, you need to create a cliffhanger at this moment that will draw the audience back after the commercial. This cliffhanger moment — where everything has gotten worse because of the *unwise decision* and the First Action that followed it — is called the **Act Break**.

If Frasier's First Action is to discredit Niles, how can that First Action backfire in a way that is organic to the series, spring from the personality of our main character and make matters worse, thus creating a cliffhanger moment for our **Act Break**?

What if Frasier makes unfair accusations against Niles in front of the opera club? Niles would be furious, wouldn't he? An embarrassing and nasty argument could break out between Frasier and Niles in front of the entire club. Here's a wonderful irony. Our snobby, ambitious characters, Frasier and Niles, are hissing like cats in front of the people they most want to impress, and the people who are least likely to tolerate their unseemly behavior. Our cliffhanger moment could be that:

(Act Break) Frasier and Niles are both disqualified from running for president and asked to leave.

At the Act Break then, Frasier's *unwise decision* and First Action have backfired and made matters worse. Frasier is now further from his First

Goal than when he started. Our reader or viewer has a rooting interest in coming back from the commercial to see how Frasier will get himself out of this mess.

What I have laid out so far is one-half of a sitcom story. I started out with a First Goal for Frasier — becoming president of the opera club. If Frasier simply ran for office and got elected president with no problems it'd be a pretty boring half-hour, wouldn't it? Because real life seldom works out so smoothly, I added an Obstacle for Frasier: His brother, Niles, is running against him for president of the opera club. Niles is an organic obstacle because it has been well-established on *Frasier* that Frasier and Niles are competitive. I am using the paints that are already in the tray. The premise of the series — about a radio personality in Seattle and his mismatched family — works with the personality of the main character — a pompous, egocentric social climber — to produce a story.

The reader or viewer reaches the Act Break eager to see how the story will be resolved.

What might the second half of our story be?

Frasier's in a real mess, isn't he? His own personality, his human frailty, has gotten him into trouble. He has been disqualified from running for president of the opera club. He is further from his First Goal than when he started. His *unwise decision* and First Action have backfired and made the Obstacle even larger. Frasier has to do something now to solve the new and bigger problem before he can ever get back to his First Goal of becoming president of the opera club.

Frasier now must clean up the mess that he created with his First Action. He can't run for president if he has been disqualified. Frasier needs to show the members of the opera club that he isn't as immature as he seemed at the meeting. We also have Niles in the same predicament. What then is a logical **Second Goal** for Frasier, given what we have established so far?

Let's say that after Frasier and Niles get done blaming each other for their mutual predicament:

4) Frasier and Niles decide that they need to work together to get back in the race.

That's the **Second Goal**.

The only way to accomplish the Second Goal is to take a **Second Action**. Since Frasier and Niles have agreed to work together as the Second Goal, it seems logical that the Second Action would be to:

5) Return to the opera club and attempt to be respectful of one another. If they can get back in the race, at least one of them has a chance at becoming president.

Just as the First Action made matters worse, the Second Action is going to complicate things even more.

Why?

For one thing, your Main Character should now be in a heightened emotional state. His original plans have gone awry. He is worse off than when he started. When we are upset we get desperate, and our behavior becomes even more illogical. Your Main Character will be desperate by the time he resorts to the Second Action. His desperation will cause him to behave even more irrationally than he did during the First Action.

One of the persistent themes of situation comedy is that human beings overreact to minor problems. We find ourselves in competition or conflict with a meddling parent, a jealous sibling, a romantic rival, an ambitious co-worker, a rebellious child or a nosy neighbor. Our survival instinct overwhelms us. We make unwise decisions based on our heightened emotions. We take action that only complicates matters, and we end up worse off than when we started. Watching characters on a sitcom dig themselves into a deeper and deeper hole is fun. It's why we tune in every week. It reassures us that other human beings are as silly as we are.

As the **Second Action**, Frasier and Niles return to the opera club in an effort to get back in the race for president. Frasier is still trying to accomplish his First Goal of becoming president of the opera club.

It's important that your Main Character never loses sight of that First Goal. He is always trying to get back to it.

Frasier and Niles make a real effort to be respectful of one another. But of course they can't pull it off. Because of the established personalities of the characters this Second Action quickly deteriorates into more bickering. Frasier and Niles not only lose the presidency, but they are kicked out of the opera club forever.

At this moment, all seems lost for Frasier. He has no chance now of accomplishing his First Goal. Because of his human frailty, he is worse off than when he started.

So what happens next?

We've played out our First Goal, Obstacle, First Action, Act Break, Second Goal and Second Action. Now the characters must reach a **Resolution**. How do we logically resolve this story?

When I was producing sitcoms, it was pretty normal for the writers to get stuck plotting out a story. Often we'd hit a point where we didn't know what the characters should do next. When that happened, I would always ask the same question: *Why are we telling this story?*

Maybe we didn't know why we were telling the story, and it was time to figure it out. Maybe we did know, and we'd just lost sight of it for a minute. Sitcom stories work best when they have a theme: when there's a reason for telling the story. If you know why you are telling a story, you never get lost. You can always figure out what the characters should do next.

Why are we telling this *Frasier* story? I ask that question at this moment because the answer is going to lead us logically to the **Resolution**.

What's this *Frasier* story about? It's partly about running for president of the opera club. But how are the premise of the series and the personality of the main character working together to produce this story?

Part of the premise of any series is the relationships of the characters. Part of the premise of *Frasier* is the relationship between Frasier and Niles. This *Frasier* episode is really about their sibling rivalry, which was mined again and again on *Frasier*. In our story, we are exploring how Frasier and Niles' similar interests have made them furiously competitive. That's the theme of the episode so far. So if the theme of the episode, at least at this point in our story development, is the relationship between Frasier and Niles, and the lengths to which the two men will go to outdo each other, then our Resolution is going to involve that dynamic.

As our **Resolution**, let's say that:

6) Frasier and Niles admit that their sibling rivalry caused the problem.

This also harkens back to the premise of the series: Frasier's human frailty — in his case, pomposity and vanity — constantly getting him in trouble.

Frasier and Niles' realization that their sibling rivalry caused their problem brings about the **Resolution**. They realize how foolish they have been. They rediscover that their relationship as brothers is more important than outdoing each other. They patch things up between them. But just so things don't get too sappy, we might end the story with Frasier and Niles vowing to form a new and even snobbier opera club in which one of them would be guaranteed the job of president.

TWO-ACT FRAMEWORK

We saw in this exercise that every sitcom story has two basic parts.

Part One includes the First Goal, the Obstacle, and the First Action, all leading up to the Act Break.

Part Two is the Second Goal, the Second Action, and the Resolution.

I'm sure you see that the two parts form **two acts**.

Situation comedies have traditionally used this *Two-Act Framework*.

As I pointed out earlier, sitcoms have two acts because there's a commercial break in the middle of the episode. The Two-Act Framework exists to serve that commercial break. As folks in television have cynically pointed out for decades, the shows are really there to fill up the space between the commercials. If networks could get away with it, they'd run commercials twenty-four hours a day and not produce any shows. Operating a network would be pure profit. Luckily for writers, actors, directors, makeup artists and everyone else who works on a TV series, networks need to fill up the space between the commercials. Thus, we have the Two-Act Framework for half-hour situation comedies.

The First Act of your story must use a First Goal, an Obstacle, and a First Action which together build to a cliffhanger at the Act Break.

We need this cliffhanger at the Act Break so the audience will come back after the commercial. So how do you get the audience to come back after the commercials and watch the Second Act of the show? You structure the First Act so that your Main Character is in a real mess at the middle, and the audience can't wait to learn how it all comes out.

If you have a Reactive Main Character, then the First Goal will instead become the First Problem that the main character has to solve. Remember the *Newhart* episode I mentioned in the last chapter where Dick Loudon discovered a body in the basement of his Vermont inn? Instead of a First Goal, that episode started with a First Problem: Dick Loudon needed a new furnace for his inn.

The Obstacle was the revelation that a body was buried in the basement, right where the furnace was supposed to go. The First Action was Dick and Joanna Loudon going to the local pastor to find out more about the woman buried in their basement. The Act Break was Dick and Joanna learning from the pastor that Mrs. Newton, the woman buried in their basement, was a witch.

The First Action made matters worse for Dick Loudon because it led to the discovery that the body buried in his basement was a witch. At the Act Break, Dick was further from solving his First Problem — the need for a new furnace — than when he started. Did Dick make an *unwise decision* by going to see the pastor? Technically, no. With a Reactive Main Character like Dick Loudon, the *unwise decision* is often the logical thing to do. But the First Action still leads to a worsening of the problem. Because Dick went to see the pastor and learned the truth about the body in his basement, the Obstacle got bigger.

Frasier is an Active Main Character. He is driving the story. He's making things happen. He's getting himself into trouble with his established personality. Lucy did the same kinds of things.

Dick Loudon is a Reactive Main Character. The story is driving Dick.

Dick is faced with a problem that he didn't create. He's doing his best to solve the problem. Ray Barone might behave in the same way.

Your story will follow a logical course based on whether your Main Character is Active or Reactive. Your first step in structuring your story is to make sure that your Main Character has a First Goal that he or she wants to achieve or a First Problem that he or she needs to solve. Your second step is to create an Obstacle that stands between your Main Character and success. That Obstacle should be organic to the series. The Obstacle can be another character like Niles or some established element in the series, like Dick Loudon's historical Vermont inn. In other words, the Obstacle exists already in the series' landscape. That's what makes it organic. You just need to pluck it out and apply it to your story.

The Second Act of your story will involve your Main Character, in a heightened emotional state, setting a Second Goal. The Main Character will then take a Second Action to achieve the Second Goal, still trying desperately to get back to that First Goal. The Second Action will make everything worse, until a logical Resolution is reached.

This is the Two-Act Framework.

Occasionally, a sitcom will use a Three-Act Framework with two commercial breaks. Don't worry. The Seven Plot Elements will still help you to structure your story.

If the series you choose to spec uses the Three-Act Framework (and it probably doesn't), watch to see where the Act Breaks fall. The first Act Break may occur with the arrival of the Obstacle. The second Act Break may occur when the First Action backfires. But the Seven Plot Elements will still be there, in the same order, even if the episode is structured into three acts instead of two.

SIX-SCENE TEMPLATE

Let's go back to the *Frasier* opera club story. I'm sure you noticed that I broke each of the two main parts of the story — the two acts — into three numbered sections.

Part One (Act One) — 1) First Goal. Frasier wants to be president of his opera club. He happily begins his campaign, confident of victory. 2) Obstacle. Frasier discovers to his horror that Niles is running against him. A rift opens between Frasier and Niles. Frasier makes the *unwise decision* to double-cross his brother. 3) First Action. Frasier tries to discredit Niles. Frasier and Niles' bickering gets them both disqualified. Act Break.

Part Two (Act Two) — 4) Second Goal. Frasier and Niles want to get back in the race. 5) Second Action. Frasier and Niles attempt to respect each other. They fall back into bickering and are tossed out of the club. 6) Resolution. Frasier and Niles realize that sibling rivalry caused the problem. They vow to form their own better opera club.

This story has a total of six sections, three in each of the two parts. In other words, the story has two acts, and a total of six scenes.

I call this the *Six-Scene Template*: Three scenes in the First Act, three more scenes in the Second Act.

When you combine the Two-Act Framework with the Six-Scene Template, you get the standard sitcom structure:

Act One: 1) First Goal or First Problem; 2) Obstacle; 3) First Action; Act Break.

Act Two: 4) Second Goal or Second Problem; 5) Second Action; 6) Resolution.

Sitcoms used to follow the Six-Scene Template almost slavishly, but since *Seinfeld*, half-hour series are rarely this symmetrical anymore. Maybe the change occurred due to decreased attention span in the audience or just boredom with the form, but I noticed that *Seinfeld* really broke the mold. Today, there may be four scenes in the First Act and only one scene in the Second Act, or nine scenes in the First Act and seven scenes in the Second Act.

But the Six-Scene Template remains helpful in plotting out your story because it allows you to integrate the Seven Plot Elements properly into your story. How can you develop the story for your spec sitcom episode using the Two-Act Structure and the Six-Scene Template?

Establish a First Goal or First Problem for your Main Character.

Establish an Obstacle that makes the First Goal difficult to reach or the First Problem a challenge to solve. The Obstacle should be organic to the series. (Frasier's Obstacle was Niles. Dick Loudon's Obstacle was a body buried under his Vermont inn.)

Your Main Character will decide on a First Action, something he or she does to overcome the Obstacle and achieve the First Goal or solve the First Problem. The Main Character's First Action will either be an *unwise decision* based on the character's established personality or a logical choice that nevertheless exacerbates the problem. When the First Action inevitably backfires or presents a new and more difficult problem, your Main Character will be further from his original goal or will face an even bigger challenge at the Act Break.

In Act Two, your Main Character is faced with a newer and bigger challenge than he or she started out with. He or she will be further from the First Goal than when the story began. Frasier wanted to be president of his opera club. Now he has been disqualified from even running. Dick Loudon needed a new furnace. Now he discovers that a witch is buried in his basement.

Your Main Character must now develop a Second Goal that he or she believes will clean up the mess and get back to achieving that First Goal or solving that First Problem. At this point in the story, your Main Character ought to be in a heightened emotional state. His original plans have gone haywire. He's frustrated and upset or more confused than ever.

Because your Main Character is now feeling desperate, his Second Action will likely be even more unwise than his First Action.

The Second Action will create even bigger problems, forcing your Main Character to suffer further humiliation or to rally his courage and convictions, eventually leading to a Resolution.

In the Second Act of our *Frasier* story, Frasier and Niles have both been disqualified from running for president of the opera club. Though they blame each other, they set a Second Goal of reentering the race. They realize that the only way that either of them has a chance to become president of the opera club is to try to work together. As pompous intellectuals,

Frasier and Niles are confident that they can overcome their petty squabbling and behave as mature men. As viewers, we know from experience that Frasier and Niles are children, and that they will regress into even more childish bickering.

Frasier and Niles' attempt at cooperation is their Second Action, but their established personalities take over and this leads inevitably to still more bickering which gets them thrown out of the opera club for good, culminating in a Resolution where the two brothers accept responsibility for their actions, but remain in character by resolving to form another, even snobbier club.

In the *Newhart* episode, Dick Loudon discovers at the Act Break that the body buried in his basement is a witch. In Act Two, Dick sets a Second Goal. He wants Mrs. Newton's name expunged from the "witch list" and her body moved from his basement to the church graveyard where it belongs.

Dick Loudon's Second Action clears Mrs. Newton's name, but relocating her body becomes a bigger problem. A kid arrives from the local mortuary and discovers that he will have to dig up a buried witch. The kid bolts.

Desperate now, Dick calls on the macabre trio of Larry, Darryl and Darryl. The three local characters frighten Dick and Joanna. Dick summons his courage and hires them anyway. Dick finds to his relief that Larry, Darryl and Darryl are happy to dig up the body, thus creating the Resolution.

The Two-Act Framework helps you to break your story down into two main parts, or two acts. Each act has to build to a climax. Your First Act builds to a climax at the Act Break. Your Second Act builds to a climax at the Resolution.

The Six-Scene Template helps you break down each of your two acts into three distinct parts. I think when you break down the elements in this way, structuring your story doesn't seem so daunting. There's logic to it; a pattern.

You still have plenty of work to do coming up with a unique and creative First Goal or First Problem for your Main Character, then adding the other elements in a clever and logical way drawing on the personality of the Main Character and the premise of the series — the paints that are already in the tray. But now you have a road map for structuring your story using the Two-Act Framework and the Six-Scene Template.

When I was writing and producing sitcoms, we used all these same guidelines every week in structuring our stories. This is the way the pros do it. You might as well do it the same way.

HOW WE DID IT ON *COACH*

Here's an episode of *Coach* that I wrote in which we used the premise of the series and the personality of the Main Character to arrive at a First Goal, the organic elements of the series to create an Obstacle, and then log-ically developed the rest of the story using the paints that were already in the tray.

Writer's credit for an episode of *Coach*.

We decided we wanted to do an episode about a poker game. A poker game made sense as a story area for *Coach* based on the premise of the series about a competitive and macho football coach. It seemed logical to us that Hayden Fox would host a weekly card game. It also seemed logical that our two supporting male characters, Luther and Dauber, played by Jerry Van Dyke and Bill Fagerbakke, would be regular players in Hayden's weekly game.

What other organic element from the series could we add to this poker game to give us a First Goal for Hayden Fox, an Obstacle, and a First Action that would get Hayden into a big mess at the Act Break?

We had established a recurring character on the series, Judy Watkins, the women's basketball coach, played by Pam Stone. Because Judy had already appeared in a few episodes, she qualified as an organic element of the series. She was Dauber's girlfriend. Judy was as competitive and aggressive as Hayden Fox. She was as tall as Hayden Fox and not the least bit intimidated by him. They hated each other. We decided that Judy Watkins was the perfect organic element from the landscape of the series to interject into Hayden Fox's weekly poker game. Judy became our Obstacle standing between Hayden and an enjoyable poker game.

Using the Seven Plot Elements, we began our First Scene with an argument between Hayden and Judy over a movie projector. Dauber entered in the middle of the argument with news that one of the other coaches couldn't make it to Hayden's regular weekly poker game that evening. Hayden was upset. He loved his weekly poker game because he won every week. Hayden's First Goal became salvaging his poker game so he could keep winning. Who else could they get to play? Dauber suggested they let Judy play. Judy was not intimidated by Hayden. She would be a formidable opponent. Judy became the Obstacle keeping Hayden from his guaranteed victory at the poker table.

Based on Hayden's established personality it made logical sense to us that Hayden would make the *unwise decision* of trying to intimidate Judy at the poker game. In the second scene, Hayden's First Action was to become more competitive than ever before because he was playing against his arch rival. He made a pot of very spicy chili to upset Judy's concentration, and upped the stakes of the poker game. Based on Judy's established personality, it made logical sense to us that Judy would be a cracker-jack poker player with a cast-iron stomach. We were using the paints that were already in the tray. Now we needed Hayden's First Action to backfire. We needed to make things even worse for Hayden and move him further from his First Goal in order to get us to a compelling Act Break.

In our Third Scene, later in the poker game, Hayden had lost every hand to Judy. Hayden's competitive drive only increased. He became desperate. In the final hand, Hayden bet his truck. Judy won. The First Action of the Main Character — his attempt to intimidate his rival by upping the stakes of the poker game — completely backfired. He suffered a humiliating defeat at the Act Break. Hayden's First Goal was to win at poker. Judy was the Obstacle standing in his way. Due to Hayden's *unwise decision* and First Action, he had now lost his truck to Judy. He was further from his First Goal than when he started. The audience was eager to return after the commercial to see what would happen next.

Coming back from the commercial, we wanted to reintroduce our story and show the consequences in Act Two of Hayden's foolish behavior in Act One. We also wanted to give Hayden the motivation for his Second Goal and Second Action in Act Two.

In our Fourth Scene at the top of Act Two, we compounded the loss of Hayden's truck with the additional indignity of Hayden having to ride to work on a child's bicycle in a rain storm. Hayden arrived at his office wet, furious, and even more humiliated, all because of his behavior in Act One. Hayden set a Second Goal of getting even with Judy. He insisted on another poker game that evening.

The point of the episode was to show Hayden's personality getting the best of him. That's why we were telling the story. Like Frasier, Hayden Fox was an Active Main Character. (Active Main Characters are usually very flawed personalities. Reactive Main Characters are funny, but closer to normal people.) As an active and flawed character, Hayden's ego and his insecurity frequently got him into trouble.

It logically followed that we would make matters worse for Hayden with his Second Action.

As the Fifth Scene opened, another poker game was under way, and already Judy had won more of Hayden's money. Hayden was now in a heightened emotional state. He was desperate. The Second Action evolved from Hayden's desperation. He makes another unwise decision that increases his troubles. Hayden bet his retirement property. The other players were stunned. They tried to reason with Hayden, but Hayden's competitive drive had overcome him. At this moment, Christine Armstrong — Hayden's girlfriend, played by the delightful Shelley Fabares — arrived at Hayden's cabin.

Christine was Hayden's conscience, his Jiminy Cricket. She loved Hayden and accepted his flaws. Hayden respected Christine and loved her. If anyone was going to get Hayden to listen to reason, it was Christine. So it made logical sense for Christine to show up at the moment of greatest peril. Like the cavalry in a Western, Christine arrived in the nick of time.

In the Sixth Scene of the episode, Christine took Hayden outside where Hayden admitted that he had made a fool of himself. Judy was a better poker player. On the series that season Hayden was suffering defeat after defeat on the football field. He confessed to Christine that the poker game was the only place where he got to win every week. Now Judy had ruined that for him. Hayden felt that his life had hit rock bottom. All seemed lost. Christine reminded Hayden that she still loved him. He hadn't lost *everything*. Hayden realized that it was time to quit. The Resolution came when Hayden went back inside, admitted defeat, and accepted his humiliation, thus showing courage that redeemed him.

This was a completely organic episode of *Coach*. There were no guest stars, only the reappearance of a recurring character. We wrote a story about the Main Character. We developed a story that exploited elements of the Main Character's personality. We drew from the premise of the series about a competitive football coach facing moral dilemmas. We used the series formula. We utilized the Seven Plot Elements and the Six-Scene Template. We found a new way to explore what had been previously established. We used the paints that were already in the tray.

GOING TO WORK ON YOUR STORY

How closely should you follow the Six-Scene Template?

When structuring the story for your spec episode, should you always put the First Goal in the First Scene, the Obstacle in the Second Scene, and the First Action and Act Break in the Third Scene?

It depends on the story and on the particular series you have chosen to spec.

In the *Coach* episode, the First Goal and the Obstacle both occurred during the First Scene. The First Action played out over the Second Scene and Third Scene. You have to feel your way through this and see what serves your story best. I suggest that you construct your story using the Seven Plot Elements only, not worrying yet about scenes.

Establish your First Goal, Obstacle, *unwise decision*, First Action, and Act Break. The Act Break will always occur at the end of the First Act in any sitcom script, but the end of your First Act might not arrive until Scene Seven.

To help you structure your story, look at the series you have chosen to spec. If the writers of the series usually include six or seven scenes in their First Act, you may need to spread the Seven Plot Elements of your story among numerous scenes. The First Goal might logically be in the First Scene. The Obstacle might show up in the Second Scene. But the First Action might have several parts and be divided up over two or three scenes. Look at the sample script that you ordered from Planet MegaMall. Maybe you were really smart and ordered several sample scripts. Great idea! Identify where the writers of that series usually place the First Goal, the Obstacle, and the First Action. We know where the Act Break is going to occur. See if there's a pattern to the way they distribute the Seven Plot Elements. Count how many scenes they usually write into each act. I'm confident that if you look for patterns in the series that you have chosen to spec you will find them. These patterns will guide you toward the proper structure for your First and Second Acts.

TURNING PLOT ELEMENTS INTO SCENES

Let's use the Seven Plot Elements from the Frasier opera club story and break those elements down into individual scenes.

The numbered sections for Act One went like this:

1) First Goal: Frasier wants to be president of his opera club. He begins his campaign with confidence.

2) Obstacle: Frasier discovers that Niles is running against him.

3) First Action: Frasier tries to discredit Niles. Bickering gets Frasier and Niles disqualified. Act Break.

If you look at these three sections, it's pretty obvious that *Element #3* is going to occur at the opera club meeting. That's a scene. The opera club headquarters will probably have to be a Swing Set — an extra set constructed specifically for this episode — but this scene might also occur in Frasier's apartment. Perhaps Frasier is hosting the opera club. For now, though, let's say that Scene 3 is going to take place at the opera club.

Element #2 likely will be another scene and also could take place in Frasier's apartment. Frasier is practicing his campaign speech for the presidency of the opera club when Niles comes over and announces that he is running, too. The two men could quarrel. Niles could exit in a huff.

Element #2 could also take place at Nervosa, the coffee bar. Perhaps Frasier enters, brimming with excitement about his candidacy, and finds Niles already at their regular table working on his campaign speech. A quarrel erupts. Frasier leaves in a huff. That sounds like a good idea, so for now let's say that Element #2 becomes Scene 2 and takes place at Nervosa.

Element #1 is now logically going to be Scene 1. Scene 1 could take place at the radio station. As Frasier finishes his radio show, he learns that the president of his opera club has died. Frasier feigns sadness for a moment, then is consumed with ambition to succeed the deceased leader. We might then convert the elements of the First Act of the *Frasier* opera club episode into scenes as follows:

Act One — Scene 1 — Radio Station — Frasier learns of the death of the president of his opera club. The presidency, an office that Frasier has coveted for years, is suddenly vacant. Frasier determines to win that office.

Act One — Scene 2 — Nervosa — Frasier enters, needing a latte to energize him for the campaign ahead, only to discover that Niles is after the same goal. A quarrel erupts. Frasier leaves in a huff.

Act One — Scene 3 — The Opera Club — Frasier follows Niles to the podium for his campaign speech. Frasier turns his speech into a vicious attack on Niles. Another quarrel erupts between the brothers. Both men are disqualified. The sergeant-at-arms tosses them out. Act Break.

Let's quickly lay out our Second Act in the same way.

4) Second Goal: Frasier and Niles want to get back in the race.

5) Second Action: Frasier and Niles attempt to respect each other. They fall back into bickering and are tossed out of the club.

6) Resolution: Frasier and Niles realize that sibling rivalry caused the problem. They vow to form their own better opera club.

Element #4 also seems to be a scene. Let's make that Scene 4 and place it back at Frasier's apartment after the opera club meeting.

Element #5 is at the opera club meeting. We'll make that Scene 5.

Element #6 might take place back at Frasier's apartment. Let's make that Scene 6.

Now our Second Act would lay out as follows:

Act Two — Scene 4 — Frasier's Apartment — Frasier and Niles return. They quarrel more, blaming each other for their predicament. They decide to be mature and work together. May the best man win!

Act Two — Scene 5 — The Opera Club — An attempt at decorum quickly degenerates into more bickering. Both men are expelled from the club.

Act Two — Scene 6 — Frasier's Apartment — The tragic aftermath. Admissions of guilt from both brothers. A vow to start a new club.

By using the Seven Plot Elements, we have been able to successfully structure our *Frasier* story and then break it down into scenes. It was all pretty logical, wasn't it?

FAMILIAR SETS

As you're thinking about how to structure your story and where to place the action of each scene, keep in mind that you want to begin your episode in one of the regular sets. You don't want to begin your spec episode in a set we've never seen before. We wouldn't want to begin our opera club episode of *Frasier* in the Opera Club set.

The Common Room set from *Newhart.*

Why not?

Writers have learned from experience that audiences prefer to have stories open in a familiar set. When an episode of *Frasier* begins, we want to be instantly comfortable and certain that it's a *Frasier*. Opening your story in a location that we've never seen before is disconcerting to a reader and to the audience. It makes it harder for the audience to get into the story if they are distracted by unfamiliar surroundings.

Your spec script is intended to demonstrate your familiarity with the series you have chosen. Starting with one of the regular sets helps you to demonstrate that you know that series well.

Where does the series you have chosen to spec usually open? *Frasier* often started at the radio station. If the series you have chosen usually starts in a particular set, you'll want to start your episode there as well. Remember that the audience is used to seeing the same sets week after week. Familiarity is part of the appeal of any television series. Viewers tune in week after week to see the same characters in the same surroundings. Sameness is reassuring to the audience. Our own lives are so full of change and upheaval that I think we gravitate to TV series for a sense of stability. Everything is always the same on a TV series. Everything always works out in the end. This comforts us. If you want to write for television, you have to enjoy playing by these rules.

Pay attention to the series you have chosen to spec. Play by their rules. Use the paints that are already in the tray. Make note of the sets they regularly use, and use those sets in your spec script. If you were writing a spec *Frasier*, you'd want to be sure to use the Radio Station, Nervosa and Frasier's Apartment in your story.

"B" STORY

The purpose of your spec script is to show producers that you understand the series you have chosen to spec. You need to demonstrate that you not only understand the Main Character, but that you understand the supporting characters as well.

Staying with our *Frasier* opera club episode, how do Martin, Daphne and Roz figure in this story? They don't yet, do they? The story is about Frasier and Niles, and a good chunk of it takes place at the Opera Club, away from the usual sets. How are we going to get the other regular characters into the episode? The answer is a "B" story — a second, usually smaller plot that parallels the main plot or "A" story.

How do you come up with a "B" story?

How your "A" story lays out will give you clues as to how to use the other characters. Sitcom is logical. Everything fits together in a pattern.

If you were writing the opera club episode which involves only Frasier and Niles, you'd need to come up with a "B" story involving Martin, Daphne and maybe Roz.

Let's look at the structure of our "A" story and let it guide us to our "B" story:

Act One — Scene 1 — Radio Station — Frasier learns of the death of the president of his opera club. The presidency, an office he has coveted for years, is suddenly vacant. Frasier determines to win that office.

Roz is Frasier's producer. She would logically be present as Frasier finishes his radio show. Roz would probably be the person to pass along to Frasier the information that the president of the opera club has died. Someone called while Frasier was on the air and Roz took the call. Having Roz in the scene gives Frasier someone to talk to. You can "get the pipe out" this way — place in dialogue the exposition that explains the story to the viewer. Roz is a blue-collar gal who is critical of Frasier's snobbishness, so you have a chance for comedy as Roz ridicules the opera club.

Act One — Scene 2 — Nervosa — Frasier enters, needing a latte to energize him for the campaign ahead, only to discover that Niles is after the same goal. A quarrel erupts. Frasier leaves in a huff.

Since Scene 3 takes place at the opera club, Scene 2 at Nervosa is our only chance to work Martin and Daphne into the First Act. Martin and Daphne were frequent customers of Nervosa, so it makes sense for them to be there. Perhaps Scene 2 opens with Martin and Daphne having coffee. Martin's birthday is tomorrow night. Daphne asks if Frasier and Niles are taking Martin someplace special. Martin says they haven't mentioned anything. Maybe they've planned a surprise. Frasier enters, bursting with the news about his campaign to become president of the opera club. Frasier mentions an emergency meeting of the opera club for tomorrow night. It's clear that in the excitement about the opera club, Frasier has forgotten Martin's birthday. Martin is a proud man. He won't allow Daphne to set Frasier straight. Niles arrives. Niles has also heard about the death of the opera club president. Frasier learns that Niles is running for president as well. Frasier and Niles quarrel. In the excitement over the opera club, both men have forgotten about their father's birthday. Both men leave, angrily passing Roz on their way out. Roz immediately wishes Martin a happy birthday. Martin storms out. Roz is left with Daphne wondering why everyone is so grumpy.

Now we have a "B" story that involves not only Martin and Daphne, but Roz, Frasier and Niles. The opera club has taken precedence over Martin's birthday.

Act One — Scene 3 — The Opera Club — Frasier follows Niles to the podium for his campaign speech. Frasier turns his speech into a vicious attack on Niles. Another quarrel erupts between the brothers. Both men are disqualified. The sergeant-at-arms tosses them out. Act Break.

This scene will not involve your "B" story.

Act Two — Scene 4 — Frasier's Apartment — Frasier and Niles return. They blame each other. They decide to be mature and work together. May the best man win.

The emergency meeting of the opera club in Scene 3 took place on the night of Martin's birthday. Perhaps we open Act Two with grumpy Martin sitting in his recliner feeling sorry for himself. He won't even eat the birthday cake that Daphne baked for him. Roz drops over with a present for Martin. Martin isn't cheered up. He's too hurt that his sons forgot his birthday. Martin, Daphne and Roz hear Frasier and Niles arguing in the hall, crossing from the elevator to Frasier's front door. In a classic *Frasier* farce, Martin insists that all evidence of his birthday be hidden from Frasier and Niles. Martin doesn't want them feeling guilty now. He's too angry at them. Daphne and Roz scramble to hide the cake, the plates and the presents in the other room. Frasier and Niles enter, quarreling. Both men try to elicit sympathy from their father. Martin, furious over being forgotten, lashes out at both of them. Martin never mentions his birthday, but he tells them both how selfish they are. "Families are supposed to stick together. You two make me sick!" Martin's outburst has the unexpected result of bringing Frasier and Niles back together. Perhaps Daphne is just about to reveal to Frasier and Niles that it's Martin's birthday when Frasier suggests that he and Niles return to the opera club and support each other as their father suggested. Niles loves the idea. They thank their father for his advice and rush out, having missed the birthday again.

Act Two — Scene Five — The Opera Club — An attempt at decorum quickly degenerates into more bickering. Both men are expelled from the club.

No "B" story here, either.

Act Two — Scene Six — Frasier's Apartment — The tragic aftermath. Admissions of guilt from both brothers. A vow to start a new club.

This scene could open with the cake and presents out in view again. Martin, more hurt than ever, still refuses to participate in his birthday. Roz is about to give up and go home. Daphne reminds Martin that she baked him a cake and bought him a present. Roz came over with a present. Maybe his sons disappointed him, but the least he can do is acknowledge the women's thoughtfulness. Martin agrees and starts to open presents when again Frasier and Niles are heard in the hallway. Again Martin insists that everything be hidden. Again Daphne and Roz must scramble to hide the evidence of the birthday celebration. Frasier and Niles enter. Both men are more upset than ever due to the fiasco at the opera club. Daphne has reached the end of her patience. She tells Frasier and Niles that they forgot Martin's birthday. Now both men feel even worse. Their selfishness and competition have not only cost them membership in their opera club, but they've hurt their father as well. Frasier and Niles apologize to Martin. They have learned their lesson. Frasier decides that instead of singing the trite "Happy Birthday to You," they should play a birthday song from one of Frasier's favorite operas. Frasier slips a CD into the stereo as Martin, Daphne and Roz groan. Niles is impressed that Frasier owns the CD for such an obscure and unappreciated opera. He points out that between Frasier's opera collection and his own they are a first-class opera club all by themselves. They get the idea to form a new and better opera club in which one of them is sure to be president. Reinvigorated, Frasier and Niles go into Frasier's room to examine Frasier's opera collection, having forgotten the birthday again.

This "B" story also makes use of the Seven Plot Elements that we used for our "A" story, even though the "B" story unfolds over only three scenes.

Act One — Scene 2 — First Goal or First Problem: It's Martin's birthday. Obstacle: Frasier and Niles have forgotten because of the opera club. Act Two — Scene 4 — First Action: Daphne and Roz remember Martin's birthday. Their efforts backfire, though, with the arrival of Frasier and Niles.

Act Two — Scene 6 — Second Goal: Save Martin's birthday. Daphne makes Martin open a present, but this backfires again with the arrival of Frasier and Niles. Second Action: Daphne rebukes Frasier and Niles for missing the birthday. Both men are mortified. As the "A" and "B" stories meet, Frasier and Niles suffer a bigger humiliation due to their human flaws. Resolution: Frasier and Niles apologize to Martin.

A "B" story like this one dovetails nicely with the "A" story. It involves all the characters, it evolves from the "A" story, and both stories come together in a common theme at the end.

It isn't always possible to blend "A" and "B" stories together so neatly, but it's always worth a try.

MULTIPLE STORY LINES

If the series you have chosen for your spec sitcom episode is an ensemble series like *Scrubs*, you may have to include a "B," "C" and even a "D" story. Sometimes an ensemble series will build an episode around a common theme. In this way, parallel stories can all be moving toward the same conclusion. If you have chosen an ensemble series for your spec episode, it may help you to find a common theme for your episode that all your story lines can follow.

An episode of *Scrubs* followed the theme of the end of residency for the doctors. J.D., Elliot and Turk were all coming to the end of an important phase in their lives. Each character had his or her own story line that sprang from the personality of the character and explored how each character was making that emotional transition.

If you are going to spec an ensemble series, I recommend following all of the guidelines that we have already discussed:

1) Study the series carefully so you "hear it in your head."
2) Choose an "A" story about the Main Character. The story should spring from the personality of the Main Character and the premise of the series.
3) Follow the guidelines specified in this chapter to structure your "A" story.
4) If your "A" story does not include all of the supporting characters, choose a "B" story. Your "B" story should evolve from the "A" story if possible, but certainly should spring from the personality of the supporting character and the premise of the series.

Follow steps 1, 2 and 3 to structure your "B" story.

Follow steps 1, 2, and 3 in developing "C" and "D" stories.

RUNNERS

Occasionally, even after working out a solid "A" and "B" story, you will still have one regular character who just doesn't figure much in either story. I'd try to avoid this circumstance in a spec episode and use all of the regular characters as fully as possible.

But if you find that one of the regular characters just doesn't have much to contribute to either your "A" or "B" stories, you can give that character a "Runner."

A Runner is a small problem or issue for a supporting character that you can plug in at the top or bottom of two or three scenes. A Runner isn't big enough to qualify as a "B" or "C" story. It doesn't require all the elements of First Goal and Obstacle and all that. It is just a running gag that keeps the character alive in the episode.

We did a Runner on an episode of *Coach* in which Luther complained that he'd been thrown out of an All-You-Can-Eat restaurant before he had eaten all he could eat. The humor came from the fact that every time you saw Luther in that episode, usually at the top of a scene, he was complaining again to some new person about how he hadn't been able to eat all he could eat.

If you use a Runner for a supporting character, find one that springs organically from the established personality of that character. Luther was established on *Coach* as a big eater and an obsessive personality, so it was organic to the series for Luther to be ranting about how he had been tossed out of the All-You-Can-Eat restaurant.

Supporting characters on sitcoms all have their little quirks that the audience knows and enjoys from week to week. Think about all the aspects of the supporting character's personality, and then try to find some little problem or attitude that will carry them through the episode.

Seinfeld used several recurring Runners for Kramer. One was Kramer's dream of opening a restaurant where you make your own pizza. Another was Kramer's idea for a coffee-table book about coffee tables.

TRUST YOUR INSTINCTS

Working out an entire sitcom episode is seldom easy. Rooms full of professional writers can spend hours, even days laboring over a story, trying to get it right.

If you find yourself struggling, don't be discouraged. If this were as easy as it looks, everyone would be doing it.

I've tried to lay out the basic structure of a typical sitcom episode as simply as I can. I've given you some rules and guidelines to help make sense of the process. I made it sound simpler than it really is to help you get your head around the formula.

When I was producing network series, and we would break a story for an episode, I had an entire staff at my disposal — sometimes as many as seven other writers all working together. All of us had experience. All of us had talent. All of us had good ideas. We had each other to fill the cup when one of us went dry.

Writing alone can be frustrating and draining. Comedy seems to thrive in a group. So when you are working by yourself, you can get discouraged, lose your bearings, doubt your ability. When I'm working alone, I pitch ideas to my wife and to my friends. Feedback really helps.

One additional piece of advice I have always given to other writers is: *Trust your instincts.* If it feels right, it probably *is* right.

The perfect story for your spec sitcom episode is out there. Once you have a story idea that feels right to you and seems consistent with the series you have chosen to spec, you can now put it together logically based on the guidelines I have provided.

When you find the right story for your spec episode and then structure it correctly, much of your work will be done. You will be standing at the top of the mountain. You will be able to see where you are going and how you are going to get there. The rest is just details.

In the next chapter, we will move on to outlining your story. You haven't done that yet. What we have done is this chapter is called "breaking the story." In structuring a First and Second Act, deciding on a First Goal, Obstacle, First Action, Act Break, Second Goal, Second Action and Resolution, we have laid out the broad strokes of the plot.

Now we have to flesh out the finer points of the story within the individual scenes and then write a Detailed Outline. We'll have to figure out specifically what's going to happen in each scene, refine our story, and solve any story problems.

When you feel confident that you have put together all the elements needed for structuring your story, meet me in the next chapter, and we will start your outline.

CHAPTER RECAP — THE ELEPHANT REMEMBERS

When you feel you have a good idea for your story, take a look at the Seven Plot Elements listed in this chapter and see if your story holds up. You will need a First Goal or First Problem for your Main Character. You will need an Obstacle standing between your Main Character and achieving his or her goal or solving the problem. Your Main Character will need to make an *unwise decision*. Your Main Character will then take a First Action toward achieving the First Goal or solving the First Problem. But because of the *unwise decision*, this First Action will backfire on the Main Character, so that at the Act Break the Main Character will find himself even further away from the First Goal or from solving the First Problem.

In Act Two, your Main Character will be frustrated that his efforts have gone awry. He or she will be in a heightened emotional state. Your Main Character will now set a Second Goal that will involve fixing the mess he or she has created and moving again toward the First Goal. Your Main Character will take a Second Action. Because of your Main Character's heightened emotional state, this Second Action will make matters even worse. Your Main Character will reach a moment where all seems lost. Your Main Character must now suffer a further humiliation and/or summon courage in order to move toward a Resolution of the story.

If your "A" story does not involve all of the regular characters on the series, you will need to come up with a "B" story to service those characters. If you are specing a series that uses multiple story lines, you will probably need a "C" and "D" story as well.

Make sure that you have all of the Seven Plot Elements covered before moving on to the Outline. It might be a good idea to try your story out on someone else. Pitch your story to friends and get their reaction. If there are flaws in your story that you haven't seen, now is the time to discover them. Feedback from another person can alert you to unseen problems. Don't be discouraged if problems crop up. They are a natural part of the process. You can revisit this chapter, fix your story problems, and then move on to your Outline.

YOUR "TO DO" LIST

1) Summarize several actual stories from your favorite shows. Identify each of the Seven Plot Elements within each episode.

2) Write the Seven Plot Elements in big letters on a whiteboard or on a large sketch pad or on note cards that you can tack up on a wall someplace. You don't have to write down any ideas yet. Just write down the Seven Plot Elements and look at them.

3) Study the Seven Plot Elements until you have them memorized. This will get you thinking properly about structure.

4) As you get ideas for each of the Seven Plot Elements, write your ideas next to the appropriate plot element on the whiteboard. You may have to mess around with this for a few days until your story starts to fall into place.

5) Challenge your ideas for each of the Seven Plot Elements:

Is your First Goal or First Problem a realistic goal or believable problem for the Main Character? Does your First Goal truly spring from an aspect of the Main Character's personality? Do we fully understand the Main Character's motivation for needing to achieve the First Goal or solve the First Problem? Is the Main Character's motivation grounded in events that we have already witnessed on the series? Do you feel a real rooting interest in your Main Character achieving the goal or solving the problem?

Is the Obstacle organic to the series? Was it already there in the series landscape? Is the Obstacle formidable enough to create a real challenge for the Main Character?

Does your Main Character's First Action involve an *unwise decision*? (Or a logical decision based on the First Problem that nonetheless makes matters worse?) Is the First Action consistent with the Main Character's established personality? How is the First Action going to backfire on the Main Character?

Does the Act Break moment leave the Main Character further from achieving his First Goal or from solving his First Problem? Does the Act Break moment leave the Main Character metaphorically hanging from a cliff? At the Act Break, are we dying to know how the Main Character is going to get out of this mess?

Is the Second Goal designed to clean up the mess created by the First Action and move the Main Character back toward achieving the First Goal? (Is the Second Problem a complication that springs from the First Action?) Is the Main Character in a heightened emotional state when he or she desperately settles on the Second Goal or confronts the Second Problem?

Does the Second Action also backfire and make matters even worse? Does the Second Action corner the Main Character, forcing him or her toward the Resolution?

Is there irony in the Resolution? Does the Main Character come to realize that either the First Goal was a false goal, and/or that it was the *unwise decision* that sabotaged his chances for success? Does the Main Character see that the First Problem could have been solved much more easily if he or she had followed a more responsible course of action? Or, is it the courage, patience, honesty or humility that the Main Character finally found by going through this ordeal that solved the First Problem and resolved the story?

When you can answer all of these challenges to your story satisfactorily, you will be ready to move on to the Outline.

CHAPTER 5

OUTLINING
YOUR STORY

We came up with an idea for an episode of *Sabrina, the Teenage Witch* in which Sabrina wrote a story for school on a magic typewriter. All of the characters in Sabrina's story then came to life and started running around her school. It was a complicated notion, even for us, because all of our actors would be playing their regular characters but simultaneously playing alter-ego characters from Sabrina's story, all with different agendas, all crossing paths in multiple scenes. I wrote up a Detailed Outline of the whole episode. It was indeed complex, but as I laid out the scenes, one after another, in outline form, I could see that the episode was going to work. It turned out to be one of our most enjoyable shows.

WHY BOTHER WITH AN OUTLINE?

For me, the outline is the essential and invaluable step between *Structuring Your Story* and *Writing Scenes*.

Even after I have decided on a story and identified my First Goal or First Problem, my Obstacle, First Action, Act Break, Second Goal, Second Action and Resolution, I am not yet prepared to write dialogue. I've done a lot of work already. But I know from experience that once I plunge into the individual scenes, I can easily get lost or stuck. I want to avoid getting lost or stuck. I want to feel confident about every detail of my story before I begin to write dialogue. I want to know not only the beginning, middle and end of my entire story, but I want to know the beginning, middle and end of each individual scene.

Taking the time to write a Detailed Outline always helps me to identify any remaining story problems. Every story idea, no matter how good it is, has at least a few wrinkles in it that need to be ironed out. The outline is the best place to smooth out those wrinkles. The outline is also the place to improve the story by giving it more depth and meaning.

I always look at my outline as a chance to "pre-write" my scenes, and see if they work. Throughout my career, I've found that I am more confident if I sketch out all my scenes in a Detailed Outline before I go to script. Then when I start writing my script, I am relaxed and focused on jokes and dialogue because I know there are no hidden land mines lurking in the landscape of my story.

Most producers of television series will demand an outline when giving out an assignment, particularly from an inexperienced writer. A wise producer wants to be sure that all the story problems are worked out before he sends a writer to script. An outline is the ideal way to make sure that the story works, and that the writer understands the story that he or she has been assigned.

If you become a professional sitcom writer, you're going to have to write outlines anyway. You might as well learn how to do it now!

The longer you spend working on your story during the Outline stage, the better your script is going to be. And honestly, the longer you work on your story — the more complete your story is when you go to script — the easier it will be to come up with jokes.

I want you to write great spec scripts that will eventually get you to your Lucky Break. When you get your Lucky Break, I want you to be prepared to write a great Outline for the producer who hires you so that the producer will relax about you, confident that he's made the right choice in giving you an assignment. I want your first professional script to be a knock-out draft that helps get you a second job and a third one. So for all these reasons, I'm including this chapter on Outlines.

Your whole future as a sitcom writer will likely hinge on how well you can write your spec scripts.

You will write better spec scripts now, and you will write better professional scripts in the future, if you train yourself to patiently go through each step of the story development process:

1) Create the right story based on the premise of the series and the personality of the Main Character.

2) Carefully structure that story, step by logical step, using the Seven Plot Elements and the paints that are already in the tray.

3) Write a Detailed Outline before you go to script so that you can work out any remaining story problems.

Then when it's time to write the script, you will be free to concentrate on dialogue and jokes.

For me, writing the Outline is the process of thinking your story through in detail.

Let's go through the Outline process together, using our *Frasier* story as an example. I will show you how to take the good ideas that we assembled in the last chapter and flesh out those ideas into a Detailed Outline that will make writing the script very much easier.

THE WHITEBOARD

If we had been pitching out our *Frasier* story in a writers' conference room, I would have written much of what we discussed on a whiteboard. The whiteboard is a wonderful visual aid because it allows all the writers in the room to see at a glance how the story is progressing.

The whiteboard was particularly useful on *Sabrina, the Teenage Witch* because we often told complicated stories and used multiple story lines. A story for *Sabrina* could have as many as forty-five scenes. With so many story lines and individual scenes to coordinate, it was easy to get confused during pitch sessions. Putting our ideas up on the whiteboard helped us to see the entire episode in a single glance. This helped us to identify holes in our stories. It reminded us to keep all our regular characters alive.

Even when you're working alone on a spec script, I suggest using a whiteboard if you have one at your disposal.

Write down the Seven Plot Elements on the whiteboard. Write them in big letters:

FIRST GOAL OR FIRST PROBLEM —
OBSTACLE —
FIRST ACTION —
ACT BREAK —
SECOND GOAL —
SECOND ACTION —
RESOLUTION —

Next to each of these Elements, write your idea for that Element:

FIRST GOAL OR FIRST PROBLEM — Frasier wants to be president of the opera club.
OBSTACLE — Niles is running against him.
FIRST ACTION — Frasier tries to discredit Niles.
ACT BREAK — Argument gets Frasier and Niles disqualified.
SECOND GOAL — Frasier and Niles decide to cooperate.
SECOND ACTION — More bickering gets them both tossed out of the club.
RESOLUTION — Frasier and Niles decide their relationship is more important.

As you continue to structure your story, use the whiteboard to convert your Plot Elements into Scenes as we did in the last chapter:

ACT ONE
Scene 1 — Radio Station — Frasier learns that presidency of opera club is open. He decides to run.
Scene 2 — Nervosa — Frasier runs into Niles. Niles is running, too. Argument.
Scene 3 — Opera Club — Frasier tries to discredit Niles. They bicker. Frasier and Niles are both disqualified. Act Break.

ACT TWO
Scene 4 — Frasier's Apartment — Frasier and Niles blame each other. Vow to work together.
Scene 5 — Opera Club — More bickering. Both are tossed out of the club.
Scene 6 — Frasier's Apartment — Frasier and Niles realize their relationship is more important. Vow to form an even snobbier club.

While still working with the whiteboard, add your "B" story (and "C" or "D" stories if you are using multiple story lines):

ACT ONE

Scene 1 — Radio Station — Frasier learns that presidency of opera club is open. He decides to run.

Scene 2 — Nervosa — Frasier runs into Niles. Niles is running, too. Argument.

"B" story — It's Martin's birthday. Frasier and Niles forget.

Scene 3 — Opera Club — Frasier tries to discredit Niles. They bicker. Frasier and Niles are both disqualified. Act Break.

ACT TWO

Scene 4 — Frasier's Apartment — Frasier and Niles blame each other. Vow to work together.

"B" story — Daphne and Roz try to celebrate birthday but Martin grumpy. Frasier and Niles interrupt.

Scene 5 — Opera Club — More bickering. Both are tossed out of the club.

Scene 6 — Frasier's Apartment — Frasier and Niles realize their relationship is more important. Vow to form an even snobbier club.

"B" story — Frasier and Niles learn that they forgot Martin's birthday.

Step back and look at your whole story on the whiteboard. It looks pretty complete. The broad strokes of a good story are there. As you glance at the entire story, ask yourself some pertinent questions:

Is the story real? Does it make sense? Is your Main Character at the center of the action? Do all of your regular characters have a part to play in this story? How does your "B" story blend with your "A" story?

If anything written on the whiteboard seems wrong, it's easy to erase. One swipe of a cloth and a bad idea is gone. You can use one color pen for your "A" story and another color pen for your "B" story.

If you don't have access to a whiteboard, but you use a script-writing program such as Final Draft, you can accomplish the same thing by making note cards on the computer and moving them around. That may work as well for you as the whiteboard.

The idea is to use the whiteboard as a visual aid to identify the Seven Plot Elements, add your ideas for each element, convert the Plot Elements into scenes, and add your "B" story.

This is the first step in outlining your story. Your ideas are organized and written down. These are the notes that you'll use to flesh out your story in a Detailed Outline on the computer.

HOW I WRITE AN OUTLINE

Once you feel that you have properly structured your story on the whiteboard, it's time to move to the Outline.

You're going to use your notes from the whiteboard or from note cards to flesh out your story in detail. It's fine to add some dialogue when it feels natural to do so, but you aren't going to be worried yet about jokes. Jokes are your last concern. If you get an idea for a joke, by all means put it in the Outline. But don't feel stress over jokes at this point. When your story makes sense and flows properly, the jokes will come. I promise.

To show you how to get started, let's organize the *Frasier* story into a Detailed Outline. Just as with every other part of story development, each step in the Outline process is logical. The clues you need are there. All you have to do is draw on your knowledge of the series. The paints are already in the tray.

Scene 1

In the opening scene of your spec script, you'll want to get off to a galloping start. You want your reader thinking: "Yeah, this sounds like the show!" You want your reader interested in the story. You want the reader rooting for the Main Character. You want to make the promise of funny scenes yet to come.

Here are the notes from the last chapter for Scene 1 of the *Frasier* story:

Act One — Scene 1 – Radio Station – Frasier learns of the death of the president of his opera club. The presidency, an office he has coveted for years, is suddenly vacant. Frasier determines to win that office.

Roz is Frasier's producer. She would logically be present as Frasier finishes his radio show. Roz might be the person to pass along to Frasier the information that the president of the opera club had died. Someone called while Frasier was on the air and Roz took the call. Roz gives Frasier someone to talk to. You can "get the pipe out" this way — place in dialogue the exposition that explains the story to the viewer. Roz is a blue-collar gal who is critical of Frasier's snobbishness, so you have a chance for comedy as Roz ridicules Frasier's snooty opera club.

You want to use your Outline to expand your notes and get a fuller sense of the scene. What exactly is going to happen? Remember that we want the scene to have a beginning, a middle and an end, even if the scene requires only five or six pages of dialogue. Sometimes the best way to get going on an Outline is to just write down the basics. Don't worry about jokes or a lot of details. Based on the notes, we want to accomplish the following tasks in Scene 1:

1) "Get the pipe out." "Pipe" means exposition — dialogue that explains the story. We want to use dialogue to explain to the reader what the story is going to be about.

2) Establish Frasier's First Goal of running for president of the opera club. Those are our tasks for Scene 1.

I might write a Rough Outline for Scene 1 of the *Frasier* story like this: Frasier finishes up his radio broadcast. Roz enters from the control room and hands Frasier a phone message. Roz thinks nothing of the message, but Frasier has a huge reaction. "My God! Arthur Lipton is dead!" Roz asks, "Who the heck is Arthur Lipton?" Frasier tells her Arthur Lipton is — or was — president of his opera club. Roz says, "Oh." She couldn't be less interested. She heads back into the control room. Frasier, highly excited, follows her in. Frasier tells Roz that while he's grieved, this is also a golden opportunity. The presidency of the opera club is vacant for the first time in ten years! Roz imagines the stampede to get on the ballot. But Frasier ignores her sarcasm. "You're right, Roz! I'll have to get my name in immediately!" Perhaps Frasier places a frantic phone call to the secretary of the opera club. Though we can see that Frasier is bursting with excitement, he feigns sorrow to the secretary. Frasier can hardly control his glee when he learns that he's the first to file his candidacy. He begins to plot his campaign. This will be a dream come true. Roz listens patiently but bored to death. Frasier, bursting with excitement, dashes out without even saying good-bye.

Even sketched out as roughly as this, we already see the beginning of a good story. We have "gotten the pipe out." We have also described Frasier's First Goal. He wants to be president of his opera club. We see opportunities for comedy based on the established personalities of the characters. Frasier is excited about another of his pompous ambitions. Roz thinks it's pretty silly.

Character Motivation

You'll want to introduce motivation for your Main Character as soon as possible, usually in this first scene. In any good story the audience or reader must understand why a character wants what he wants. This is where rooting interest comes from. How can we root for a character to achieve his goal or solve his problem unless we understand why it is so important to him? So before we move on, let's ask ourselves why Frasier wants to be president of his opera club. Besides his ego, what is motivating Frasier's desire? What can we cull from our knowledge of the series to help us test the premise and explore fresh territory not yet covered on the series?

In other episodes of *Frasier*, we've seen the Main Character vie for leadership of his wine club and the tenants association of the building where he lives. Can we use those past stories, the paints that are already in the tray, to better understand Frasier's motives in this story?

When Frasier has gone after things in other episodes, be they awards or other forms of recognition, he seldom achieves his goal. He is usually thwarted by his ego and his ambition. That has been part of the premise of the series and the series formula. Perhaps all of these past failures have affected Frasier. Perhaps he wants to run for president of his opera club, but he worries that he'll fumble the election. Perhaps Frasier confesses to Roz how much the club means to him. Perhaps he's vulnerable in front of Roz. Perhaps Roz is surprised by Frasier's vulnerability. Perhaps she tells

Frasier that even though she thinks an opera club sounds pompous and silly, she is moved by how much the club means to him. She suggests that rather than give one of his usual stuffy speeches, maybe he'd be better off if he shared his true feelings with the club just as he did with her. She tells him that she'd vote for him just because of how much it means to him. Buoyed by Roz's support, Frasier decides to run.

Frasier's motivation adds a stronger theme to the story. Frasier is going to drop his usual pomposity and go for sincerity. Aren't we rooting for him a little more because of that? Perhaps we can exploit this theme in subsequent scenes.

Motivating Your Main Character

In the first scene of your spec sitcom script, think about the personality of your Main Character, as he or she faces the First Goal or First Problem. Can you find a way to make this First Goal or First Problem mean something special to the Main Character? Has your Main Character pursued a similar goal or faced a similar problem in a previous episode of the series? If so, how did the Main Character handle that earlier goal or problem? How might the past affect the present? Remember how I used Hawkeye's established anti-war feelings to heighten the drama in my spec episode of *M*A*S*H*?

If you are writing a spec episode of *Two and a Half Men*, ask yourself how Alan or Charlie might pursue the goal you have given him or react to the problem you have created based on his behavior in previous episodes. Try to find a way to make the First Goal or First Problem mean something special to Alan or Charlie based on his established personality and the experiences he has endured already in the series.

Let's incorporate these new ideas about motivation for the Main Character into our *Frasier* outline. Since we are still working in outline form, it's easy at this point to improve our story.

Our revised Outline for Act One, Scene 1, might read as follows:

Frasier finishes up his radio broadcast. Roz enters from the control room and hands Frasier a phone message. Roz thinks nothing of the message, but

Frasier has a huge reaction. "My God! Arthur Lipton is dead!" Roz asks, "Who the heck is Arthur Lipton?" Frasier tells her Arthur Lipton is — or was — president of his opera club. Roz says, "Oh." She couldn't be less interested. She heads back into the control room. Frasier, highly excited, follows her in. Frasier tells Roz that while he's grieved, this is also a golden opportunity. The presidency of the opera club is vacant for the first time in ten years! Roz hopes Frasier won't be too disappointed if he loses. She reminds him that he ran for president of his wine club and failed. He ran for president of his condominium board and failed. He was nominated for awards and lost. He gets all worked up over these petty honors, and then something always goes wrong and he ends up disappointed. Roz asks, "Why do you care so much? It's just a stupid club for snobs." Frasier is hurt. He tells Roz that he realizes that opera may sound pompous to some people, but his mother introduced him to opera as a young boy, and he loved it. Maybe he loved it because of how much *she* loved it. Frasier and his mother used to listen to opera together on rainy afternoons when he was a child. Now every time he goes to the opera or goes to a meeting of his club, he's reminded of how close he was to his mother, how she appreciated him for who he was, and how she encouraged him to be himself. "Opera keeps her alive for me," Frasier confesses. Roz is moved. She tells Frasier that she'd vote for him based on what he just said. Frasier is surprised by Roz's reaction. "You shared a part of yourself with me, Frasier, instead of giving one of your usual endless stuffy speeches. I was moved. It made me love you even more. It made me want to support you. Maybe the snobs will be moved in the same way." Buoyed by Roz's encouragement, Frasier calls and nominates himself.

There is a comic element to Frasier's motives that we can enjoy, but his real emotions add rooting interest to the story and make it stronger and deeper. Frasier's First Goal is now easier to understand, which gives it weight and makes us want him to succeed.

Scene 2

Let's move on to our second scene and see if we can exploit the theme even more. Here are the notes for *Scene 2* compiled in the previous chapter:

Act One — Scene 2 — Nervosa – Frasier enters, needing a latte to energize him for the campaign ahead, only to discover that Niles is after the same goal. A quarrel. Frasier leaves in a huff.

Scene 2 opens with Martin and Daphne getting some coffee together. Martin's birthday is tomorrow night. Daphne asks Martin if Frasier and Niles are taking him someplace special for his birthday. Martin says they haven't mentioned anything. Daphne wonders if Frasier and Niles have planned a surprise. Frasier enters, bursting with the news about his campaign to become president of the opera club. Frasier mentions an emergency meeting of the opera club for tomorrow night. It's clear that in the excitement about the opera club, Frasier has forgotten Martin's birthday. Niles arrives. Niles has also heard about the death of the opera club president. Frasier learns that Niles is running for president as well. Frasier and Niles quarrel. In the excitement over the opera club, both Frasier and Niles have forgotten about their father's birthday. Both men leave, angrily passing Roz on their way out. Roz immediately wishes Martin a happy birthday. Martin storms out. Roz is left with Daphne wondering why everyone is so grumpy.

Based on the notes, we have three tasks to accomplish while outlining *Scene 2*:

1) Introduce the "B" story about Martin's birthday.

2) Keep Frasier focused on his First Goal of becoming president of the opera club.

3) Introduce the Obstacle, which will be Niles running against Frasier.

From the notes, we know how to reveal our "B" story about Martin's birthday. But can we incorporate Martin's birthday, and the mix-ups we've planned for later, more cleverly into the theme of our story? We might try this: When Daphne asks Martin about plans for tomorrow night, she mentions that he never wants to make a big deal out of his birthday. He never allows any fuss at all. Daphne asks if it's just Martin's policeman machismo at work. Martin confesses that the boys always made a big fuss over their mother's birthday because they were much closer to her than they were to him. Martin says he loves his sons, and he knows they love him, but he doesn't expect the same attention that they gave to their mother. As long as the boys don't forget his birthday completely, Martin is satisfied.

Here we're adding to the back story about Frasier's late mother established in other episodes and mentioned by Frasier in *Scene 1*. We're using the paints that are already in the tray. We imagine that Martin would likely appreciate a little attention from his sons, but by downplaying the importance of his birthday Martin is simply trying to protect his own feelings. He was never as close to his sons as they were to their mother. We have added *rooting interest*. As viewers or readers, we'd love to see Martin get the attention he deserves on his birthday.

Now let's build some more on the theme that we've begun in *Scene 1*. Frasier always loses elections, and the other characters are well aware of it. We are using the paints that are already in the tray. We might try:

Frasier rushes in for a latte, bursting with the news about running for president of his opera club. Martin reminds Frasier about his past failures and how upset he gets when he inevitably loses, just as Roz did.

This adds to the comedy. Everyone is aware that Frasier loses these elections.

Frasier assures Martin that he has stumbled on an entirely new approach to campaigning: sincerity. Frasier says there's an emergency meeting of the opera club for tomorrow night. It's obvious to Martin and Daphne that Frasier has forgotten Martin's birthday.

Frasier forgetting Martin's birthday has more meaning now. We have used facts established in past episodes of *Frasier* and reconfigured them to enrich our story. We've also added sympathy for Martin, haven't we? In previous episodes of *Frasier*, it was well established that Frasier and Niles were more like their cultured mother and had little in common with their policeman father. Throughout the series, Frasier, Niles and Martin have struggled with this issue. It's touching and funny. Incorporating it into our story demonstrates knowledge of the series.

Daphne tries to remind Frasier about Martin's birthday, but Martin won't let her.

The occasion of Martin's birthday now takes on added poignancy.

Our last task in outlining this scene is to establish Niles as our Obstacle. We want Frasier to find out that Niles is running against him for president of the Opera Club. We want a quarrel to erupt between the brothers. And we want to keep the issue of Martin's birthday alive. Let's try this:

Niles arrives at Nervosa. He and Frasier acknowledge the death of Arthur Lipton. Frasier tells Niles he's running for president. Niles reminds Frasier of his bad track record running for office.

We get added humor here because both Roz *and* Martin warned Frasier of the same thing.

Frasier, encouraged by his conversation earlier with Roz, says he has a secret new approach. Niles tries harder to discourage Frasier from running, reminding him of how upset he gets when he loses. Frasier realizes what Niles is up to. "You ninny! *You're* running!" Niles admits he's been waiting ten years for this opportunity.

Our Obstacle is now neatly in place. Faced with this unforeseen Obstacle, the emotions of our Main Character are heightened and will lead to an *unwise decision*.

Niles warns Frasier that he hasn't a chance of winning. Niles considers himself a greater opera expert, and he's been currying favor with the members for years. Daphne suggests that neither of them run, and they spend tomorrow night with their father instead.

This keeps our "B" story alive.

But by now Frasier and Niles are caught up in sibling rivalry. Niles tells Frasier he'll crush him in the campaign. Frasier says he has a tactic that will trump Niles and his shameless bribery. Both men storm out. Roz enters and wishes Martin a happy birthday. Martin, upset over being forgotten by his sons, barks at Roz and leaves.

We've improved our story considerably by working it out in detail in the Outline before we started writing the script.

Our revised Outline for Act One, Scene 2, would now read like this:

Act One - Scene 2 — Nervosa — Scene opens with Martin and Daphne getting some coffee together. When Daphne asks Martin about plans for tomorrow night, she mentions that he never wants to make a big deal out of his birthday. He never allows any fuss at all. Daphne asks if it's just Martin's policeman machismo at work. Martin confesses that the boys always made a big fuss over their mother's birthday because they were much closer to her than they were to him. Martin says he loves his sons, and he knows they love him, but he doesn't expect the same attention that they gave to their mother. As long as the boys don't forget his birthday completely, Martin is satisfied. Frasier rushes in for a latte, bursting with the news about running for president of his opera club. Martin reminds Frasier about his past failures and how upset he gets when he inevitably loses, but Frasier assures Martin that he has stumbled on an entirely new approach to campaigning: sincerity. Frasier says there's an emergency meeting of the opera club for tomorrow night. It's obvious to Martin and Daphne that Frasier has forgotten Martin's birthday. Daphne tries to remind Frasier about Martin's birthday, but Martin won't let her. Niles arrives at Nervosa. He and Frasier acknowledge the death of Arthur Lipton. Frasier tells Niles he's running for president. Niles reminds Frasier of his bad track record running for office. Frasier, encouraged by his conversation earlier with Roz, says he has a secret new approach. Niles tries harder to discourage Frasier from running, reminding him of how upset he gets when he loses. Frasier realizes what Niles is up to. "You ninny! *You're* running!" Niles admits he's been waiting ten years for this opportunity. Niles warns Frasier that he hasn't a chance of winning. Niles considers himself a greater opera expert, and he's been currying favor with the members for years. Daphne suggests that neither of them run, and they spend tomorrow night with their father instead. But by now Frasier and Niles are caught up in sibling rivalry. Niles tells Frasier he'll crush him in the campaign. Frasier says he has a tactic that will trump Niles and his shameless bribery. Both men storm out. Roz enters and wishes Martin a happy birthday. Martin, upset over being forgotten by his sons, barks at Roz and leaves.

Our story has gotten considerably stronger in the Outline stage, and this is as it should be. Fleshing out your scenes in an Outline without having to worry yet about dialogue and jokes allows you to think creatively about your story. It allows you to dig deeper and make the story more meaningful.

After just two scenes we have a rooting interest in the First Goal of our Main Character, a formidable Obstacle, a solid "B" story that dovetails nicely with our "A" story, and we have four of our regular characters in a heightened emotional state.

Scene 3

Let's look at our notes for the next scene:

Act One — Scene 3 — The Opera Club — Frasier follows Niles to the podium for his campaign speech. Frasier turns his speech into a vicious attack on Niles. Another quarrel erupts between the brothers. Both men are disqualified. The sergeant-at-arms tosses them out. Act Break."

We don't have many notes for our third scene, so the Outline provides us with the perfect opportunity to flesh out what we have into a solid scene.

Based on the adjustments we've made to the previous two scenes, we may want to rethink this scene slightly. Writing a Detailed Outline can help you to identify and solve problems and/or strengthen your story before you begin writing your script.

We'll stick to our basic idea for this scene, but we'll make it even better in Outline form.

Frasier's First Goal, as identified in *Scene 1*, is to be president of the opera club. His Obstacle is Niles running against him. Frasier's First Action has changed from our original idea. This is normal in story development. Don't be concerned as you work on your Outline if you discover a better First Action or a stronger Second Goal for your Main Character. This is what the Outline is for. You are testing your story before you begin writing your script to see if the story will hold up. If you find problems or come up with better ideas, you're doing your job as a writer!

Frasier was encouraged by Roz to try sincerity. We came up with that while outlining *Scene 1*. Speaking from his heart about his mother's influence on him has now become Frasier's plan to overcome the Obstacle of Niles and achieve his First Goal of winning the presidency of the opera club. Sincerity is Frasier's new First Action.

As we open *Scene 3*, it has been a while since Frasier talked to Roz and devised his "sincerity" plan. We were busy in *Scene 2* setting up our "B" story and establishing Niles as Frasier's Obstacle. It would be wise then to begin our *Scene 3* by reminding the reader and the audience of Frasier's First Action plan.

Perhaps we open *Scene 3* at the opera club with Frasier talking to a female club member:

The meeting hasn't started yet. Members mill about with coffee. We hear Frasier trying out some of his "sincere" story on this female club member.

Frasier is cleverly pre-screening his speech to see if it is going to play. (This reminds a reader or the audience of the First Action plan.)

The female club member is visibly touched by Frasier's story about his mother introducing him to opera. She tells Frasier that he has her vote. Frasier is now certain that his First Action is going to work. Niles arrives. Frasier, brimming with confidence, approaches Niles. Niles nervously reviews what appears to be a voluminous speech. Niles hides the speech from Frasier, but admits he was checking some oblique opera reference in his text. Frasier, more certain than ever of victory, offers an olive branch to Niles. He reminds Niles of the years of enjoyment that opera has brought to both of them. Niles reminisces for a second about their mother. Frasier's First Action seems to be working even on Niles. The meeting is gaveled to order, and after a few remarks, a Moderator invites the two candidates to speak.

Our original idea for the *unwise decision* and First Action was to have Frasier try to discredit Niles. We've moved away from that notion because the story seemed to gain more meaning if Frasier tried to defeat Niles with sincerity. Now Frasier is brimming with confidence. What if his hubris now dictates his *unwise decision*? That's what hubris usually does. What if we change the *unwise decision* to:

Frasier generously offers to let Niles speak first.

Frasier's motives are of course selfish. As always, we are drawing on the established personality of our Active Main Character. Frasier knows that Niles has written a dreary speech full of dry history and obscure facts — just the sort of speech Frasier might have given if he hadn't opened up to Roz in *Scene 1*. Frasier is certain that his "heartfelt" and "sincere" speech will be even more effective if delivered *after* Niles' boring speech and right before the vote. So Frasier makes the *unwise decision* to let Niles go first.

What can we do now to make Frasier's First Action backfire, perhaps as a result of his *unwise decision* to let Niles speak first? You may have noticed that I planted the seeds of Frasier's destruction in the previous paragraph. Frasier reminded Niles of their mother. What if that now comes back to haunt Frasier as follows:

Niles, to Frasier's surprise and horror, dumps his dreary speech and decides to speak from his heart. The result is that Niles extemporaneously makes the same speech that Frasier had planned. We even hear Niles use some of the exact phrases that Frasier used on Roz and on the female club member. Niles speech amounts to only a few sentences, but it is tender and moving, just as Frasier's speech might have been had he gone first. The membership applauds loud and long. They dry their tears. Niles would seem to have the presidency in the bag! Frasier approaches the podium like a dead man. His speech has been usurped. His plan is dashed. His hopes are destroyed. Frasier's frustration over all the losses in all the previous elections for wine club and condo board now spills out.

As a reader or audience, we completely understand where Frasier's rage is coming from. Frasier accuses Niles of stealing his ideas and his observations about opera and using them to suck up to their mother when they were kids. "He stole the love of our mother that was rightfully mine!" Niles, offended and furious, shouts back at Frasier. Old wounds are opened. The meeting dissolves into chaos. The sergeant-at-arms is called. Act Break.

Frasier's First Action has completely backfired, and he is now further from his First Goal than when he started.

In outlining our First Act, we've made some adjustments to our original notes, but I believe the story is stronger, more compelling, and more cohesive. This is what an Outline is for. We are testing our story, ironing out the wrinkles, making the story stronger before we begin to write dialogue. We are following the rules for a successful spec script.

We are combining our knowledge of the series, the premise, the formula, and the established personality of the Main Character to produce a story that sounds like the show.

Scene 4

Let's look at our notes for *Scene 4*:

Act Two — Scene 4 — Frasier's Apartment — Frasier and Niles return. They blame each other. They decide to be mature and work together. May the best man win.

The emergency meeting of the opera club in Act One, Scene Three took place on the night of Martin's birthday. Perhaps we open Act Two with grumpy Martin feeling sorry for himself. He won't even eat the birthday cake that Daphne baked for him. Perhaps Roz drops over with a present for Martin. Martin isn't cheered up. He's too hurt that his sons forgot his birthday. Martin, Daphne and Roz hear Frasier and Niles arguing in the hall as they get off the elevator. In classic *Frasier* style, Martin insists that all evidence of his birthday be hidden from Frasier and Niles. Martin doesn't want them feeling guilty now. He's too angry at them. Daphne and Roz scramble to hide the cake, the plates and the presents in the other room. Frasier and Niles enter, quarreling. Both men try to elicit sympathy from their father. Martin, furious over being forgotten, lashes out at both of them. Martin never mentions his birthday, but he tells them both how selfish they are. Families are supposed to stick together. Frasier and Niles are well rebuked. Perhaps Daphne is just about to reveal to Frasier and Niles that it's Martin's birthday when Frasier suggests that he and Niles return to the opera club and support each other. Niles loves the idea. They thank their father for his advice and rush out, having missed the birthday again.

Based on the notes, here are our tasks as we outline *Scene 4*:

1) Show how Martin's birthday has been ruined because Frasier and Niles forgot.

2) Put Frasier and Niles into conflict with Martin.

3) Establish Frasier's Second Goal of getting back in the race.

Our audience knows that Frasier and Niles have been disqualified, but Martin, Daphne and Roz do not. Usually you don't want to repeat information that the audience already has, but in this case it's going to throw fuel on the fire of Martin's forgotten birthday.

Let's outline *Scene 4* as follows:

Frasier and Niles report that they've both been disqualified from the presidential race. Frasier blames Niles for stealing his speech. Niles claims he was merely speaking from his heart. Frasier counters: "That's what *I* was supposed to do!" Daphne and Roz search for a way to bring up the birthday. Frasier says: "Dad, I had a very touching remembrance to share of our dear mother and the bond that she and I forged because of our mutual love of opera, but Niles sullied it with a lot of cheap, greeting card sentimentality." Niles: "How dare you! I was every bit as close to her as you were, if not more! No two people ever loved *Die Zauberflöte* as much as Mother and me!"

Martin would of course be hurt by these comments. His sons have not only forgotten his birthday, but they unwittingly pour salt on the wound by reminiscing about their mother. But Martin is too proud to reveal his true feelings. He covers his injury by chastising Frasier and Niles:

"Your mother loved both of you equally! She had a special bond with each of you. One that I'm sorry to say I was never able to match. This is no way to honor her memory." Martin exits to his room. Daphne scowls at Frasier and Niles. "Now look what you've done! You've hurt your father's feelings! And on this of all days!"

Frasier and Niles would, of course, miss the hint from Daphne about the birthday and fall back into their characteristic ambition and self-absorption:

Frasier admits that Martin is right. This is no way to honor their mother. Daphne: "Your mother? What about your father?!" Niles: "Frasier, we owe it to Mother's memory to go back down there and apologize." Frasier: "I was thinking precisely the same thing. I don't suppose there's any chance of getting back in the race." Niles: "Perhaps if we both humbled ourselves…" Frasier: "Yes! We'll dazzle them with our humility!" Niles: "I love it!" Daphne: "Have either of you glanced at a calendar?" Frasier: "Selfless, dedicated to a higher cause. We'll have

them eating out of our hands." Niles: "Mother would be proud." Frasier and
Niles exit, leaving Daphne and Roz.

Frasier has identified his Second Goal of getting back in the race, and
has taken Niles along with him as an ally.

Our revised Outline for *Scene 4* would now read as follows:

Act Two — Scene 4 — Frasier's Apartment — Scene opens with grumpy
Martin feeling sorry for himself. He won't even eat the birthday cake that
Daphne baked for him. Perhaps Roz drops over with a present for Martin.
Martin isn't cheered up. He's too hurt that his sons forgot his birthday. Martin,
Daphne and Roz hear Frasier and Niles arguing in the hall as they get off the
elevator. In classic *Frasier* style, Martin insists that all evidence of his birthday be
hidden from Frasier and Niles. Martin doesn't want them feeling guilty now.
He's too angry at them. Daphne and Roz scramble to hide the cake, the plates
and the presents in the other room. Frasier and Niles enter, quarreling. Frasier
and Niles report that they've both been disqualified from the presidential race.
Frasier blames Niles for stealing his speech. Niles claims he was merely speaking from his heart. Frasier counters: "That's what *I* was supposed to do!"
Daphne and Roz search for a way to bring up the birthday. Frasier says: "Dad,
I had a very touching remembrance to share of our dear mother and the bond
that she and I forged because of our mutual love of opera, but Niles sullied it
with a lot of cheap, greeting card sentimentality." Niles: "How dare you! I was
every bit as close to her as you were, if not more! No two people ever loved
Die Zauberflöte as much as Mother and me!" Martin shouts: "Your mother
loved both of you equally! She had a special bond with each of you. One that
I'm sorry to say I was never able to match. This is no way to honor her memory." Martin exits to his room. Daphne scowls at Frasier and Niles. "Now look
what you've done! You've hurt your father's feelings! And on this of all days!"
Frasier admits that Martin is right. This is no way to honor their mother.
Daphne: "Your mother? What about your father?" Niles: "Frasier, we owe it to
Mother's memory to go back down there and apologize." Frasier: "I was thinking precisely the same thing. I don't suppose there's any chance of getting back
in the race." Niles: "Perhaps if we both humbled ourselves…" Frasier: "Yes! We'll
dazzle them with our humility!" Niles: "I love it!" Daphne: "Have either of you

glanced at a calendar?" Frasier: "Selfless, dedicated to a higher cause. We'll have them eating out of our hands." Niles: "Mother would be proud." Frasier and Niles exit, leaving Daphne and Roz.

It's a better scene now. We've advanced our "B" story and brought the "A" and "B" stories into concert with one another.

Scene 5

Let's check the notes for *Scene 5*:

Act Two — Scene 5 — The Opera Club — An attempt at decorum quickly degenerates into more bickering. Both men are expelled from the club.

Our tasks while outlining Scene 5 are:
1) Show Frasier's Second Action of trying to get along with Niles so he can get back in the race.
2) See the Second Action backfire as Frasier and Niles return to bickering.

We don't yet know precisely what is going to happen in this scene, so we have some plotting to do. How do we figure out what should happen? The answer is always the same: Your characters will guide you.

Because we know Frasier and Niles so well, we can anticipate that any attempt at humility will quickly turn into a contest. These two brothers are hopelessly competitive. The paints are already in the tray. Of course the scene will end up being about who can be the most humble!

Let's try this:

Frasier interrupts the meeting and asks if he and Niles might be allowed to apologize for their earlier behavior. They realize that they made everyone uncomfortable before. Frasier says that he and Niles both want what is best for the opera club. Niles agrees. "We're both very sorry," says Frasier. "Both *equally* sorry," says Niles.

Let the games begin.

Remember to keep the Main Character focused on his First Goal, even to the bitter end. Frasier, at this moment of contrition, still wants to be president of the opera club. He's going to take one last stab at it. He's in a heightened emotional state. He's desperate. He can't help himself.

Frasier: "I got carried away because all I've ever wanted to do since I first became a member is serve this club as its humble president."

Niles' radar lights up at this.

Niles: "I've wanted the same thing!"

Now come the thrust and parry:

Frasier: "Opera has guided me through some of the greatest challenges of my life." Niles: "Mine as well." Frasier: "Except for the time you let your season tickets lapse." Niles: "I was going through a divorce, and they were *her* tickets!" Frasier: "Ah! Never even bothered to buy your own subscription…" Niles is incensed. "How dare you!" The beleaguered sergeant-at-arms again leaps to his feet.

By using our knowledge of the characters, it was pretty easy to find our way through this scene. We knew that Frasier and Niles wouldn't be able to avoid competing with each other, even as they attempted to apologize.

I've added quite a bit of dialogue to the Outline. These lines will serve as placeholders until it's time to write the actual scene. The dialogue in the Outline will act as a road map. We know what feelings and ideas we want the characters to communicate. When it comes time to write the scene, we can use the dialogue from the Outline as a starting point. We'll then be free to concentrate on jokes, and make the dialogue even better.

Our revised Outline for *Scene 5* would read as follows:

Act Two — Scene 5 — Opera Club: Frasier interrupts the meeting and asks if he and Niles might be allowed to apologize for their earlier behavior. They realize that they made everyone uncomfortable before. Frasier says that he and Niles both want what is best for the opera club. Niles agrees. "We're both very sorry," says Frasier. "Both *equally* sorry," says Niles. Frasier: "I got carried away because all I've ever wanted to do since I first became a member is serve this club as its humble president." Niles: "I've wanted the same thing!" Frasier: "Opera has guided me through some of the greatest challenges of my life." Niles: "Mine as well." Frasier: "Except for the time you let your season tickets lapse." Niles: "I was going through a divorce, and they were *her* tickets!" Frasier: "Ah! Never even bothered to buy your own subscription…" Niles is incensed. "How dare you!" The beleaguered sergeant-at-arms again leaps to his feet.

More dialogue will be needed when the scene is written, but again we have a road map for writing the scene. We know what feelings and ideas will be expressed by the characters.

Scene 6

Let's look at our notes for Act Two, *Scene 6*:

Act Two — Scene 6 — Frasier's Apartment — The tragic aftermath. Admissions of guilt from both brothers. A vow to start a new club.

This scene could open with the cake and presents out in view again. Martin, more hurt than ever, still refuses to participate in his birthday. Roz is about to give up and go home. Daphne reminds Martin that she baked him a cake and bought him a present. Roz came over with a present. Maybe his sons disappointed him, but the least he can do is acknowledge Daphne and Roz's thoughtfulness. Martin agrees and starts to open presents when again Frasier and Niles are heard arguing in the hallway. Again Martin insists that everything be hidden. Again Daphne and Roz must scramble to hide the evidence of the birthday celebration. Frasier and Niles enter. Both men are more upset than ever. Daphne has reached the end of her patience. She tells Frasier and Niles that they forgot Martin's birthday. Now both men feel terrible. Their selfishness and competition have not only cost them membership in their opera club, but they've hurt their father as well. Frasier and Niles apologize to Martin. They have learned their lesson. Frasier decides that instead of singing the trite "Happy Birthday to You," they should play a birthday song from one of Frasier's favorite operas. Frasier slips a CD into the stereo as Martin, Daphne and Roz groan. Niles is impressed that Frasier owns the CD for such an obscure yet unappreciated opera. Niles points out that between Frasier's opera collection and his own they are a first-class opera club all by themselves. They get the idea to form a new and better opera club in which one of them is sure to be president. Reinvigorated, Frasier and Niles go into Frasier's room to examine Frasier's opera collection, having forgotten the birthday again.

Our tasks in outlining *Scene 6* are to:
1) Resolve our "A" story.
2) Resolve our "B" story.

3) Try to resolve both stories together in a way that provides a satisfying ending.

As I look over the notes, the only place where we're thin is Frasier and Niles' return from the opera club.

We can flesh this out by saying:

Frasier and Niles enter sheepishly. They confess that they both feel embarrassed by their inexcusable behavior this evening. Daphne tells them it's about time they realized it. Niles asks Daphne how she could possibly know that they were expelled from the opera club.

This would be the first time we've heard for sure that Frasier and Niles were expelled. Rather than play that out in the previous scene, it can be handled more quickly here in one line of dialogue.

Frasier and Niles' reaction to the news that they forgot their father's birthday can be fleshed out. Since we have woven the back story about their mother into this episode, we can use that issue to resolve both our "A" and "B" stories:

Frasier and Niles apologize to Martin. "Dad, we're so sorry." Martin pretends that it's no big deal. Martin: "I barely even noticed, did I, Daphne?" But Frasier and Niles know Martin is lying to protect their feelings. Frasier confesses: "We got carried away with our own foolish ambitions." Frasier and Niles beat themselves up for their insensitivity. Martin can see how bad the boys feel. As a loving father, he wants to comfort them. Martin: "Maybe I never said it, but I always admired your ambition. You boys always tried to be the very best that you could be in whatever you were doing. You were never satisfied to be vice-president of a club. You always wanted to be president. You wanted to be first in your class in school. I respected that." Frasier and Niles are surprised to hear this. "We thought only Mom was proud of us." Martin: "I was always proud. Okay, so ambitious people get carried away sometimes as you two did with the stupid opera club..." Frasier and Niles patiently absorb the shot from Martin. Martin goes on: "But ambitious people are also the ones who make a difference in this world." Frasier and Niles are thrilled to hear that their father is proud of them. Frasier: "In all my vain attempts to gain recognition for myself at the opera club or the wine club or the condo board or at award ceremonies, I think all I ever really wanted was your approval. Until this moment, I was never sure I had it." Martin: "You always had it, son. You both did." Niles is in tears by now. Niles: "We never wanted any other father but you." Martin: "That's the best present you could have possibly given me." "Happy birthday, Dad." "Thank you, boys. That's really all I needed to hear."

From here we can go back to our notes. Frasier insists on singing an opera song instead of "Happy Birthday To You." Frasier and Niles scheme to form a new opera club of which they can be in charge.

This scene has a great deal more depth and emotion now, doesn't it? Our "A" story has made our "B" story stronger, our "B" story has strengthened our "A" story, and both stories have dovetailed into a very satisfying resolution in which our three characters, Frasier, Niles and Martin, have overcome petty ambition, competition and jealousy — all very real and very recognizable emotions — and have grown closer in the process. Roz and Daphne have played an important supporting role.

By taking the time to outline your story in this way, I know that you will improve the story, work out any obvious problems, and hopefully give your story more substance.

Please don't be afraid to add real emotion to your spec sitcom stories. You don't have to be sappy or maudlin, but it has been my experience that producers — and readers in general — are more interested in a story that is about real feelings. A reader is much more likely to finish a script in which he or she has a rooting interest. A rooting interest is much easier to cultivate if the story somehow touches the reader's heart.

Now look back over the Detailed Outline. As we went through the Outline process in this chapter, you saw me make changes in the notes that I had jotted down in previous chapters. You saw the story expand and improve as I worked it over during the Outline process.

I have often written outlines for real sitcom scripts that were 10, 15 or even 20 pages long. I wrote such Detailed Outlines for my own protection, so that I could be sure that I had solved every story problem before I tried to write dialogue. I wanted to be certain that each scene advanced the story, and that each scene had a beginning, middle and end. I wanted to be certain of what feelings and ideas the characters would express in each scene. I wanted to be certain that I had given all of the regular characters an important role to play in the story. I wanted to be confident that my "A" and "B" stories complemented each other.

I have found throughout my career that the more detailed I made my outlines, the better my scripts turned out. And the more fun I had writing the script when I had a complete and thoughtful outline to work from.

You don't want to confront story problems when you are writing scenes. You want to be able to put all of your energy and imagination into dialogue.

The more you think about your story before you begin writing dialogue, and the more you question your story and try to improve it, the easier it will be to write scenes, and the better your script will eventually be.

CHAPTER RECAP — THE ELEPHANT REMEMBERS

Creating a Detailed Outline is a great way to pre-write your script without worrying about jokes or dialogue. You are working only with story now, challenging your ideas, making sure that your story is real and makes sense. Use the Outline process to expand and enrich your story. Most of your work on the story should be completed in the Outline.

Convert your ideas for the Seven Plot Elements into scenes on the whiteboard. Do this after you have listed the Seven Plot Elements, written your ideas for each plot element, and challenged your ideas.

List the tasks that you need to accomplish with each scene: Introduce Obstacle. Add supporting characters. Add "B" story.

Add your "B" story (and "C" and "D" stories if your series uses multiple story lines) while still working with the whiteboard or with cards. When the whiteboard is full of notes, and all of the story problems that you can see have been solved, turn on your computer and start your Detailed Outline.

Don't worry if your story evolves during the Outline process. We're interested in improving the story at every stage of development.

Stay in story mode throughout the Outline process. Don't worry about jokes or dialogue. Jokes will flow like water when your story is complete and makes sense!

If you have ideas for dialogue, of course stick them in. But don't get bogged down. I happily put terrible dialogue in an Outline just to serve as a placeholder.

Plumb the depths of back story, character and motivation while working on the Outline. Use the paints that are already in the tray. Think about how your story might affect the emotions of the characters based on what has happened to them in previous stories.

Remember that your reader has to care about the story you are telling and have a rooting interest in the outcome. Compelling stories are always about emotions. Reach down to the marrow of who these characters are.

YOUR "TO DO" LIST

1) If you're feeling uncomfortable about your outline, or are fighting with the impulse to rush ahead to the script, try pitching your story to a friend or family member. This is a trick to build your confidence and slow you down. I'm trying to keep you in Outline mode because I know the value of writing a Detailed Outline. Record your oral pitch, and transcribe what you said to the computer. Now you have the start of an Outline. Read over what you pitched. Do you find holes in the story? Now's the time to fill those holes! Can you make the story richer, more compelling, or more emotional based on your knowledge of the series? Now's the time to dig deeper into the premise, the characters, the back story!

2) If you're struggling with one of the Seven Plot Elements, don't worry. You'll fix it! Stop and ask yourself, why am I telling this story? (And don't say, "Because I want to be rich and famous.") Sure, that's the real motivation, but why did you choose this particular story to tell? What basic human emotion are you trying to explore with your story? Is it a story about jealousy or greed or fear or self doubt or devotion or lust? If you are sure of why you are telling the story, you'll be able to solve any

story problem.) Reread my definitions for each of the Seven Plot Elements. Are you adhering to the definition? If you're stuck, ask yourself, what do I need to do now to move the story forward toward the Resolution? You know the Main Character very well. Based on your knowledge of the Main Character's personality, what would he or she do now?

3) Reread some of the sample scripts you ordered from Planet Megamall. Take an actual scene from a sample script and write the Outline version of that scene. In doing this, you will likely develop a deeper appreciation for what that scene is really about. There's more to every scene than just jokes and plot. What are the characters feeling in this scene? How does this scene relate to other scenes in other episodes? How is this scene part of the fabric of the entire series? You'll realize that there's a lot going on below the surface of a scene. The more you understand all the layers of a scene, the more complex and interesting you will be able to make your own scenes!

CHAPTER 6

WRITING SCENES

Once on *Newhart*, we wrote an episode in which our Main Character, Dick Loudon, played by Bob Newhart, was hosting a TV show about books. Dick's guest author cancelled just before air time. Dick was desperate for a replacement guest. Dick's producer, played by Peter Scolari, arrived with an author who had written a book about a canoe trip up the Amazon River. Greatly relieved, Dick went on the air immediately. The guest was fascinating. It looked as if Dick's worries were over. About halfway through his story, however, the author began to describe his encounters with dinosaurs and flying saucers. The author was obviously insane.

When the network executives read our script for this episode, they threatened to shut down the show. They said the script wasn't funny. The executives particularly objected to the scene between Dick Loudon and the Amazon author. What the network executives hadn't thought about when they read the script was that the real humor of the scene was not in jokes written on the page, but rather in Bob Newhart's priceless reactions to what the author was saying. Dick Loudon's honest predicament and his realistic and heroic efforts to make the best of a very embarrassing yet believable situation would make the scene memorable and enjoyable for the audience. We explained this to the executives. With Bob's gracious support for our script, the executives skeptically let us go forward.

When the scene was finally shot on Friday night, the studio audience split their sides with laughter at Bob Newhart's brilliant reactions. Those same executives who had hated the script all week approached us with smiles on their faces and said, "You should do episodes like this one more often!"

MOVE THE STORY FORWARD

All well-written scenes, whether in a novel, a play, a screenplay or a TV script, have one thing in common: Their primary purpose is to move the story forward. Think of a scene in a script as a stair on a staircase. Each stair moves you one step closer to the top.

In Chapter Four, I identified Seven Plot Elements in order to help you structure your story and keep it moving forward.

Each scene in your spec sitcom script must serve one of the Seven Plot Elements. This is how the scene moves the story forward. If the scene doesn't serve one of the plot elements, the scene doesn't belong in the script.
In our *Frasier* story, every scene serves one of the plot elements. The First Scene identifies Frasier's First Goal. The Second Scene introduces the Obstacle that will keep Frasier from achieving his goal. The Third Scene serves two plot elements. It shows us Frasier's *unwise decision*, and his First Action toward achieving his First Goal. In that same scene, his First Action backfires, and at the Act Break he is even further from his First Goal than when he started. In the Fourth Scene, Frasier identifies his Second Goal. In the Fifth Scene he initiates his Second Action, which also backfires. In the Sixth Scene, there is a Resolution of the story.

There are no wasted scenes. Each scene moves the story forward by serving one of the Seven Plot Elements.

Your story may require more than six scenes, depending on the formula of the series you have chosen to spec. Your First Action, for example, may be divided into several parts and play out over three or four scenes. You might be writing a spec episode of *Scrubs*. Your First Action might involve J.D. trying to get a day off so he can be with a new girl friend. J.D.'s First Action might be to track down several of the other characters — Elliot, Turk, etc. — over the course of three or four scenes to see if he can convince one of them to cover for him.

No matter how many scenes your story may require, every scene in your script must serve one of the Seven Plot Elements. Every scene in your script must move the story forward.

There are no scenes in our *Frasier* story where Frasier and Niles just sit around sipping coffee and saying clever things to each other. Every moment is designed specifically to move our story forward. Some moments move our "A" story forward, and some moments move our "B" story forward. All the moments advance some aspect of the story.

By developing our *Frasier* story using the Seven Plot Elements, then translating the ideas for those elements into scenes, and fleshing out each of those scenes in a Detailed Outline, we have kept our story moving forward toward the Resolution.

MUCH OF THE WORK IS ALREADY DONE!

If you look back over our Detailed Outline, you'll see that much of the work of writing the script is already done. Each scene moves the story forward. Each scene has a beginning, a middle and an end. We know where the scenes are going to take place. We know which characters are going to appear in each scene. We know the characters' motivations within the story and within each individual scene. We even have a pretty good idea of what each character is going to say in each scene.

Because we have prepared so carefully, we can now concentrate entirely on dialogue and jokes. We have a great road map for writing our script. There's no mystery. All we have to do now is connect the dots within each scene through the characters' conversation.

When you have completed all these steps with your story, you will be ready to write scenes for your spec sitcom script. You'll be able to concentrate entirely on dialogue and jokes because your story is properly structured and completely outlined. Your story problems are solved.

A DIFFERENT WAY OF WRITING SCENES

Now it's time to start writing scenes.

If you're confident of your ability to write dialogue, especially jokes, I imagine that you will be raring to go.

On the other hand, you may feel a little wary. Some of the best comedy writers I have worked with over the years were nervous about writing jokes. If you're insecure about jokes, let me reassure you. First of all, you're not alone. Everyone is afraid of not being funny. No one wants to pitch or write a joke that falls flat. Secondly, the people I've worked with who were the most confident about jokes, the "Joke Men," were usually the least talented writers. I'd much rather work with an introspective writer who can give me a solid scene that makes sense and is true to the characters and to the premise of the series, than have to endure some joke-meister who is going to hand me eight pages of generic gags, totally unrelated to the series we're doing, that he'd shoehorn into any script that he was writing.

I want to offer you a different approach to writing scenes for situation comedy that I know will help you now and will continue to help you throughout your career as a professional sitcom writer. My method is logical, just as every other step in sitcom writing has been logical. If you feel that you're a strong joke writer already, indulge me for a few pages. If you're concerned about jokes, your concerns are about to diminish.

For many years now I have believed that coming up with the jokes is the easiest part of sitcom writing. I believe this partly because I have learned from experience that the *hardest* part of sitcom writing is developing a good story and structuring that story properly. Without a good story that is properly structured, even the cleverest jokes are going to fall flat. When a story is fake or forced, when the characters behave as fools or do and say things that no one would ever do or say, the audience doesn't care. When the audience doesn't care, they don't laugh. With a good story that is properly structured, in which the characters behave in a way that is honest and authentic if slightly exaggerated, the jokes will flow like water from a tap. When the audience is engaged, they laugh. I guarantee it.

I have learned from experience that if you understand the characters and the premise of the series, you instinctively know what the characters are going to say. It's logical. If you know how the characters think and feel and react, based on how they have behaved and what they have said in other episodes, you will know what they should say in *your* script. The paints are already in the tray.

So how should you get started writing scenes for your spec sitcom script? What is my magic method for writing scenes that is different and better?

WRITE IT AS A DRAMA FIRST

Allow me to share with you now one of the best pieces of advice I ever received about writing a scene for a situation comedy: Write it as a drama first!

Sound crazy? Or like a waste of time?

Bill Idelson, a wonderful writer who imparted a great deal of wisdom to me, gave me this advice at the very beginning of my career. I have tested Bill's theory again and again, and it has held up beautifully over the years. Write it as a drama first.

Why?

Write each scene in your spec sitcom script as a drama first because you want each scene to be real. You want each scene to make sense. You want the characters to speak to one another as human beings actually speak. Human beings in real life do not speak to one another in set-ups and jokes. Human beings in real life do not speak to each other in one-liners and wise cracks. Human beings in real life speak to one another with *feelings* and with *ideas*!

FEELINGS and IDEAS are what you want to get down on paper first, before you move on to the jokes!

You want your characters to speak to each other in a way that sounds natural and real. That's what good writing is. You do not want your characters to speak to each other in a way that sounds contrived or "written." The best way make sure that the final draft of your scenes sounds natural and real, as well as funny, is to make sure that the scenes sound natural and real from the beginning. The best way to insure that your scenes sound natural and real from the beginning is to write those scenes as drama first.

ROUGHING OUT A SCENE AS DRAMA FIRST

Let's take the first scene from our spec *Frasier* outline and write it out in script form with dialogue. We're going to write it as a drama first. We are not going to worry about jokes.

We are going to write the first scene as a drama because we want to be certain that our dialogue is natural and real. We are going to write the scene as a drama first so that we are sure that our characters are speaking to one another in feelings and ideas, not in set-ups and jokes.

Here we go…

The first sentence of our outline reads as follows: "Frasier finishes up his radio broadcast."

This is a pretty typical opening moment for a *Frasier* episode, isn't it? And that's good. You want your reader's first thought to be, "Okay, this sounds like the show."

When you are plotting the first moment of your spec sitcom script, think about the series you have chosen to spec. Do episodes of that series usually start in a certain way: In a particular set? At a particular time of day?

If you were writing a spec episode of *Two and a Half Men* you would probably open your story at Charlie's Malibu beach house, wouldn't you? You might start in Charlie's kitchen or in his living room, but you'd start at Charlie's house. That's the main set for the series. That's where most of the action takes place. That's where most episodes of *Two and a Half Men* begin. If you start your spec script in a way that is consistent with the series, then right away the reader is in familiar territory. He or she is comfortable. It sounds like the show. You seem to know what you're doing.

"Frasier finishes up his radio broadcast."

The instinct here is to immediately try to think of something funny that Frasier can say to his radio listeners so you can start your script with a joke. That instinct is correct. Of course you are eventually going to want to start this scene with a solid laugh. But bear with me. We're going to write one draft of this first scene without worrying about jokes. We're going use this first draft of the first scene to make sure that our characters speak to one another in feelings and ideas, not set-ups and jokes. The set-ups and jokes will come later. Set-ups and jokes will be much easier to construct if our scene lays out naturally and truthfully first.

Just to get this first moment out of the way, let's have Frasier sign off his broadcast. We want to get Roz in as quickly as possible so we can get our story going:

>   FRASIER
>   This is Dr. Frasier Crane saying,
>   good-bye and good mental health.

We've got a placeholder here. No jokes. This isn't the final draft. We'll spruce it up later.

Let's move on with our outline:

"Roz enters from the control room and hands Frasier a phone message."

Let's flesh out that sentence as a stage direction and as dialogue:

Frasier removes his ear phones as Roz enters from the control room. She hands some slips of paper to Frasier.

>   ROZ
>   Here are your phone messages.

Frasier glances at the messages.

>   FRASIER
>   Anything important?

>   ROZ
>   I just take the messages. I don't
>   evaluate them. Listen, I wanted to ask
>   you about tomorrow night. Daphne said
>   it's your father's birth—

I brought Roz in with an agenda. She just talked to Daphne. Roz has learned about Martin's birthday tomorrow night, and she wants to talk to

Frasier about it. This teases our "B" story right here on page one. In the next scene, when Daphne and Martin discuss the birthday, the subject will have already been introduced, so it won't seem like it's arriving from nowhere. It also gives Roz something to be concerned about. It involves her immediately in a story that will unfold throughout the rest of the episode. It is important in your spec script to give all of your characters an agenda, something to be concerned about. The more you can weave the characters' agendas into the fabric of your story, the better. I could have had Roz talk about her daughter or her love life or wanting a raise, but since Roz is going to be involved in the "B" story about Martin's birthday, why not start her involvement right here?

Back to our outline: "Roz thinks nothing of the message but Frasier has a huge reaction."

Let's translate that into the following stage direction and dialogue:

```
Frasier stares in surprise at one of his phone messages.
                    FRASIER
        My God, Arthur Lipton is dead!
```

This little moment accomplishes several things. Frasier isn't listening to Roz. That's typical of self-absorbed Frasier. We're writing the Frasier that we know. We're using the paints that are already in the tray. Roz's reference to Martin's birthday tomorrow night isn't heard by Frasier because he cuts her off before she can finish, distracted by the news in the phone message. That's good! The reader or audience now has a tidbit of information that Frasier knows nothing about. We've planted a tiny sense of mystery which helps to hook the reader.

Back to the outline: "Roz asks, who the heck is Arthur Lipton?"

Roz can ask the same question in dialogue, but do so with a little more attitude and edge. I'm going to get in the neighborhood of a joke here, but again, bear with me:

```
                     ROZ
        I saw that, but since I had no idea
        who he was, my reaction was more muted.
```

She's sarcastic here, and that's Roz. It's her character as we've seen it in countless episodes already. It's also an invitation for Frasier to give Roz information that the audience needs. He's going to explain to Roz — and more importantly, to the audience — who Arthur Lipton was and why his death is important. Information that the audience needs in order for them to understand the story is called exposition. A slang term for putting exposition into a TV script is "laying pipe." You get the picture, I'm sure. "Pipe" is expository information that you need to provide so your audience understands what's going on.

Writing good exposition, "laying pipe" skillfully, is very, very important. A reader or viewer can lose interest fast if the expository information is presented in a way that sounds clunky. A lot of writers really stink at exposition. I had the great privilege early in my career of working with the Emmy-winning sitcom writer, David Lloyd. David wrote for *The Mary Tyler Moore Show* and for *Taxi, Cheers,* and *Frasier.* He was as good at laying pipe as any writer I ever knew. I learned from David Lloyd that writing good exposition, "laying pipe" skillfully, is really a matter of making sure that one of your characters really needs to hear this information or that one of your characters really needs to provide it. In this case, Roz couldn't care less about Arthur Lipton, but Frasier is going to respond to Roz's sarcasm with information that is very important *to him*, and also happens to be information that the audience needs to hear.

Let's add the following dialogue:

> FRASIER
> Arthur Lipton was president of my opera
> club.

> ROZ
> Uh huh. So anyway, Daphne said that
> tomorrow night was —

Roz doesn't care about Arthur Lipton, but Frasier does! Roz is back to her agenda, trying to find out about Martin's birthday. Frasier isn't interested in Roz's agenda. He is consumed with the news about Arthur Lipton because it means a great deal to him. So he plunges ahead with more information that we need to hear but that Roz doesn't care about.

From the outline:

"Frasier tells her Arthur Lipton is — or was — president of his opera club. Roz says, 'Oh.' She couldn't be less interested. She heads back into the control room. Frasier, highly excited, follows her in. Frasier tells Roz that while he's grieved, this is a golden opportunity. The presidency of the opera club is vacant for the first time in ten years!"

It seems unnatural now to have Roz exit to the control room. We've added an attitude for her that wasn't in the outline. This is normal. Each time you rethink a scene, hopefully you'll come up with some new ideas. Now we have Roz trying to find out about Martin's birthday. But Frasier, excited, keeps interrupting. That serves us quite well. It's always fun to have characters working at cross purposes. Let's have Frasier interrupt Roz's query about the birthday party with musing about Arthur Lipton:

> FRASIER
> I'm grieved of course. Who wouldn't
> be? Arthur Lipton guided that club for
> ten years. On the other hand, this means
> that for the first time in a decade the
> presidency is vacant.

The pipe has been laid. We know that the presidency of the opera club is vacant. We suspect that Frasier is interested.

We can move on now to establishing Frasier's First Goal. The outline reads: "Roz hopes Frasier won't be too disappointed if he loses. She reminds him that he ran for president of his wine club and failed. He ran for president of his condominium board and failed. He was nominated for awards and lost. He gets all worked up over these petty honors and then something always goes wrong and he ends up disappointed. Roz asks, 'Why do you care so much?'"

This is a mouth full of information for Roz. We certainly don't want to pile it all into one speech. When you have to transmit a lot of information like this, you also need to keep the dialogue natural. You don't want your characters speaking the way people do on TV commercials: "Gee, Phyllis, when Harry is irregular I always buy Ex-Lax." We can do better than that. Let's see if we can get out this information in a more conversational way:

```
Roz forgets her agenda for a moment and looks
skeptically at Frasier.
                    ROZ
         You're not thinking of running for
         president, right?


                  FRASIER
         Why wouldn't I consider it?


                    ROZ
         Because whenever you go after one of
         these silly honors you always get your
         heart broken.


                  FRASIER
         I'm sure I have no idea what you're
         talking about.


                    ROZ
         You ran for president of your wine club
         and lost. You ran for president of
         your condo board and lost. You get
         nominated for awards and you always
         lose. And then you mope around here
         for weeks feeling sorry for yourself.

Frasier hangs his head. He knows that what Roz is
saying is true.
```

```
                    ROZ (cont'd)
      Why do you care so much? It's just a
      stupid club for snobs.
```

Candor like this is consistent with Roz's character. She's a no-nonsense gal, quite the opposite of pretentious Frasier. This is a moment that many of us can relate to. In an effort to try to protect the feelings of someone we care about we end up pointing out their shortcomings. Their feelings get hurt anyway.

We are just a page or two into our script and already an interesting story has started. The reader doesn't have to wait long to discover what the story is about or to develop a rooting interest in its outcome.

You'll want to do the same thing with your spec script.

Get your "A" story going as soon as possible, on the first page if you can. Your reader isn't going to read page after page waiting for the story to start. If your reader is a Hollywood big-shot, she or he is busy, skeptical and impatient. You've got to hook your reader fast as we have here.

Let's get back to our outline: "Frasier is hurt. He tells Roz that he realizes that opera may sound pompous to some people, but his mother introduced him to opera as a young boy, and he loved it. Maybe he loved it because of how much she loved it. Frasier and his mother used to listen to opera together on rainy afternoons when he was a child. Now every time he goes to the opera or goes to a meeting of his club he's reminded of how close he was to his mother, how she appreciated him for who he was, and how she encouraged him to be himself. 'Opera keeps her alive for me,' Frasier confesses."

Once again we're faced with a lot of exposition. But this is important dialogue in the opening scene. Remember that we want our characters talking to each other in feelings and ideas, not set-ups and jokes. We are writing real and natural dialogue in this first draft.

Everything in this section of the outline expresses Frasier's deepest feelings. It reminds us of who he is, and creates sympathy for him. He loved his mother and he misses her. This humanizes Frasier and helps to explain and justify the comical behavior he will demonstrate later.

When a character on a sitcom is about to pursue a goal and/or make an *unwise decision* that will get him into trouble, it is very important for the audience to understand why the goal is being pursued and why the unwise decision is being made. The dialogue we are about to write will explain Frasier's First Goal. He wants to be president of his opera club not just because of his ego, but because it helps him to reconnect with his mother. Having Frasier express his feelings will help everyone in the audience to understand Frasier's motives and to root for him to achieve his goal.

As you introduce a First Goal or First Problem for the Main Character in your spec sitcom script, make sure that you add dialogue which helps the reader to understand why the character is pursuing the goal or why the character wants so badly to solve the problem. Once we understand the character's motives and believe that the motives are legitimate and consistent with the character and with the premise of the series, we will then accept and enjoy even the most outrageous behavior later.

Comedy hinges on setting everything up believably. That's another reason I'm asking you to leave jokes out of your first draft. If your story plays believably as a drama, then you can be confident that it will play believably as a comedy. Comedy is just believable and recognizable human behavior that is exaggerated to comic heights. If we understand why a character is doing something, we will accept almost any behavior no matter how outrageous.

Frasier's reminiscences about his past are called "back story." That means you are introducing facts that happened prior to the action in the scene. We are not adding new elements to the Frasier character or reinventing the series. It was well-established on the *Frasier* series that the character of Frasier Crane was close to his mother and that she was very cultured, so it is consistent with the series and with the character to add these new details about Frasier's life. (We aren't giving him a former wife that we've never seen or a former job that we've never heard about. We've heard about all of these feelings and ideas before.)

Let's now put Frasier's reminiscences about his mother — his motives for wanting to be president of the opera club — into dialogue, without worrying about jokes:

```
                    FRASIER
    Perhaps opera does seem pompous to you,
    Roz. But my mother introduced me to
    opera when I was a small boy. We used
    to listen to opera together on rainy
    afternoons, just the two of us, on the
    living room sofa in front of a roaring
    fire. It was so peaceful and soothing.
    I felt safe and happy. Those are some
    of the most cherished memories of my
    life. It pleased my mother that I
    enjoyed opera as much as she did. It
    made me feel important to her, and it
    made me feel comfortable with myself.
    I loved my mother, and every time I
    listen to opera or talk about opera, it
    helps to keep her alive for me.
```

This speech is heartfelt and honest. It certainly isn't funny yet, but it's real. I will show you in the next draft how you can easily add jokes that will liven it up. But right now let's keep working from our outline: "Roz is moved. She tells Frasier that she'd vote for him based on what he just said. Frasier is surprised by Roz's reaction. 'You shared part of yourself with me, Frasier, instead of giving one of your usual endless stuffy speeches. I was moved. It made me love you even more. It made me want to support you. Maybe the snobs will be moved in the same way.'"

Roz Doyle is caustic and blunt, but she has a heart, as was demonstrated over and over on the series. And she genuinely likes Frasier. In revealing his deepest feelings to her, it's completely believable that Roz would be flattered and moved by Frasier's honesty. He's such a pompous phony much of the time that seeing him so vulnerable would easily disarm Roz. Let's have her express all that to Frasier in dialogue:

                    ROZ
What a lovely memory, Frasier. Thank
you for sharing that with me.

                    FRASIER
Seriously?

                    ROZ
Yeah. Instead of boring me to death
with one of your usual stuffy speeches,
you opened your heart. I was moved.

                    FRASIER
You were?

                    ROZ
I don't know about the other snobs in
your club, but if I was a member, and
you told me that story, I'd sure vote
for you.

We'll get to the jokes in the next draft. We've laid all the ground work for them and they're going to be easy to insert. But for right now, let's talk about why we wrote the scene this way.

When a character states a First Goal or encounters a First Problem in a sitcom episode, it is common to have another character present to witness the moment and to comment. First of all, you can't have the Main Character talking to himself. Secondly, the Supporting Character is going to play a pivotal role in where the story goes from here. This Supporting Character will very often warn the Main Character that the course of action on which he or she is embarking is dangerous or ill-advised. How often did Jerry Seinfeld warn George or Elaine or Kramer that a scheme they were hatching in the first scene was going to go awry? Monica would warn Rachel. Debra warns Ray. Carrie warns Doug. Charlie warns Alan. If a character is about to make an unwise decision, it's important that someone else be there to warn that character of the potential danger. The Main Character is going to make the unwise decision no matter what the Supporting Character says, but the warning is there to foreshadow the trouble that is sure to follow. This conscious foreshadowing is a way for the storyteller to say to his listeners, "Look, I know that what this character is about to do is wrong, but watch what happens because it's going to be enlightening." Nod, nod, wink, wink, we both know this is crazy, but let's watch anyway because we'll learn a valuable lesson.

Sometimes the Supporting Character is there not to warn but to validate what the Main Character has in mind. Joey might endorse a crazy idea that Chandler has. Often the Supporting Character is recruited to join in the plan. Lucy enlists Ethel in one of her nutty schemes.

In our *Frasier* episode, Roz warns Frasier not to run for president, but is moved by Frasier's memory. She then validates his desire to run for president. Roz is there both to warn Frasier and to nudge him forward, to help set the story in motion.

In your spec sitcom episode, your Main Character will come upon a First Goal or encounter a First Problem hopefully in the very first scene. He or she will then decide on a First Action to achieve that goal or solve that problem. Once you have established the Main Character's motives for wanting or needing to achieve the goal or solve the problem, you'll want another regular character present to either warn your Main Character that he or she is headed for trouble, or to validate the plan and perhaps even get involved in it. We've used Roz to warn Frasier about chasing after false glory but also to encourage him to share his feelings with his opera club.

Let's go back to our outline:

"Buoyed by Roz's encouragement, Frasier calls and nominates himself."

Let's add the following dialogue:

> FRASIER
>
> Thank you, Roz. Well, I haven't made
> up my mind what to do. I'd be honored
> to serve, but on the other hand I have
> been hurt far too often to face another
> disappointment. No need to rush into
> anything. Poor Arthur Lipton's body
> isn't even cold. Perhaps I'll mull it
> over on the drive home.

Frasier exits the studio casually, then as soon as he is out of Roz's sight, he whips out his cell phone and dials.

> FRASIER
>
> This is Frasier Crane calling... Yes, I
> just heard. I'm heartsick. What will
> we do without dear old Arthur?... I
> was wondering... when precisely will the
> club be accepting nominations?

We end our scene with our Main Character in motion toward his First Goal with no Obstacle yet in sight. We know something is going to go wrong, but we have no idea what, so there's an element of excitement for the Main Character and mystery for the reader. We understand why Frasier wants so badly to achieve his goal. He's been thwarted in the past and he wants to reconnect with his dead mother. All the ingredients for a solid story are here. This is a serviceable first draft of our first scene.

I strongly suggest that you write the entire first draft of your spec sitcom script in this way. If your story works as a drama, it will work as a comedy.

Even if you feel comfortable writing jokes, until you have mastered the sitcom form I suggest training yourself to write with feelings and ideas first. Sketching out your first draft as a drama will help you to focus entirely on honest and believable dialogue. Writers who are comfortable with jokes are often more interested in the "funny" than in the "real." Well, if it ain't real, it ain't gonna be funny! Don't just take my word for it. Test out my theory. Watch a good comedy, either a movie or a sitcom. If it works, it works because it's believable. Then watch a bad comedy. If the jokes fall flat, if you're embarrassed for the poor actors, it's because the behavior and dialogue of the characters isn't believable. Comedies fall flat or are embarrassing to watch (and we've all seen plenty of them) because they are not grounded in reality. That's why I want you to write your script as a drama first. Have enough respect for your story to make it work as a drama. Once you've done that, it is easy to add humor.

If you're not confident about your ability to write jokes, then writing your scenes as drama first is going to be a huge help to your self-esteem. Once you have a draft of any scene or script, you already have something on paper. You haven't allowed your fears or doubts to stop you from writing. You have completed a draft. Good for you! You can enjoy a sense of accomplishment. You know now that you have a solid scene that is real and believable and moves your story forward. You've introduced your First Goal or First Problem. You are well on your way. So just keep writing. Work from your Detailed Outline and write your entire first draft as a drama. Have faith that the jokes are going to come because I'm going to show you how to find them as soon as you're ready.

Great! We have a scene! It makes sense and it's real. We resisted the temptation to get bogged down with jokes. We have dialogue that plays with authenticity. We're off to a good start.

NOW FOR THE JOKES

Now comes the easy and fun part — the jokes. And if you don't believe me yet that jokes are the easy part, wait until you've read through this section. I'm going to demystify jokes for you in the same way that I demystified all the other parts of constructing a solid spec sitcom episode. I'm going to show you how it's all logical. I'm going to show you how you will use your knowledge of the series, your understanding of the series premise, your understanding of its formula, and your understanding of the personalities of the characters to guide you to the jokes that are there waiting to be written. The paints are already in the tray. All you have to do is dip your brush and apply it to the canvas.

Let's rewrite the first scene of our spec *Frasier* and add some jokes. We'll start with the opening moment.

Frasier had a tradition of opening episodes with a caller on the line. There'd be a quick joke and then the story would start. We only want to hear a sentence or two from the caller. But by opening our spec script in the same way that most *Frasier* episodes began, we are demonstrating our knowledge of the series. You'll want to open your spec episode in the tradition of the series you have chosen.

Our caller's problem can be about anything. These caller moments on *Frasier* were often "stand alone" jokes that had nothing to do with the actual story. But to help focus our thinking, could our caller have a problem that is at least thematically consistent with our story? When you stay focused on the theme of your story, you'll find that jokes are easier to come by. Our theme has evolved into one about Frasier losing sight of what really matters to him — his strong connection to his family — and focusing instead on external accomplishments like becoming president of his opera club.

Let's try giving similar grandiose dreams to our Caller:

                    CALLER
        I just feel that if I could become
        pope, I could help solve so many of the
        world's problems.

                    FRASIER
        Your heart is in the right place,
        Kevin. And I envy your sense of
        spiritual calling. But often we have
        to set aside our dreams, at least
        temporarily, in order to attend to
        personal matters staring us in the

```
        face. In your case, that means
        returning the six dollars you stole
        from your sister, passing that Spanish
        test, and graduating from middle
        school.
```

Roz indicates to Frasier that it's time to sign off.

```
                        FRASIER
        Well, I see we're out of time. Until
        tomorrow this is Dr. Frasier Crane
        wishing you good-bye and good mental
        health.
```

Our set-up line is funny by itself. A caller wants to be pope. It's consistent with our theme. Frasier, the competent and compassionate radio host, offers responsible advice, also consistent with our theme about priorities. The joke comes when we realize that the caller is fourteen years old.

We have our first jokes, and they weren't that hard to come by, were they? We found them in our theme and from the established personality of our Main Character. Let's revisit our first draft:

```
Frasier removes his ear phones as Roz enters from
the control room. She hands some slips of paper to
Frasier.
                        ROZ
        Here are your phone messages.
Frasier glances at the messages.

                        FRASIER
        Thank you, Roz. Anything important?
```

```
                    ROZ
     I just take the messages. I don't
     evaluate them. Listen, I wanted to ask
     you about tomorrow night. Daphne said
     it's your father's birth—
```

Frasier stares in surprise at one of his phone
messages.

```
                  FRASIER
     My God, Arthur Lipton is dead!
```

```
                    ROZ
     I saw that, but since I had no idea who
     he was, my reaction was more muted.
```

We can give Roz a more biting response here.

```
                    ROZ
     I saw that, but since I had no idea who
     he was, I was able to hold myself
     together.
```

This line has more life to it but with the same idea. Often creating or
improving a joke involves simply giving the character more attitude.

```
                  FRASIER
     Arthur Lipton was president of my opera
     club!
```

```
                    ROZ
     Uh huh.
```

Again, we can improve Roz's response. She isn't going to care who
Arthur Lipton was, and she's going to want Frasier to know that she doesn't
care so she can get back to her agenda. That's the logic of the joke we want
to find. How do we word it? Perhaps we can go back to what Roz said in
her previous speech and continue the theme:

> ROZ
>
> Still holding together. So anyway,
> Daphne said that tomorrow night was —

Back to our first draft:

> FRASIER
>
> I'm grieved of course. Who wouldn't
> be? Arthur Lipton guided that club for
> ten years. On the other hand, this
> means that for the first time in a
> decade the presidency is vacant.

This is important information that we want to pass on to our reader. There is also a joke already there waiting to be mined. Frasier expresses grief that Arthur Lipton is dead, but in the same breath sees an opportunity to succeed him. That's very human. We all are guilty of this kind of thinking from time to time. Such an attitude shift is called a "turn," and it's a standard form of joke. We can polish this line into a joke simply by exaggerating the turn. We'll give Frasier a bigger reaction to the news, and sharpen his selfish motives so that they stand in greater contrast to his professed grief:

> FRASIER
>
> This is a profound shock. I'm deeply
> grieved. Arthur Lipton was the heart
> and soul of that club. He guided it
> with passion and mastery for ten
> memorable years. On the other hand, if
> the old coot has finally croaked then
> the presidency is at last up for grabs!

The content of the line is the same as in the first draft. All I've done is exaggerate Frasier's attitudes, which are consistent with Frasier's established character. Characters on sitcoms often speak more candidly than you or I might in real life. That's what we love about Larry David on *Curb Your*

Enthusiasm. He says out loud what most of us would never admit to thinking. This is a common practice on sitcoms and a great source for jokes.

Let's get back to our first draft:

```
Roz forgets her agenda for a moment and looks
skeptically at Frasier.

                    ROZ
      You're not thinking of running for
      president, right?


                    FRASIER
      Why wouldn't I consider it?
```

We can improve these two lines in the same way by exaggerating the attitudes:

```
                    ROZ
      Oh, God, Frasier. You're not thinking
      of running, are you?


                    FRASIER
      What the hell do you care? The closest
      you've come to seeing an opera is Elmer
      Fudd singing "Kill the Wabbit."
```

Roz knows from experience that Frasier is headed for trouble just as we do. And because I can hear Roz in my head, I know that the actress will make the line even funnier. Frasier fires back, snobbishly dismissing Roz. This is typical of the by-play between these two characters throughout the series. Roz constantly cut through Frasier's pomposity, and Frasier belittled her lack of sophistication. When writing the characters in your spec sitcom script, draw on the history that the characters have together and you will find the humor.

Back to the first draft:

> ROZ
>
> Because whenever you go after one of
> these silly honors you always get your
> heart broken.

Frasier's last line was a shot at Roz, so we can heighten the emotion of Roz's line in response:

> ROZ
>
> I care because whenever you go chasing
> after one of these silly honors you
> always get your heart broken, and then
> I get stuck picking up the pieces.

Roz makes the same point as she did in the first draft, but now a little more vividly. Back to the first draft:

> FRASIER
>
> I'm sure I have no idea what you're
> talking about.
>
> ROZ
>
> You ran for president of your wine club
> and lost. You ran for president of
> your condo board and lost. You get
> nominated for awards and you always
> lose. And then you mope around here
> for weeks feeling sorry for yourself.

The first three sentences of Roz's speech are fine. Let's make the last sentence more descriptive:

> ROZ
>
> And then we end up with two weeks'
> worth of crappy, listless shows while
> you mope around here feeling sorry for
> yourself.

Back to the first draft:

> Frasier hangs his head. He knows that what Roz is
> saying is true.

I'm going to give Frasier a line here instead of this stage direction. I think Frasier can be hurt by what Roz said and fire back at her:

> FRASIER
> Well, thank you very much for your
> merciless recounting of my failed
> attempts at recognition. I apologize
> for the extent to which you have been
> inconvenienced by my humiliation!

Back to the first draft:

> ROZ
> Why do you care so much? It's just a
> stupid club for snobs.

Roz's line is already a joke, but Frasier's next speech is a real mouthful:

> FRASIER
> Perhaps opera does seem pompous to you,
> Roz. But my mother introduced me to
> opera when I was a small boy. We used
> to listen to opera together on rainy
> afternoons, just the two of us, on the
> living room sofa in front of a roaring
> fire. It was so peaceful and soothing. I
> felt safe and happy. Those are some
> of the most cherished memories of my
> life. It pleased my mother that I
> enjoyed opera as much as she did. It
> made me feel important to her, and it
> made me feel comfortable with myself.

```
I loved my mother, and every time I
listen to opera or talk about opera, it
helps to keep her alive for me.
```

I don't want to interrupt Frasier's reverie with sarcastic responses from Roz. That would spoil the impact of the dialogue. But a long speech like this never looks good on the page. What I can do is make the dialogue a little more conversational and break up the speech with a few stage directions that indicate that Roz is being won over. I'd rewrite it as follows:

```
            FRASIER
I imagine a club for music lovers does
seem a bit pompous to someone with
season passes to Motocross Mania.

Roz sneers.

            FRASIER (Cont'd)
But I learned to love opera from my
mother. We'd listen together on rainy
afternoons. Just the two of us. Those
are some of the most cherished memories
of my life.

Roz softens as she listens to Frasier.

            FRASIER (Cont'd)
It pleased my mother that I enjoyed
opera as much as she did. It made me
feel important to her, and it helped me
to feel comfortable with myself. I
loved my mother, and every time I
listen to opera or talk about opera, it
keeps her alive for me.
```

When you're faced with a long speech for one of your characters, try to break it up. If it's appropriate to add dialogue from the other characters please do so. But if you're writing a speech like Frasier's that is intended to have an emotional impact, remember that the character who is listening — in this case, Roz — is also reacting. By adding a stage direction or two that notes the reaction of the other character, you break up the long speech and keep the other character alive. You guide the reader through the emotions of the moment.

Let's return to our first draft:

```
                    ROZ
      That's a lovely memory, Frasier. Thank
      you for sharing that with me.


                  FRASIER
      Seriously?


                    ROZ
      Yeah. Instead of boring me to death
      with one of your usual stuffy speeches,
      you shared what was in your heart. I
      was moved.
```

The thought is right here, but we can adjust these lines to make them sound more like the characters and to add some humor. Let's rewrite these speeches as follows:

```
                    ROZ
      Wow. That's a really lovely memory,
      Frasier. Geez. Thanks for sharing
      that with me.

Frasier is surprised.


                  FRASIER
      You weren't appalled by my gilded
      sentimentality?
```

                    ROZ
Of course I was, but usually you're
boring me to death with one of your
stuffy speeches. This was from your
heart. I was moved.

Let's look at the rest of the scene from our first draft:

                    FRASIER
You were?

                    ROZ
I don't know about the other snobs in
your club, but if I was a member of the
opera club, and you told me that story,
I'd sure vote for you.

                    FRASIER
Thank you, Roz. Well, I haven't made
up my mind what to do. I'd be honored
to serve, but on the other hand I have
been hurt far too often to face another
disappointment. No need to rush into
anything. Poor Arthur Lipton's body
isn't even cold. Perhaps I'll mull it
over on the drive home.

Frasier exits the studio casually, then as soon as
he is out of Roz's sight, he whips out his cell
phone and dials.

                    FRASIER
This is Frasier Crane calling... Yes, I
just heard. I'm heartsick. What will
we do without dear old Arthur?... I was
wondering... When precisely will the
club be accepting nominations?

When writing a scene, always look hard at what your characters are saying and doing. Does it make sense? Is it real? Is the dialogue consistent with the attitudes that you want your characters to have? Roz tells Frasier that if she belonged to his club and he gave that speech she'd vote for him. Do we really want her to say that? As I look this scene over, I know that Roz needs to be moved by Frasier's memory so that Frasier will be motivated to use this memory in his run for president of the opera club, but should Roz be moved so much that she now advocates his running for president? Can she be moved and still hold on to her original attitude that he'll just get his heart broken?

As you're writing, you're always making adjustments. You're always looking for a better way to construct a scene. The more you have prepared your story, and the more real you have made the feelings and ideas of the characters, the easier it is to concentrate and make improvements. Now that I think about it, I'd rewrite these last few speeches so that Roz does not advocate Frasier running:

> FRASIER
> Really? My extemporaneous
> vulnerability made an impression.

> ROZ
> It did. But not so much that I'm
> suggesting that you should run for
> president. I'm touched but not crazy.

> FRASIER
> I wasn't thinking about running. You
> make an excellent point, Roz. Every
> time I go after recognition I'm
> invariably crushed. I've learned my
> lesson. I'm simply pleased that I
> could make you understand what opera
> means to me. There's more than
> sufficient reward in that.

                         ROZ
        Good.

    Frasier starts for the door.

                       FRASIER
        I'll see you tomorrow then.

    Frasier exits the studio casually, then as soon as
    he is out of Roz's sight, he whips out his cell
    phone and dials.

                       FRASIER
        This is Frasier Crane calling... Yes, I
        just heard. I'm heartsick. What will
        we do without dear old Arthur?... I
        was wondering... When precisely will the
        club be accepting nominations?

This last line is called the "blow" or "blow-off" to the scene. It's the final joke, and it ought to accomplish several things. It needs to end the scene on a solid laugh. It needs to propel us into the next scene by promising more comedy to come.

I ended the scene with Frasier doing another "turn." First, he professes to Roz that he has no intention of running for president. But the moment he's out the door, he calls and nominates himself. We're not necessarily surprised by Frasier's turn. The brighter members of the audience will have seen this turn coming. But that's okay. Audiences love it when they can predict a character's behavior. It makes them feel in on the joke and more attached to the series.

The "blow" to our first scene works because Frasier makes a predictable yet funny turn, and because the "blow" promises more comedy to come. We now know that Frasier is going to run for president of the opera club. We are eager to discover what will happen next.

Would the writers of *Frasier* have written the scene this way? Almost certainly not. That's why you never send your spec sitcom script to the producers of that series. You send it to the producers of another series. But I think that by writing the scene as a drama first, and then deriving the humor from what we already know about the characters, we have constructed a believable scene that identifies the First Goal, builds rooting interest in the character and in the story, and sounds like the show.

MAKING THE HUMOR EASIER TO FIND

I hope that by writing a draft of this scene as a drama first, you have seen the value of establishing the attitudes of the characters in a believable and authentic way prior to worrying about jokes. I also hope this exercise has demonstrated a way to find jokes from the established personalities and relationships of the characters. You don't have to pluck the humor from thin air. If you can hear the characters in your head, you will instinctively know what they ought to say. The humor will therefore be relatively easy to find.

Writing good scenes, and writing jokes, is not mysterious. If you prepare yourself by properly structuring your story and outlining your scenes in detail, then use your knowledge of the series and of the characters, finding the humor is no more difficult than an Easter egg hunt. The treasure is right in front of you. All you have to do is look.

PAGE COUNT

How many pages should your spec script be? It depends on which series you have chosen to spec. If you can afford it, order several sample scripts for the series you have chosen. Note the page count for these actual episodes. Use these sample scripts to guide you to the proper page count for your spec script.

In general, if you are writing a spec episode for a multi-camera comedy like *Two and a Half Men*, you'll want your script to be no less than forty-two pages and no more than fifty. Less that forty-two pages will look as if you didn't try hard enough. More than fifty pages can look as if you can't edit yourself. Producers want to read as few pages as possible, but your script must look as though you have made the proper effort.

For a single-camera series like *My Name Is Earl*, your spec script should probably run about thirty pages. Single-camera series are usually written in one-hour or screenplay format. The dialogue and stage directions are single-spaced, and that's what creates the lower page count. Again, get a hold of some sample scripts. If the series is very visual, the actual page count may be in the high twenties. If it's a talky series, the scripts may run a few pages into the thirties. Dialogue takes up more page space than stage directions. A talky but fast-paced series like *Scrubs* will likely have scripts that run slightly longer than a slower-paced series like *Earl*. Sample scripts will show you the normal length of scripts and the script format that the series uses. Do they start each new scene on a new page? You'll need to know that.

Keep in mind that a half-hour sitcom episode contains only about twenty-two minutes of program content. The rule of thumb in Hollywood has always been: About a page a minute for single camera, and about two pages a minute for multi-camera. But a spec episode of a single camera sitcom should be at least twenty-five pages. A spec script for a multi-camera series should not be more than fifty-two pages. Part of what you are demonstrating with a spec sitcom script is your ability to work within the format. Producers will have no respect for writers who don't write enough, and are always impatient with writers who write too much. Beyond the obvious constraints of time, there is a good reason why most sitcom scripts run in the range of forty-two to fifty pages. (Or in the low thirties for single camera.) Sitcom scripts just work best at this length. Take it on faith. It's true.

Structure your story so that the Act Break comes as close to the middle of the script as possible. If you write a forty-five-page script, your Act Break should arrive at about page twenty-two or twenty-three. It looks more professional to write a balanced script. Professional sitcom writers will sometimes end up with a rough draft in which the first act is thirty pages and the second act is only twenty. That writer will then rewrite and edit his script to balance the two acts.

Why is balance so important? It isn't just anal. Constructing a good story for a sitcom requires you to put your Main Character through a two-part ordeal. In the First Act of our *Frasier* story, Frasier is trying to put a strategy into action to achieve the goal of becoming president of his opera club. The First Act is balanced so that two-thirds of the act, Scenes 1 and 3, are centered on developing and implementing that strategy. Only Scene 2 focuses on Frasier's family. But the episode is just as much about Frasier's relationships with his family members: his idealized relationship with his deceased mother and his current and difficult relationships with his father and brother.

Act Two moves the story forward and makes it deeper and more meaningful. Act Two literally "brings Frasier home" from his adventure in Act One. He learns to put his emphasis on family and not on achieving meaningless external goals. Act Two is also about showing that Frasier can't live in the past. He has to learn to appreciate and get along with the family that he has now. Act Two is therefore conversely balanced so that two of the three scenes in Act Two are about Frasier's relationship with his family and just one scene, Scene 5, is about the opera strategy. Both acts are needed to put the Main Character through the ordeal so he can learn the lesson of the story. Both acts are of equal importance in telling this story. Both acts require equal weight. Keeping your two acts balanced and giving each act a slightly different emphasis in advancing the theme of your story is part of what good storytelling is all about. Good storytelling is what keeps the reader interested.

Just practically speaking, you may have noticed as you channel surf that if the sitcom you are watching goes to commercial and you try to flip to a sitcom on another network, that sitcom will probably also be on its commercial break. This is no accident. The networks want to discourage flipping, so they try hard to make sure that all series run their commercials at approximately the same time. Producers are encouraged to edit their episodes so that the commercial breaks for their series come at the same time as the commercial breaks for the competition.

You can't write for television if you resent the rules. You might as well start playing by the rules now. If you want your script to look professional, edit your scenes so that your two acts are about the same length. Write your entire spec script to about the same length as the sample scripts for the series you have chosen to spec.

CHAPTER RECAP — THE ELEPHANT REMEMBERS

Writing comedy should be fun! Makes sense, doesn't it? You're trying to make people laugh. You should be laughing, too! You should be having a good time while you're writing!

Writers who struggle with comedy do so not because they lack a sense of humor but because they lack confidence about what they're doing. You build confidence by being properly prepared. Comedy is always logical. If you follow the logical steps in constructing comedy, your scenes will always be funny.

That's why I strongly suggest that you write your sitcom scenes as drama first. If your characters speak to each other with feelings and ideas, if they speak as human beings actually speak, then your scenes will be real and will make sense.

When a scene is real and makes sense, it is always easy to find the humor.

Humor comes from exaggeration. Sitcom characters are just exaggerations of real people. Most sitcom characters are created without the "self-edit button" that inhibits all the rest of us. Sitcom characters aren't as good as we are at pretending to be mature and rational. Sitcom characters are therefore more honest with their emotions and less inhibited about expressing them. Sitcom characters act more impulsively than real people. Sitcom characters have big reactions to problems and situations that real people can take in stride.

Imagine that someone butts in front of you in line at the supermarket. Are you going to make a big scene about it? Of course not. You're going to take a deep breath and let it go. But what would George Costanza do? Or Lucy? They'd make a scene, wouldn't they?

Take away that part of you that has been trained to act rationally and with maturity. Listen to the little kid voice in your head that wants to cry and scream and be jealous and get attention and eat ice cream before dinner. And then write from that uninhibited childish voice. That's what situation comedy is all about.

You don't have to make the characters in your spec script funny. They're already funny! The creators of the series did that work for you. You know how they think and how they react. All you have to do is take what you already know about the characters and use that knowledge in your story. That's why jokes are not that hard to write. Jokes flow naturally from the established personalities of the characters. Think about who the characters are. You know them very well! Use your knowledge to guide you to what they should say to each other. Hear them in your head.

YOUR "TO DO" LIST

1) Remember how I wrote that "turn" in the *Frasier* scene? I took a humorless speech and made it funny simply by slightly exaggerating Frasier's attitudes. I did the same thing with Roz. After you write a scene as drama, look at the individual speeches. Make them funny by exaggerating the attitudes of the characters. Turn off the "self-edit button" and make your characters speak with brutal honesty or with childish selfishness.

2) Once you've written a scene as drama, go back and pull out all the stops. Let the characters speak to each other with no "self-edit button" at all. Your next draft may be too uninhibited, but you can always pull it back. Find humor in a scene by letting emotions fly.

3) After you've written a scene as drama, think about what makes each of the characters funny. With Frasier we knew about his social ambitions. We also knew that Roz was sarcastic and brutally candid. What makes the characters in your sitcom funny? Write their dialogue from the funny quirks and attitudes that you know about already.

4) You may have heard or read somewhere that there need to be four jokes per page in a sitcom script or six or some other arbitrary number. Please

don't worry about this. Yes, you'll need humor on every page. Construct your story and your scenes properly, and the opportunities for humor will automatically be there. When you're sure you can't find any more jokes in a scene, put it aside for a day or two. Go do something else and forget about it. Reread the scene later when you're feeling refreshed. First thing in the morning is a great time to reread a scene if you've gotten a good night's sleep. After a meal is also a good time. I promise you that when you come back to a scene refreshed, you will always be able to find additional humor.

At this point, we're done with the first part of the book. I've shared with you everything I've learned over the course of my career about writing a solid spec sitcom script.

If you're getting ready to write your first spec sitcom script, choose a series that you love and know well. Come up with a story that evolves organically from the premise of the series and from the personality of the Main Character. Structure your story using the Seven Plot Elements. Flesh out your story in a Detailed Outline, using the formula for the series. Write your scenes as a drama first, then find the humor from what you already know about the regular characters.

In order to build a portfolio of several spec scripts, you may have to write scripts for one or two series that you don't know or like as well. I am certain that after you have written spec scripts for the series that you enjoy the most, you will have the confidence to try writing for other series. Taking a shot at less familiar sitcoms will be good practice for when you are a professional writer. Undoubtedly, you will someday have to write an episode of a brand new series, or of a series that you don't know well. Study an unfamiliar series for a few weeks. Look at the website. Order some sample scripts. Figure out the premise, the formula and the personality of the Main Character. Treat this spec exercise as if it were a professional writing assignment. The more you prepare yourself now, the less likely you are to endure a rocky start later.

PART TWO

GETTING OFF TO A GREAT START AS A PROFESSIONAL SITCOM WRITER

CHAPTER 7

YOUR FINISHED MASTERPIECE: NOW WHAT?

"Okay, Sheldon. I've written a spec script of my favorite sitcom. I'm working on story ideas for two more so I'll have my 'portfolio of spec scripts.' You said in the Introduction that you'd help me make some Hollywood connections. Okay! I'm waiting for those connections! Who are they? Where do I find them? Who do I call? Is this where you give me your cell phone number, or take me to lunch at the Polo Lounge, or hook me up with someone at CAA? Come on, man. I've got rent to pay! Let's go!"

NOW WHAT?

I don't blame you for being impatient. If you're feeling antsy and eager and ready for me to pony up on some of those fancy promises I made to you, fine. Good place to be. You won't get any criticism from me.

Speaking of criticism, let's broach that subject briefly.

(Am I stalling? Yeah. But it's my book. What choice do you have?)

Look, when you do finish a draft of a spec script, I want you to do something very important *first*, before we call the William Morris Agency.

I want you to savor the moment of satisfaction.

When a writer finishes any piece of work, be it a poem, a play, a short story, a cartoon caption for the *New Yorker*, a screenplay or a spec episode of *The Office*, it is very important to recognize that you have accomplished something difficult and real. Most people never try to write anything. Most of those who try never finish. Writing is a lot about talent, and it is also a lot about following the rules and doing the preparation, but writing is every bit as much about finishing. If you don't finish, you aren't a writer. If you do finish, you *are* a writer!

If you've finished a spec sitcom episode, then you're a writer! Maybe not a writer who's getting paid yet, but you're a writer nonetheless. Writers finish. So please pat yourself on the back for getting this far.

Now that you've finished a draft of a spec script, and you've given yourself a little praise, maybe even taken yourself out to dinner and a movie as a reward, there are some additional critical steps to take between typing "The End" and cashing a check from Universal.

The second thing you are going to do AFTER the praise but BEFORE the Hollywood connections is *give your script to other people to read*.

"WHO CARES WHAT *YOU* THINK?!"

Nobody, and I mean *nobody*, writes a script and gets it perfect on the first draft. Not David Mamet or Aaron Sorkin or Shane Black or anyone. And neither will you.

All scripts, even sitcom scripts, have story problems and dialogue problems and certainly punctuation problems. I worked with a professional writer who had no idea how to use a comma. So she just stuck them anywhere, with no rhyme or reason, as if she were gluing plastic butterflies on a sliding glass door. Made me nuts to read her stuff!

There are going to be problems in your script that you don't even know about yet. But they are problems that a Hollywood big-shot is going to notice right off the bat. You want to get those problems solved now, long, long before your script is lying on some desk at Warner Brothers. You're going to need some feedback.

To get feedback, you're going to have to send your masterpiece out into the world.

Now, which part of the world do you send it to first?

Do you mail your very first draft of your very first spec sitcom episode to a Hollywood agent?

Oh, my God, *NOOOOOOOO!!!!*

Don't you dare send that script to an agent until I tell you to! And I'm not ever going to tell you to, so don't even worry about agents until the agents chapter which is coming up four chapters from now.

So where do you get this feedback? To whom do you send your script?

SOMEONE WHO IS ACTUALLY GOING TO READ IT

Give your script to someone who is actually going to read it... and is actually going to read it right away!

If that someone is your girlfriend or boyfriend or roommate or spouse or best buddy, fine. If they will read it right away, give it to them by all means.

Don't give your script to someone who is *not* going to read it right away!

After all the work that you've done to write a script, you don't need the agony and the humiliation of waiting and waiting for a reaction from someone who has left your script on the kitchen table for two weeks while you churn your guts out about why you haven't heard, then having to call that person after way too much time has gone by and meekly inquire, "Did you have a chance to look at that script I sent you?"

To hell with that person! Don't give your script to anyone who never pays their parking tickets or can't ever get anyplace on time or hasn't returned your copy of *The Da Vinci Code* for seven months.

There are plenty of people in your life who will agree to read your script and then *not read it*! Stay away from them! You need feedback, not neglect.

The best person to give your script to for that initial reaction is the person who is going to read it right way. You know who that person is. They go to the dentist every six months. They change their car's oil after three thousand miles. Maybe they don't know much about writing. Maybe they've never read a script before in their lives. But if they'll read your script this weekend and tell you what they think, that's better than sitting around for months waiting for some scofflaw to remember what backpack they left it in.

Now, if you have access to someone who will read your script right away *and* actually knows something about writing, this is the ideal person to send your script to!

If you have a writing teacher, or a writer friend, and you feel that they truly have time to read it, give your script to them. If you're afraid of your teacher, or the teacher is an idiot, then give the script to one of your classmates. And not the one who you know will like it. Give it to the classmate whose work *you* admire. Give it to the classmate who says the smartest things in class.

As I mentioned, I gave my spec sitcom scripts to Bill Froug, who was my graduate screenwriting professor at UCLA. Bill gave harsh notes. But he read my stuff right away, and all of his notes were valid and insightful. Some of his notes were devastating. I'd hate him afterward. But his notes were always smart and correct. And when I listened to him, my work always got better.

"I REALLY LIKED IT EXCEPT FOR THE PART WHERE..."

When someone reads your script, they are going to have a reaction. There are going to be parts of your script that they liked more than other parts. You need them to tell you all of that so you can start to figure out what you need to fix. If they read your script and all they have to say is, "I really liked it," then having them read it was a waste of your time and theirs. This is someone who didn't read the script carefully, or has serious problems with reading comprehension, or can't be bothered to give you an honest reaction. If you don't get some real notes from your first reader then give your script to the next person and see what they say.

Criticism is awful. We've all gotten it. It hurts. I don't know about you, but criticism almost always makes me angry. You feel stupid for the mistakes that you made. Or you vehemently disagree. You feel certain that all of the choices you made were correct, and the person giving you notes is an ignorant sot. It is okay to feel bad about criticism. It's okay to be angry. It's okay to feel resentful. Just don't express it. Keep your rage to yourself, for Heaven's sake. You may want this person to read something else someday. But go ahead and feel as bad as you need to. Of course you're ticked off or humiliated or both. You worked hard on that script and now someone is pointing out the parts of it that they don't like? How dare they!

If you have a hard time with criticism, it is *not* because you are a weak person or a prima donna. It is because you care about the work you did. I don't trust anyone who takes criticism easily. I've worked with professional writers who would take network notes with a big fat smile on their face and then go back to the office without being upset at all. I hated those guys. And I didn't think much of their work either. If criticism doesn't hurt then I don't believe you care very much about what you wrote. It's the hack writer who takes criticism happily. He didn't know what he was doing in the first place. He's grateful for the criticism because he was completely lost to begin with.

Just know that once you put your script out into the world for judgment, the people who read it are going to have criticisms. Your ego is going to be bruised, your patience strained, and your mettle tested.

But here is maybe the smartest thing that Barry Kemp ever said to me:

"THERE IS TRUTH IN EVEN THE DUMBEST NOTE"

Painful though it may be, and after the initial shock, most of the criticism you get about your spec script is eventually going to make sense to you. Honest. It really will. Here's why: What parts of a script do people most often criticize? They criticize the parts that you had doubts about yourself! You know where the lousy jokes are. You know where the story has holes. You know the places where you fudged a little or didn't work as hard as you needed to. Well, those are the spots that are going to get nailed. But sometimes you need to get nailed in order to get motivated to go back and fix it. Most criticism is like getting caught snoozing in the break room. Deep down, you knew you weren't supposed to do what you did. Now someone has pointed it out. So you'll suck it up, admit your mistake, and go back and make things right.

But sometimes notes feel like they're from the moon.

When I was writing and producing sitcoms we used to get network notes that were so stupid you wanted to throw a rotting pumpkin at the mallet head who was giving them to you, or you wanted to dunk your own head in a bowl of ice water so it wouldn't melt. On *Newhart* and on *Coach*,

Barry Kemp and I would regularly get notes that were so foolish or off the wall that I'd come back to the office and rant for an hour. You should've been there. I'm really funny when I get going. Those were some classic rants. I'm like Lewis Black when I go off.

But Barry always said, "There's truth in even the dumbest note."

Now, some notes *are* from the moon, and those you eventually ignore, but Barry's point was that no note, no criticism, should ever be dismissed out of hand. We got plenty of notes that we discussed, spat on, and then discarded. But we did consider them. And every once in a while we'd be enduring some crazy criticism that made no sense to us at all, when all of a sudden we'd discover some flaw in the script that we didn't even know was there.

The best notes are going to come from other writers, because writers know how to talk to each other. People who aren't writers don't know how to give notes. They'll stammer and stutter and say stuff that makes no sense at all. But just because their notes are confused or inarticulate doesn't mean they're wrong.

If you believe me that there is some kernel of truth in every criticism, then sit with all the criticism you get. Think it over. Sit with it until you stop being angry or insulted. Then think about it again. You may find a big piece of help in what sounded like a really stupid observation.

Give your script to someone who will read it fast and, if possible, who knows something about writing. Listen to their criticism. Get angry. Feel embarrassed. But take the criticism seriously. Then go back and work on your script some more.

THREE OR FOUR PEOPLE

I suggest getting a reaction to your spec script from at least three or four different people. I expect, and you should expect, that you are going to do four or five drafts of your spec sitcom script before you are ready for someone who is actually in show business to read it. You don't want to blow what may be your one and only link to "The Inside" by handing the Insider a script that isn't ready. When everyone that you know who *isn't* in show business loves your script and thinks it's a work of genius, then you're ready to give it to the pros.

So finish your spec script. Give it to someone that you know. Get some criticism. The criticism may upset you and discourage you, so give yourself time to calm down. Realize that most of the problems are ones you knew were there already. Get feedback from two or three other people. Go back to the script and start rewriting. If you're confused, you can review the previous chapters of this book to see where you got off track.

When you finish your second draft, you'll get more feedback. You'll do another draft. You'll find someone new to read that draft, and you'll get some more notes.

Finally, lots of feedback and several drafts later, you'll want to get your script to someone in show business.

Okay, we're getting closer to me telling you how to get your script to someone in Hollywood. But I'm going to stall some more.

"WHAT ELSE HAVE YOU GOT?"

When you get so lucky that someone in show business reads and actually likes your spec script, what are they going to say to you? Do you remember from Chapter One? They are going to say, "What else have you got?" And when they ask you what else you've got, you better be able to give them three or four other scripts to choose from.

So when you have finished your first spec sitcom script, and you've given it to three or four people to read, and they've all given you criticism, and you've done four or five rewrites of that same script, and then you've given it back to those people or maybe even given it to three or four new people, and everyone is falling all over themselves telling you what a genius you are, what are you going to do now?

You are going to write another spec script! And go through the same process with that one. And then you're going to write another one. *And another one.* **And another one!** And if you are rolling your eyes right now and cursing me under your breath, see how far you get with your one paltry little spec episode of *How I Met Your Mother*. You aren't going to get very far.

I want you to have three or four spec scripts in the drawer before you approach anyone in show business. Because if they like what they read, and they ask you, "What else have you got?" I want you to be able to reach into that drawer and pull out another script for them to read that is just as good as the first one. If they like that second script as much as the first one, you'll have your chance at a job. If they like that first script but you *don't* have another script ready to give them, that person may not be around in two months when you finally finish that second script.

And what about that second spec? And the third one?

I told you to choose a series that you know and love for your first spec script. If you want to be a professional sitcom writer, I'm going to count on the fact that there are several sitcoms that you love or at least know very well. So if the very first spec script that you write is an episode of *My Name Is Earl* because that is your favorite show, what should your second script be?

If your first *Earl* sucks, and after reading this remarkably helpful and insightful book you now gratefully realize that you understand the process better, and you have a much funnier story idea than you did the first time, then chuck the first script and write another *Earl*. But once you have nailed *Earl*, move on to your second favorite sitcom and write an episode of that. After a few months of work, I'd like you to have four different spec scripts, all of them in great shape. By your fourth spec script, you should really be feeling confident. And by having more than just two specs to show, you give yourself variety and dimension and insurance and wiggle room. If somebody in show business reads your *Earl*, and loves it, and says, "What else have you got?" and you say, "Well, I have an episode of *The Office*," and they say, "I haven't watched too many episodes of *The Office*. Have you got anything else?" I want you to be able to say, "Yes! I do! I have this *Two and a Half Men*!"

I want you to have enough scripts banked that you are going to be able to hand someone that solid *second* script that they want to read. Once you've got a toehold, you don't want to lose it. Preparation! That's what is going to get you in the door and keep you in the door.

But okay. Let's say that you now have four different solid spec scripts, or five, or eleven. And everyone who has read them loves them. Everyone thinks you're the next Chuck Lorre. *Now* you're ready to give one of your scripts to someone in show business. *Now*, after much stalling, I have to at last deliver the goods and tell you how to meet that Hollywood connection.

MAY I HAVE THE ADDRESS OF THAT SHOW BIZ CONTACT, PLEASE?

If you have an uncle at Paramount... Well, if you *do* have an uncle at Paramount then you don't need this book. If you *don't* have an uncle at Paramount, how are you going to get a spec script to someone in Hollywood who can give you a job?

Again, let me tell you what you are *not* going to do! You are *not* going to put your scripts in an envelope and mail them unsolicited to a Hollywood agent.

No agents! Why?

Because Hollywood agents don't give out jobs! Hollywood agents accept offers from Hollywood studios for Hollywood people who *already have* Hollywood jobs.

Have you seen the movie *Tootsie* with Dustin Hoffman? If you have never seen that movie, do yourself a favor. Go rent it. It now ranks as an "old movie" and a "classic," but you can find it at NetFlix or at Blockbuster. Sidney Pollack directed this movie, but he also acts in it. He plays Dustin Hoffman's agent. And there's a scene in Sidney's office where Sidney explains to Dustin — and to the world — what agents actually do. Wait for that scene between Dustin Hoffman and Sidney Pollack that takes place in Sidney's office. It is the best explanation of the role of agents ever given in a movie or anyplace else. It is amazing how many people in Hollywood don't know the simple truth that is revealed in this scene. Sidney, the agent, says to Dustin, the client, "My job is to field offers."

Other than the fact that agents lie nearly 100% of the time, that statement — "My job is to field offers" — is the most important thing you will ever need to know about agents, and it is the reason why you are *not* going to send your spec script to an agent.

Agents do not get people jobs. Agents field offers.

For many years, I was represented by a boutique literary agency in Hollywood. This agency handled some of the top writers and producers and directors in all of the Sitcom Universe. They were "the sitcom agency." And one of the hundreds of jokes that went around about that agency was that there were no dials on the telephones. In other words, there were no outgoing calls. Only incoming. These guys were not out getting jobs for their clients. They didn't have to. The jobs came to them. All they did was field offers.

There are no offers to field for someone just trying to break into show business. How could there be? No one knows who you are.

Even if a Hollywood agent actually reads your spec script (and he won't — he'll have some assistant read it, and give him coverage) and, miraculously, the assistant likes it *and* the agent likes it (and this is in the realm of likelihood akin to an alien space ship landing at Burger King), that agent already has a bunch of other sitcom writers as clients who, like you, aren't working, and who are calling him six times a day demanding a job. For the few jobs that are available at any time for sitcom writers, an agent is pushing the clients that he already has, who, unlike you, have track records and are hot. He isn't going to by-pass those established clients, who, if he can get them hired will bring him ten times the commission that you will, to push your little spec script.

Don't waste your time with agents. You need a friend. You need to find someone who is going to get excited about helping you get your Lucky Break.

"*So who is that person?!*"

Okay. I'm really done stalling now. I'll tell you…

YOUR FRIEND IN SHOW BUSINESS

I gave my spec scripts to Bill Froug. Bill had friends in Hollywood. He gave one of my specs to the ex-wife of a well-known sitcom writer named Bill Idelson. Bill eventually read my script, and liked it, and called me. I went to see Bill at his office at NBC in Burbank. Bill's first question to me was, "What else have you got?" I gave him other scripts. He liked all of my

scripts and gave them to his producer, Arnold Margolin. Arnold was looking to hire a new writer on the show. Arnold liked my scripts, was pleased
to toss a break to a green young kid, and hired me. That was *My Big Big
Lucky Break*!

I have no idea where your Lucky Break is going to come from. But it's
out there somewhere. So let's find it.

Look, if I knew a secret formula for getting your spec sitcom script to
the right people or for getting you closer to your Lucky Break, I'd give that
formula to you. I'd do it happily. Why not? You bought my book. I owe
you that.

The most useful thing that you can do to help yourself get a job as a
sitcom writer is to write three or four or eleven solid spec sitcom scripts. I
believe that the information I passed on to you in the previous chapters can
help you to write a better spec script.

Once those scripts are written and rewritten and vetted by a few well-
chosen critics, your next goal is to get those scripts to someone who can
help you get a job.

Getting your scripts to an agent isn't the answer unless that agent is a
family friend. An agent spends some of his or her time fielding offers and
promoting the clients that he or she already has. The agent spends the rest
of his time trying to steal other hot clients away from rival agencies.
Breaking ground for a new, unknown, untested writer is not something
most agents are interested in doing, nor do they have the time.

So you've got your spec scripts in hand. You need to find a friend who
can help you get your Lucky Break.

How do you find *your friend in show business*?

Yes!! That's what you've been waiting for me to finally tell you for
chapters and chapters and pages and pages!

This question brings me, however, to the important point that if you
want to write for sitcoms, sooner or later you are going to have to move to
Los Angeles.

Stalling again. I know. I hate myself.

Los Angeles is where they make the sitcoms. They don't shoot TV sitcoms in Pennsylvania, and nobody that I know earns a living writing for television from their home in Pennsylvania. This may sound obvious to you. I'm sure it does. But a woman from Pennsylvania contacted me while I was producing *Newhart* for CBS. She wanted to write an episode of our show. She had a typewriter and a TV set, and she saw no reason to move to Los Angeles. I pointed out to her that if she wanted to be a sitcom writer, she was going to have to move to L.A. I explained that even if I loved her spec sitcom script, we didn't give out assignments over the phone or through the mail. She needed to be in Los Angeles so she could come to a meeting at our office. At that meeting, she would pitch us some ideas. If we liked any of her ideas, we'd work out a story for her, and then send her off to write an outline. After she turned in her outline she'd come back to the office for more notes before going off to write her script. When she turned in her first draft, there'd be still more notes, etc. This was not work we could do over the phone or through the mail. She wouldn't budge and neither would I. I imagine that she's still in Pennsylvania.

To have a career as a Hollywood sitcom writer you have to physically be in Hollywood. You have to be available to go to meetings and to place yourself at Writers Guild seminars or at the right branch of Starbuck's where you have a shot at making some contacts. This is the part about helping Opportunity to find you.

If you live in Pennsylvania or anyplace outside of L.A., and you want to get paid someday to write sitcoms, it is perfectly okay to stay home until you've written a few spec scripts and gotten some positive feedback. But eventually, you're going to have to get yourself to L.A.

Okay. We've gotten you to L.A. Now, finally, at last, without further ado, let's talk about making that connection.

THE SITCOM UNIVERSE

Putting yourself in Los Angeles puts you in the orbit of the people who can hire you. You'll only be a few miles, maybe only a few blocks away from someone who might be able to give you a job. Preparation is most of "everything." Proximity is the rest of "everything."

Where specifically in L.A. do you go when you get here?

Well, you'll want to put yourself inside the Sitcom Universe.

The Sitcom Universe is the part of Los Angeles where sitcoms are made and where sitcom people can be found.

The Sitcom Universe is bordered on the west by Brentwood, Santa Monica, Pacific Palisades and the Pacific Ocean. The West Side is where a sizeable chunk of the people who matter in the Sitcom Universe — the producers, executives and agents — live. UCLA is also there. UCLA Extension offers sitcom writing classes that are often taught by former writers who still know a few people. You won't be able to live in this neighborhood yet. It's too expensive. But you can buy a mocha latte there.

Sheldon Bull discusses a scene with star Melissa Joan Hart while directing an episode of *Sabrina, the Teenage Witch.*

The Sitcom Universe is bordered on the east by Van Ness Avenue in Hollywood. Paramount Studios is at the corner of Melrose and Van Ness. Across the street are Raleigh Studios and nearby is Ren-Mar Studios. A few other studio lots are in that area including the

Sunset/Gower Studios which once was Columbia Pictures. There is no show business east of Van Ness. The only thing east of Van Ness is, you know, the rest of the United States.

The Sitcom Universe is bordered on the north by Ventura Boulevard in the San Fernando Valley. Ventura Boulevard is the Miracle Mile of Situation Comedy. This area includes Studio City, where a lot of sitcoms are shot at the old CBS lot on Radford Avenue, and at Universal City Studios. This area also includes the Walt Disney Studios and Warner Brothers

Studios in Burbank, where even more sitcoms are shot. All these northern sitcom power points are within a few ounces of gasoline from each other. You can get a relatively inexpensive meal at restaurants in this quadrant of the Sitcom Universe such as Dupar's Coffee Shop, Art's Deli and Jerry's Deli, all on Ventura Boulevard. These places are like the bar in *Star Wars*. They're frequented by space travelers who know the Sitcom Universe. Actually, some of the waitresses look a lot like the characters from the movie.

The southern border of Sitcom Universe is the Sony lot in Culver City and the Fox lot on Pico in Century City. Century City is a euphemistic term for a bunch of office buildings full of lawyers. Culver City is full of green and blue buses and modest homes. Sony and Fox are distant moons in the Sitcom Universe, sort of the Titan and Io of show business, miles away from everything except the thousands of hard-working decent people who live around them. On the other hand, if you have a job at either place, you can afford the gas to get there.

WHERE TO GO IN THE SITCOM UNIVERSE

If you live in L.A. or move to L.A., your chances of running into a sitcom producer on the street are pretty slim. You are much more likely to be run over by a sitcom producer who is racing through a red light in his BMW while reading a script and talking on his cell phone. If you are struck down by a sitcom producer, and he doesn't flee the scene, you might be able to hand him your spec script while you wait for the paramedics.

But there are all kinds of events that you can attend and regular places you can go within the Sitcom Universe where you might meet the friend who can help you. As I said earlier, you can take a sitcom writing class at UCLA Extension in Westwood or at USC (which is the Pluto of the Sitcom Universe, just south of downtown L.A. and light years from anywhere).

The Writers Guild of America, West, at the corner of Third and Fairfax, has seminars all the time that you can attend for free. I've sat on panels at the WGA with other producers and writers. Most of us are pretty nice and pretty accessible. To find out what the WGA has scheduled, look on their website at *www.WGA.org*.

The Museum of Television & Radio in Beverly Hills has events. The Museum often does tributes to TV shows. The actors and producers show up. It's a fun evening, and you might make a friend while you're fawning over Eva Longoria. Look on their website at *www.mtr.org.*

All these places (UCLA, USC, WGA, the Museum) may also have information about other places you can go to meet people who might be able to help you. Life is like the Web. You start at one site and then you click on the links.

FISH OFF THE COMPANY PIER

Women I know have come out to L.A. and gotten entry-level jobs at production companies or postproduction houses. You don't have to be a beauty, but a slim, well-groomed young female with no visible tattoos can almost always find a job answering the phone and handing out parking validations at the reception desk of some company that does business in Hollywood. There are hundreds of these places. You can find them in the Hollywood Directory. Guys can occasionally get these jobs, too, but let's be real. A pleasant-looking girl is going to have the inside track.

For guys, you may have to take any job that you can get when you move to L.A., like waiting tables at The Cheesecake Factory, and then meet the friend who can help you in a pick-up basketball game in Santa Monica or at the 24-Hour Fitness in Sherman Oaks.

FARMER'S MARKET

The point of all this is to put your life in Los Angeles and then put your body out in circulation within the Sitcom Universe, at writing classes, Writers Guild events, entry-level Hollywood jobs, screenings or any place where you might just get lucky and meet somebody who knows somebody who could someday hire you.

If you're the shy type, don't worry. I am, too. You don't have to be a pest to make a connection. You undoubtedly know somebody in L.A. already. A distant cousin. A friend of a friend from college. Look them up first. Get them to go with you to something — a yoga class in Brentwood, for instance. Pay their way so you know they'll show up. Go to an outdoor farmer's market on the weekend in Santa Monica or the Palisades, or the one every Sunday on Larchmont Avenue near Paramount Studios. Larchmont is full of show-biz types on Sunday.

Don't be a pest. Don't get a job driving for an L.A. limo company and ask every single person that you schlep to LAX if they could read your spec script. The limo company will fire you the next day.

Almost *everyone* in L.A. knows someone who is in show business. Six degrees of separation. Within the boundaries of the Sitcom Universe, the odds get even better. Put your bod in L.A., and then hit the streets. After that, it's up to Fate.

And while you are out there searching for the friend who can help you, keep writing, writing, writing, and getting better, better, better so that when the Lucky Break comes, you're ready.

Once you find the friend who can help you, you will give them your scripts to read. You will suffer their notes. You will do still more rewrites, and you will wait for them to pass your spec scripts along to the person who can actually hire you.

Let's be honest. You aren't applying for a barista job at The Coffee Bean and Tea Leaf. You're trying to break into show business. So is half the country. Why do you think *American Idol* is so hot? Because everyone has the same dream! This is a gigantic crap shoot. It's trying to hit 17 at roulette. And only Fate knows if you're going to get your Lucky Break. But you'll *never* get your Lucky Break if you aren't hanging around the neighborhoods where Lucky Breaks happen.

CHAPTER RECAP — THE ELEPHANT REMEMBERS

If I had the name of a particular sitcom producer or development executive who I knew would be happy to read your spec script, I would of course give you that name.

Yes, I know people in Hollywood. I've worked there for thirty years. I have gotten scripts from new writers to the right people. I've helped start a few careers.

All of the people I have helped had a portfolio of solid spec scripts. I knew someone who knew them. Several times I ended up being the producer who was in a position to hire them.

Your Lucky Break is out there waiting for you. Once you're inside the Sitcom Universe with your portfolio of solid spec scripts, you will make your Hollywood connection. I promise. I just don't know exactly how or when it's going to happen.

A young fellow whom I met by chance at a resort wanted to write for sketch shows like *Saturday Night Live*. I didn't know how to help him because I had no connections in that world. But we kept in touch because I was rooting for him. He ended up getting into grad school in New York City. He put himself inside the Sketch Show Universe. This young writer had no New York connections at all. He had only his talent and his determination. He kept writing sketches on spec and making videos while he went to grad school. Someone that he met in New York was able to hook him up with somebody else who worked on one of the late-night talk shows. This young writer eventually got hired on one of those talk shows and is working there right now writing jokes and sketches. He isn't yet making Elephant Bucks, but he's doing just fine, thank you very much. His dream came true because he took the time to compile a portfolio of spec material, and then he put himself inside the Sketch Show Universe. He was ready when his Lucky Break came along.

YOUR "TO DO" LIST

What am I going to tell you? Go to Sports Club L.A. with your spec scripts and wait for Ray Romano to walk in? Get a job waiting tables at The Grill in Beverly Hills and keep a spec *How I Met Your Mother* under your apron?

Here are some things you really can do to help yourself get a Lucky Break:

1) Keep writing. Yeah, yeah. But honestly, it's the absolute best thing you can do to get yourself that Lucky Break. The more scripts you have, the stronger your chances.

2) Keep trying. So maybe you don't make that Hollywood connection during your first week in L.A. So get a job at Starbuck's and keep at it. Determination, remember?

3) Be creative. I didn't have some genius plan for breaking into show business, but maybe you will. Maybe you'll get your Lucky Break from joining The Groundlings and becoming an improv actor. Maybe you'll try your hand at stand-up comedy. Lots of clubs in L.A. have open mike nights. Maybe you'll end up as a nanny to some Hollywood big-shot, or you'll date some girl who works at Disney. I gave you *my* ideas. What about *your* ideas?

4) Have faith. Anyone who knows me will tell you that I am no pie-eyed optimist. I *never* think things are going to work out, and yet they always seem to. When I was trying to break into show business, I was really afraid that I was making a mistake. People kept offering me regular jobs and I kept turning them down, worried that I was going to end up homeless and humiliated. I figure that if this bug to be a sitcom writer was put inside me and you by some Cosmic Force, then that Cosmic Force owes it to us to make it all happen. I think that what the Cosmic Force demands is that we meet it halfway. Write your spec scripts. Get inside the Sitcom Universe. Give your Lucky Break the best possible chance to happen, and it will.

CHAPTER 8

YOUR FIRST PITCH MEETING

When I went in to pitch at *M*A*S*H* for the first time, I was beyond nervous, as you can imagine. I don't even know how I managed to drive over to 20th Century Fox. I must have found the place by instinct. This was one of my favorite shows, and now I was in their offices with a chance to write an episode. I knew a couple of the *M*A*S*H* writers already, and the guys gave me quite a hazing, which broke the ice and allowed all of us to relax. When I was working on story ideas to pitch at *M*A*S*H*, I used the same approach that I'd used for all of my spec scripts. I tried to test the premise by putting one of the main characters in a difficult situation that was organic to the series and sprang from the personality of the character. I noticed that they didn't do too many stories about Colonel Potter, so I figured maybe they'd like to hear one. Col. Potter was a man of high integrity and honor, so I thought, What if a senior Army nurse, a female colonel, came to MASH 4077 for an inspection? What if she and Col. Potter really hit it off? What if Col. Potter were tempted to stray from his marital vows? It was the kind of dicey story that I loved to tackle in my spec scripts. The story was human and real, with a lot of emotional impact. Well, the *M*A*S*H* writers and producers loved it, and hired me to write the episode. They helped me a lot with the story. I wrote a line of dialogue in that episode when Col. Potter explains to the nurse, whose name was Lil, that he can't be unfaithful to his wife. He tells her, "Not while there's a girl at home with my picture on her piano." I got the line from a Paul Simon song. For some reason, producer Burt Metcalfe loved that line, and kept complimenting me on it for years after.

YOUR LUCKY BREAK HAS ARRIVED!

You found your friend who could help you get your Lucky Break. See? I told ya.

The friend liked your spec scripts. The friend got your spec scripts to someone who could hire you. That someone also liked your spec scripts.

Your Lucky Break is here at last!

Someone is finally willing to give you your first job!

My first job in Hollywood was as an apprentice writer on a sitcom staff. They hired me for very little money, but it was the most valuable learning experience of my career.

If you aren't initially hired on a staff as I was, then your first shot at a writing job on a sitcom will likely be a freelance assignment.

Freelance writing assignments in Hollywood are as scarce as parking spaces on the lot. The producers of every TV sitcom are supposed to give out at least two freelance assignments per year — only two out of 22 or 24 episodes produced for a full season. The percentages stink for the freelancer. The rest of the scripts for the season — the other 20 or 22 — are usually written "in-house," meaning that the writers working on the staff of the series crank out the vast majority of the episodes. This makes it even more challenging for a new writer to break in because how can you show them what you can do if they won't let you show them what you can do? See what I mean? It's Catch-22, but that's the way it works. It is just easier for writing staffs to manufacture scripts themselves. The finished drafts are always closer to what the producers want than anything that can be written from the outside. It isn't fair to writers who are trying desperately to get a break, but you're entering into show business, and "fair" is a concept you better get really flexible about.

When you have finally impressed a producer of a sitcom with your spec scripts, you will likely be asked to come to a "pitch meeting." In that meeting, you will be given the chance to "pitch" story ideas for that series. If you can pitch them a story that they like, you will be given an assignment to write a freelance script for that series.

I've been the freelance writer coming in to pitch on sitcoms many times. I still attend pitch meetings to this day at the networks and studios for pilots and feature film scripts. I know what it's like to walk into a room full of development executives or comedy writers and try to sell them an idea. I also have a fair amount of experience in the producer's chair. Countless freelance writers have come in to pitch to me.

Okay. You're going in to pitch on a real Hollywood sitcom. Relax. Let me walk you through the process. If I can do it, *you* can do it!

THEY'RE DOING *YOU* THE FAVOR!

Let's say you've got a meeting to go in and "pitch" to the producers of *My Name Is Earl*. The first thing you do when you get that magic phone call inviting you to come in is agree to meet at any time that they suggest. If they want to meet you next Wednesday at 10:00 a.m., or if they want to meet two weeks from Thursday at 7:30 in the evening, you say, "Yes!"

I don't care if you have already scheduled a dentist's appointment at the same hour, or you've landed the hottest date of your life, or if you have plane tickets to fly home for your mother's birthday. You happily agree to whatever time they suggest, and you never even hint that there might be a conflict. Producers of a sitcom who are inviting you in to pitch to them are doing you the most enormous favor of your life. You do not want to risk spoiling this once-in-a-lifetime opportunity by being difficult about the time. It's their time that is valuable, not yours, so you will cash in the Jet Blue tickets, get the day off from Rite Aid, reschedule the laser surgery, and get in there when they want you!

PREPARING FOR THE MEETING

Prepare for this first pitch meeting — and for every pitch meeting that you will ever attend in Hollywood — in the same way that you prepared to write your spec scripts. Hopefully, you will be intimately familiar with the series that you are going to pitch. Do yourself a favor. Watch every sitcom on TV because who knows which show is going to give you your Lucky Break? I got called in to pitch on a show called *Carter Country*. It was new. I'd never even seen it. I did a crash course in their offices watching tapes. Watch shows that you hate, because, as a comedy writer, you know something about irony. The show you can't stand will be the one that gives you a shot!

Even if you're going in to pitch on a series that you watch every week, learn as much as you possibly can about it. Go to their website. Make sure you know the names, and the correct spelling, of all the characters, and the names of all the actors who play those characters. Learn the names of all the writers and producers. You may not know ahead of time which staff members are going to be in your pitch meeting. Whoever ends up listening to your pitches, make sure you know who they are!

There are usually multiple websites for every series where you can find out the back stories on all the characters, and maybe even get a hint about what episodes have yet to air. Study every episode that they have done so far. You want to pitch them the kinds of story areas that they like to do, but you don't want to pitch them a story they have already done.

I don't know how much time you'll have to prepare for your pitch meeting, but I imagine you will have at least a few days. If for some reason they ask you in tomorrow, don't freak out. Take your own crash course on the Web, buy a few cans of Red Bull, come up with six ideas, and then get in there!

SIX STORIES, SIX NOTIONS

Once you have crammed every bit of information possible about the series into your head, you'll need to prepare at least six complete stories to pitch. Yeah. Six! Why six? Because eight is too many, and four isn't enough. Six is the number. I think six stories says, "I respect your series, and I really want this job!"

Use the same formula for these six stories that you used to come up with your spec script stories. Use the premise of the series and the personality of the Main Character.

Your six complete stories should be worked out enough that you know all of the Seven Plot Elements: the First Goal or First Problem, Obstacle, First Action, Act Break, Second Goal, Second Action and Resolution. Know these seven elements for all six of your stories!

Be sure you have some funny moments and jokes to pitch as well.

You'll want to block out a few free days or evenings to work out the details of your pitch. Write everything down. Take your notes with you. You don't want to get lost during a pitch. But the more you can commit your ideas to memory the more impressive your pitch will be.

After you have worked out six complete stories to pitch, try to work out six more "notions" or "springboards." A "notion" or "springboard" is a story idea that isn't worked out entirely but shows potential to be a complete story. An example of a good "notion" or a "springboard" would be something like, "Earl has to baby-sit for an old girlfriend and worries that one of her kids is his," or "Charlie and Alan Harper end up on the same jury." There is fertile ground for a story in each of these notions, but the whole idea hasn't been worked out.

Why six complete story ideas and six notions? Producers have a limited amount of time to meet with you. You'll be lucky if they have time for you to pitch them three ideas, much less six, but you need six complete ideas in case you get cut off fast on some of your stories. Freelance writers cannot know what stories are in the pipeline on a series. You may pitch them two or three story ideas that they are already working on. If this happens, don't worry about it. Move on to the next story. I always would compliment writers who pitched me story ideas that we were already working on. It meant that they understood the series.

You may not sell them any of your six complete story ideas. Don't feel bad if you don't. Selling a story idea to a producer is like hitting a bull's eye in the fog. When you work on staff you still have to pitch ideas to the producers, and you never know what they are going to respond to. Even when you work with a producer every day, you never know when they are going to say yes to an idea. If you don't sell any of your six complete ideas, then go to your notions. I have flamed out during pitch meetings in ten or fifteen minutes with all my best ideas. I've seen it happen to other writers. That's why you prepare six notions as well. Your notions give you six more quick shots at selling them something before the meeting is over.

HOW TO PITCH A STORY IDEA

Pitch your best idea first. Start with a one-sentence synopsis of your story

— a log line. Think about the little blurbs they put in *TV Guide* to describe an episode of *Two and a Half Men*. Try to boil your story idea down to one snappy sentence and begin your pitch with that. Producers are smart and experienced. They can see the potential of your story idea better than you can. If they don't like the idea, or it's similar to something that they are already writing, they'll let you know after that first sentence. This way you don't waste their time or yours. Remember, the clock is ticking. You only have so much time for your pitches. The producers have a million other things to do that day, so the more concise you can be the more they will like you.

If the producers respond positively to your log line, then you can pitch them the complete story. Again, be as concise as possible. Don't bore them with every little detail. Tell the story as if you were describing an episode of the series to a friend who only had a few minutes to listen. Give them the Seven Plot Elements (First Goal, Obstacle, etc.). Give them the gist of each scene and a joke or two, but just enough so they understand what you mean. You ought to be able to pitch a complete story idea in about five minutes. Time yourself before you go in. It's always a good idea to practice pitching all of your story ideas before the meeting and then rehearse them again in the car on your way to the meeting.

When you finish pitching, you'll know right away if they liked your idea. Don't worry if you forgot some details. If they like your idea they will ask some questions. Be prepared to answer them. Have some information and some jokes in reserve that weren't in the pitch. You should know about twice as much detail as you actually pitch.

If they don't like your idea or they feel it's close to something they are already working on, take the news in stride and move on, even if you've just lost your best idea.

The producers may not respond to any of your six complete story ideas. As I've said before, it's very hard for an outside writer to come up with a story idea that producers haven't already thought of or aren't already working on.

If you flame out with all six of your complete story ideas, ask if you can pitch them your notions really fast.

If they don't respond to any of your ideas or notions, it'll be up to them to decide what to do next. If they like you, if they're feeling magnanimous, if they feel you got close, they may invite you to come back and pitch again. If they do, ask for guidance. Ask if they are looking for stories for a particular character on the series or if there is a subject or theme that they would like to explore. Any information they can provide to help focus your thinking will give you a better shot next time.

Occasionally, producers will give a complete story to a writer. After I finished my first assignment at M*A*S*H, they asked me back to write another script. I didn't have to pitch the second time. They gave me the whole story.

Once, when I was working on *Coach*, we worked out a story for a freelance writer while the writer was there. We didn't respond to any of her story ideas, but we liked the writer and wanted to give her a shot, so we came up with a story for her.

YOU DON'T NEED PERFECT PITCH!

You are a writer, not a carnival barker. I hate pitching. Some writers love it. Some writers are much better at pitching than they are at writing. In fact, the best pitch artists are often just that. Pitch artists. They aren't really writers. And when it's time to put pen to paper, that's when they crumble. I knew a writer who sold everything that he pitched. But his career eventually flamed out because he couldn't deliver the goods after he made the sale.

Some writers are natural-born salesman and actors. But don't get down on yourself if you're nervous, or if you don't feel uncomfortable pitching your ideas. Very few writers like pitching. Most of us would much rather be in a room typing.

The best way to be as relaxed and confident as possible in a pitch meeting is to be prepared.

If you have six solid story ideas, and you have spent time working them out carefully, and you have your six notions in reserve, and you have rehearsed your pitch a few times before the meeting, and again in the car on your way to the meeting, you will do fine. Don't worry. You don't need perfect pitch.

Producers and staff writers are smart. If you have a good idea that they can use, they'll get it, even if you don't pitch it perfectly. Producers' ears are acutely attuned to good ideas. If you've got some good ideas, and I know you will, the producers will hear them even in a cacophony of confusion.

Prepare. Rehearse. Relax. You'll do fine!

PITCH MEETING SUPPLIES

So that you *will* be prepared, *take the following items with you to your pitch meeting*:

1) **Your six complete story ideas**. Bring them with you, written down. You can have them on cards or on a legal pad. Don't bring a lap top. It looks too nerdy. Your notes should just be talking points – key words or phrases that can quickly refresh your memory if you lose your train of thought. If you can pitch from memory, great! The meeting will go more smoothly. You will look more professional if you can pitch out of your head. But just in case your memory is faulty, or you find that you're too nervous to think straight, have the notes at your side. It is better to stop a pitch and check your notes than to get completely lost and fall into a panic.

2) **A legal or letter pad**. This is for you to take notes in case the meeting goes very well, they like one of your story ideas, and they start pitching back to you. Don't take notes until they make it clear that they like your idea and want to pursue it. Sometimes producers will pitch with you just to explore an idea for themselves, then later reject it. But if they respond to one of your ideas and want to start pitching with you right now, you'll want a note pad handy so you can write down what they say.

3) **Several pens or pencils**. You can borrow a pencil or pen, but you will look so much more professional if you have your own supplies. Just don't put the pens and pencils in your shirt pocket. You're there to pitch ideas, not fix the copy machine.

4) **A digital recorder or tape recorder**. If you take a bag of some kind to the meeting, stick a recorder in it. Like the letter pad, this is also in case the meeting goes well, and they want to pitch on one of your ideas. Ask them if it's okay to record, then run the machine. Bring a machine that works! Don't borrow some piece of junk from your roommate. If you don't already own a recorder when you get invited to your first pitch meeting, go out and buy one. You'll find the money somehow. Bring extra batteries, extra tapes or extra memory. You don't want your recorder to shut down in the middle of a meeting. You're a pro now. Act like one.

I have this old leather bag that I've been lugging with me to work and to meetings for years. I got it at a horse show of all places. It looks like a saddle bag. I can put all my stuff in there and not look like I'm some tax attorney or Ricoh technician.

Bring your supplies and be ready just in case the pitch meeting goes exceedingly well, and you sell a story right there in the room! Hey, it could happen!

KEEP IT IN PERSPECTIVE

If your spec scripts were good enough to get you into one pitch meeting, they are good enough to get you another one. So if your very first pitch meeting does not result in a sale, don't shoot yourself or think you have blown your one and only chance at success.

Unless you are pitching to the producers of a brand new series, it is very difficult to sell a story in a pitch meeting. A series that has been on the air for a while has already done most of the best stories, and they've rejected dozens of others. If you are familiar with the series, you are much less likely to pitch them an idea they have already done, but I've been in plenty of meetings where freelance writers pitched ideas that we already had in the pipeline. I've been in meetings where *every single idea* that the freelance writer pitched was already in the pipeline.

Producers (Show Runners) also tend to love their own ideas above all others. It's often nearly impossible even for members of the writing staff to sell an idea to the Show Runner because the Show Runner is madly in love with his or her own ideas and *only* his or her own ideas. Most Show Runners have fought their way up through the ranks to get to this lofty perch. They have suffered the egos of other Show Runners for years before landing a series of their own. So now it's time for them to get their way every minute! This series is their vision, and they secretly (or not so secretly) believe that they, and only they, are talented enough and dedicated enough to do this series justice. It takes a robust ego to become a Show Runner and survive at it, and it is often very difficult for those egos to believe that anyone else but them is capable of a good idea.

Keep it in perspective.

Once you start getting invited to pitch meetings, you are more than half way home! If they're asking you in to pitch, you have proven that you are good enough to be a pro. So now it's just a matter of time before you hit it big. I mean it. So feel encouraged!

CHAPTER RECAP — THE ELEPHANT REMEMBERS

Your role in a pitch meeting is part salesman, part actor. Now, neither of these "characters" may come naturally to you. Many writers are shy. That's why they became writers. Try to keep in mind that at least you'll be pitching to other writers. The producers and staff writers in the room for your pitch meeting know that pitching is a challenge. They will most likely be on your side and pulling for you to succeed.

Be prepared.

Learn as much as you can ahead of time about the series you are going to pitch. Check their website. Get sample scripts. Learn the names of the characters, the actors, the writing staff.

Bring six story ideas and six notions to your meeting.

Rehearse your pitches ahead of time. Make your pitches concise. The clock is ticking.

Be prepared to answer questions.

Bring a note pad, pens and pencils, and a recording device in case you sell something, and they want to pitch.

YOUR "TO DO" LIST

1) Just for practice, even though there's no pitch meeting in your future at this time, try coming up with six complete story ideas for a currently running sitcom that you know and like. You know why this is a good idea even now? Because it may help you nail down that perfect story for your spec script! See if you can come up with six story areas and then identify the Seven Plot Elements for each story. Don't spend days doing this. See what you can come up with in a couple of hours. If you really spark to one of your ideas, you may want to develop that idea into a spec episode.

2) Take twenty minutes, and just off the top of your head fire off as many story notions as you can for a sitcom that you know and like. Don't stress about it. Come up with as many notions as you can as quickly as possible. On writing staffs, we call this "spit-balling" or doing "springboards." It's a great way to train your brain to think about story ideas.

3) If you've tried pitching sitcom story ideas to friends or in a class, then you've already had some practice for your first pitch meeting. If you haven't tried pitching yet, now is a great time to get in some practice. Try pitching the idea for your spec sitcom episode to a friend or classmate. See how well you do as you go along. Are they following your story? Do they stay interested? Are they laughing? If you can pitch your idea successfully, then you can be sure that you'll be able to write it. If you find yourself fumbling, or if your listener loses interest, this is a great way to discover those story problems that you still need to address.

CHAPTER 9

YOUR FIRST ASSIGNMENT

When I got my first paying assignment to write an episode of a TV sitcom, I was already working on the staff of that series as an apprentice writer. Until the moment when I was assigned a script to write, I spent my days — and evenings — in the Writers' Room with the rest of the staff pitching jokes and doing group rewrites of scripts written by other people.

Now, suddenly, I was entrusted with my very first professional script. I was nervous. "Really? You? Nervous?" But I was also ready. I was blessed because I had the support of the rest of the staff. If I got confused or stuck, I could walk next door to Lloyd Garver's office or down the hall to Bill Idelson's office or to Carol Gary's office, and they'd help me.

After my script was shot, Arnold Margolin, the executive producer, and the rest of the writing staff, presented me with the writing credit title card for that episode. It was just a simple black 8x10 card with "Written By Sheldon Bull" printed on it in white ink. It was framed. As the years passed, I was given my "Developed By" and "Produced By" title cards from *Newhart*, and my producer title card for *Coach*. I have my Emmy nominations, and some wonderful cast and crew photos from some of the series that I worked on. But no keepsake from my career means more to me than that very first credit on that simple black card.

THE STORY MEETING

Your first assignment will begin with your first story meeting. That meeting may occur spontaneously at your pitch session. They loved one of the ideas that you pitched. They want to immediately expand it into a full story. If so, pull out your note pad and recorder and start writing things down.

The story meeting will likely be scheduled on another day after your pitch meeting. In either case, you are going to get most of the information and guidance that you'll need to write your outline and your script in your story meeting. Most producers will give you a good story meeting. It's in their interest to do that. They want you to come back with a good outline, so they are going to give you the material that you need to write one.

Here are my tips for making the most of your story meeting:

1) *Once it's sold, it's theirs*

If the producers like one of your ideas, they will most likely want to make significant changes in your story. It's up to you now to write the story the way they want it.

Let them change your story however they want to. Remember, it's their series. They know the series better than you do. **They know what works and what doesn't work**. So don't argue and don't look upset if they start tossing out huge chunks of your well-crafted story and replacing your ideas with their own ideas. There's about a 99% chance that they are going to do that. Let them. It's their story now!

When I sold my first story idea to M*A*S*H, I thanked the writers and producers and went happily home. The staff writers took my idea and developed the story themselves without me there. I came back about a week later. The writers had a rough outline for me. We discussed it. I took some notes, then I went home again to write a more complete outline. The M*A*S*H writers had changed my story significantly from the pitch meeting. I was a little surprised by some of the changes, but I didn't argue. I was going to tell the writers of M*A*S*H how to write their own show? I don't think so. I worked with their revised story and did my best to flesh it out in a detailed outline. The fact was, the changes made my story better. It was their series. They knew M*A*S*H better than I ever could because they worked on it every day. They knew the actors and the actors' needs. They knew from experience what worked and what didn't. They made my story stronger and better, and I was grateful for the help.

If the producers start changing your story (and they almost certainly will), happily go along with everything that they suggest.

2) *Write down everything they say!*

When I was a producer on *Newhart* and *Coach*, Barry Kemp and I would work out every detail of a story in the story meeting. We never sent a writer home with holes in his or her story. We'd pitch a million jokes. I used to say that if a freelance writer really paid attention in our story meetings, and wrote down everything we said, all he or she had left to do was go home and type up the notes. The whole script was already there.

On *Coach* and *Newhart*, we knew what worked. We knew how we wanted the scripts written. We gave the writer everything he or she needed to turn in a usable script. **The smart writers listened, wrote down what we said, typed it all up, and gave us back exactly what we had pitched to them in the story meeting**. If they did that we were happy. We'd want that writer back for another assignment.

The inexperienced writers wouldn't understand that we were giving them the entire script. Maybe their egos were offended by all of our ideas. Maybe they felt that it was all too easy, and they should be coming up with their own ideas. Either way, too often they'd ignore our ideas and our jokes. They'd come back with an outline that was different from what we had pitched in the story meeting. We'd read their outline and ask, "Where the heck did this come from?" And guess what would happen? They'd get cut off at outline. We'd thank them very much, pay them off, and write the script ourselves.

If you sell an idea to producers who are willing to work out the entire story with you in your story meeting, you'll want to get down everything that the producers say. That's why I strongly urge you to use a recorder and to take notes at the same time. The recorder will insure that you don't miss anything. Sometimes when you're busy taking notes, you don't hear every comment. The recorder serves as back-up. Take the most complete notes that you can during the meeting. Write down everything that the producers or writers pitch to you. When you get home, listen to the recording of the meeting and compare it with your notes. Fill in any details, ideas or jokes that you forgot to write down.

If producers pitch a joke, they will expect to find that joke in your outline. Write it down verbatim and put it in.

As a producer, I felt much more confident about a freelance writer if I saw them take out a recorder and a note pad. That insured me that they were going to pay attention to what we said. If you use a digital recorder, make sure it has enough memory for a long meeting. Story meetings can last all day. If you use micro-tapes, bring plenty of extras. If your recorder uses replaceable batteries, bring fresh batteries. Check your recorder periodically throughout the meeting to make sure it is still working.

I cannot stress to you enough how important it is to take complete notes!

3) *Write the story the way they want it written!*

When producers or staff writers pitch ideas to you, they aren't just making suggestions. They expect those ideas to end up in your script.

It drove me crazy as a producer when freelance writers either didn't pay attention in the story meeting or went into business for themselves once they left. Ideas and jokes that are pitched to you by producers and staff writers are the tablets from Mt. Sinai. Moses didn't rewrite the Ten Commandments. **Don't change the story!**

When you are a freelance writer in a story meeting with producers and staff writers, you are not an equal. You are a stenographer. Write down what they say and put it in your outline and in your script.

It is perfectly okay to pitch with them. If you have an idea, share it. If they don't like it, they'll tell you. But their ideas are more important than yours are because *it's their show*!

4) *Don't be afraid to stop and ask questions!*

As a producer, I want the freelance writer to leave the story meeting feeling confident. If you get confused during your story meeting, don't be embarrassed. Stop the meeting and ask questions! Sometimes story meetings can get frenetic. Writers are often extroverts and performers. They get on a roll, and it's hard to shut them up or get a word in edgewise. Sometimes two or more staff writers will pitch conflicting ideas at the same time. If that happens, you may not know which idea to write down. Producers don't always keep order in a meeting. If the meeting gets out of hand, or you get lost or confused, just **ask them to clarify what they want**. The producer will take charge and tell you what to do.

Also, expect a lot of ribbing in a story meeting. Staff writers are used to arguing with each other and making jokes at the other writer's expense. A sitcom Writers' Room can be a free-for-all. It's a combination of nursery school and a frat house. Imagine an entire room full of class clowns. That crazy atmosphere supplies the energy and fuels creativity, so enjoy it. I always did.

5) *Let them do the work*

Staff writers are always trying to impress the Show Runner. A staff writer may pitch his brains out in your story meeting in order to demonstrate to the producers that he is a better writer than you are. That's his insecurity spilling out. Be grateful! Use it to your advantage! Let the staff writers pitch all they want. Write down their ideas. That's less work for you. Honestly, **if they'll write your whole script for you in the story meeting, let them**, for Heaven's sake!

You want the staff writers on your side. Remember, at least some of them will probably be reading your outline and your first draft. If they don't like you, they are going to trash your work to the producers no matter how good a job you do. Get them on your side by laughing at their jokes, writing down what they pitch, and including their ideas and jokes in your outline and in your script. Comedy writers are all children. We are neurotic, insecure, paranoid, competitive and egomaniacal. But we respond like Golden Retrievers to flattery and praise.

6) *Like riding a roller coaster*

A story meeting, especially your first one, can be an emotional thrill ride. It can be a challenge to stay focused in one of these meetings. Several people are talking at once. Everyone is pitching jokes. Conversation is either moving so fast that you can't keep up, or the writers are goofing off, straying from the business at hand, and you worry that you'll never get your story worked out. Relax. **Just keep taking notes**. Keep your recorder running.

Keep smiling. Laugh at their jokes. Act as if you love the experience. You probably will love it. Who wouldn't want to be in a room full of funny people? Eventually, your story will be worked out and you will be ready to go home and write your outline.

When your story meeting finally ends, your head may be spinning. The story you sold them — the story you thought you were going to write — has changed so much that you barely recognize it anymore. They may have added a "B" story, but you may not be sure yet where or how the "B" story fits with the "A" story. There may be a joke that they loved that you know goes somewhere, but you can't remember where. The whole story may feel like a jumble. You can't imagine how you are ever going to turn all these confusing notes into a coherent outline.

Don't worry. You'll get it sorted out.

7) *Identify your contact person*

As you are leaving, ask, **"If I have any questions, who should I call?"** They'll make a joke about it, but they'll give you a name and phone number of one of the staff writers who was in the meeting. Save that number. That person is your contact. Don't be afraid to call them later.

8) *Stick to your due date*

Ask the producers when they'd like to have the outline. They'll make some joke about wanting it tomorrow or later this afternoon, but then they'll finally give you a real due date. Expect to get a week or two weeks to work on the outline. That'll be plenty of time.

9) *Take home sample outlines*

Ask them for a couple of sample outlines to take with you. You'll want your outline to look like the outlines written by the staff writers. Most writing staffs are happy to share their outlines and scripts with freelance writers. Take home several sample outlines if you can. Study them. Do the staff writers write long outlines or short ones? Do they put a lot of jokes in the outlines or leave that until later? The more your outline reads like one written by a member of the writing staff, the happier the producers are going to be with your work. You will definitely want to write a longer and more detailed outline as a freelance writer. You'll want to use your outline to reassure the producers that you understand all of the scenes, remember all of the story details, and know where the jokes go. Plan on writing a more detailed outline than the staff writers would turn in. Their sample outlines will help you to write an outline that reads like the ones that the producers are used to reading.

GETTING HOME

I've gone home after story meetings and thought, "What just happened to me? I'm so confused that I have no idea where to start." You may feel that way, too, especially after your very first story meeting. Don't worry. This is normal!

Here are my tips for what to do when you get home:

1) *Look over your notes right away*

When you get home from your story meeting — and after you make yourself a very strong cocktail — **take out your notes and look them over right away**! Don't wait until tomorrow. Take out your recorder. Play the meeting back. Do it while you're downing a beer or mixing a martini. Skip past the parts of the recording where everyone is just goofing around. That could be three-fourths of your tape, so you may do a lot of fast-forwarding.

I've learned from experience to go over all of my notes while the meeting is still fresh in my mind. You probably also had a few new thoughts in the car on the way home. Write your latest ideas down before you forget them.

You will likely be exhausted from the meeting, but go over everything as best you can as soon as you get home. It's okay to take a few minutes to tell your girlfriend or boyfriend or wife or husband about the meeting. They'll be excited for you. But don't let too much time go by before you review your notes and the recording of the meeting. Going over your notes will give you confidence that you have the material you need to write your outline. There *is* a complete story there. There's a First Act and an Act Break and a Second Act. You *are* going to be able to write it. There is no need to panic. If merely going over your notes and controlling your emotions is as far as you get, fine. I want you to stay confident. Going over your notes right away will keep you confident.

2) *Make happy talk to your agent*

If you have an agent at the time of your first story meeting — or at the time of your second meeting or your third one — he or she will undoubtedly want you to call after the meeting and describe how it went. No matter how you feel about the meeting, **tell the agent that it went great**. That is all the agent wants to hear. If you are even a little bit confused after your meeting, *do not* share that with your agent! Tell the agent that the story meeting went extremely well, and that you are very confident and eager to get to work. If you tell the agent that you are even a little bit frazzled (and who wouldn't be?), the agent may fly into a panic and make you upset. A fellow writer once told me, "Every time I talk to my agent, he makes me feel like I've done something wrong." An agent will not comfort you or reassure you if you are worried. In fact, it's usually your job to comfort them. So if you have to lie, lie. Your agent has already lied to you a hundred times, even if you've only been with him for a week. Lying back to him is just you evening the score a little. Your agent is also probably going to make a follow-up call to the producers of the series right after he hangs up with you. You want your agent to tell the producers how happy and excited you are. So even if you are a little dazed and confused after your story meeting (and again, this is normal — who wouldn't be?), don't tell the agent! Tell him it's the happiest day of your life.

3) *Remember that it's going to go fine*

I sincerely hope, and I sincerely believe that your first story meeting is going to go very well. I am confident that you are going to come out of the meeting excited and eager to get to work. But I know writers. I am one. Most of my friends are writers. I've been around writers for over thirty years. Most of us are brilliant and insightful and supremely competent at what we do. But we are also insecure basket cases too much of the time. We panic easily. (Well, I certainly do!) We fall into despair at the drop of a hat.

We doubt ourselves. We're paranoid and self-loathing. If you don't believe me, wait 'til you attend your first Writers Guild meeting.

Your first story meeting is going to go fine! **You are going to write a good outline and a fine script!** But if you come out of your story meeting feeling anxious, I just want you to know that feeling this way is normal, so don't let it throw you.

Coming out of a story meeting can be like coming out of a rock concert. Your ears are ringing. You're feeling drunk or high. You're tired. And you can't remember where you parked. Again, don't panic. This is normal.

When you get home, go over your notes just enough to ease your troubled mind. You are going to be able to do this!

4) *Organize your notes*

If you have any energy left, turn on the computer and begin to organize your notes. See if you can figure out right away the First Goal or First Problem, Obstacle, First Action, Act Break (that should be obvious,) Second Goal, Second Action and Resolution. You don't need to use these terms in the story meeting, but make sure that you are confident about all of the Seven Plot Elements as soon as possible after the meeting. **If you know your Seven Plot Elements, you are not going to get lost!**

If you really have some energy, see if you can organize your notes into a very rough outline. Just lay out the broad strokes of each scene and make sure it all makes sense to you. You'll sleep much easier that night if you are confident that you can get this outline written.

5) *Make sure you understand all of your notes!*

This is probably my major reason for asking you to go over your notes as soon as you get home from your story meeting. You don't want to be staring at notes tomorrow, unable to remember what you meant when you wrote them down. **Make sure that you understand all of your notes before you go to bed that night**.

If you find something in your notes that confuses you, write down the problem. Don't panic. Just write it down. It's going to get cleared up.

DAY TWO

Go over your notes again the next morning. The places where you were confused yesterday may now be clearer to you. But if you still have a few points that don't make sense to you, work around those for a little while. Just put your worries on hold for the first few hours as you start your outline. This is all going to work out. I promise.

If by the afternoon of Day Two you are still confused about some aspect of the story, don't worry. It's okay. Look, producers and staff writers are human. They often forget to sew up all the holes in a story. **If you get home and discover some aspect of your story that doesn't seem to work, or if you have some questions, call your contact person at the series.** Don't hesitate. It's their job to take your call. No one is going to think you are stupid if you have a question. They are going to be glad that you called to clear up your confusion.

DAY THREE AND BEYOND

Write your outline the same way that you wrote the outlines for your spec scripts. Maybe you'll see a new reason why I spent all that time laboriously taking you through every step of an outline. Now you know how to do it! You can take your notes and turn them into a solid outline.

Use Chapter Five as your guide to writing the outline for your first assignment.

You probably won't have to figure out the scenes. That will undoubtedly be worked out in your story meeting. My guess is that everything is going to fall neatly into place. Use this time to lay out every last detail of the story. Your outline should read almost like a complete script written in narrative form.

If the producers did their job and really worked with you on your story, the outline process should mainly be an exercise in organizing the notes. Producers want to read an outline just to make sure that you were listening and got down everything that was pitched. They also want a last glance at the story to make sure it holds up. Any flaws in the story will be apparent in the outline and can be addressed at your next meeting. Again, if you find a flaw in your story, call your contact person and talk it over with them. You may be able to work the problem out together on the phone. Or your contact may say, "Hey. You're right. That doesn't work. Let me call you back with an answer." Or they may say, "Don't worry about that. We'll fix that in the next meeting."

Remember that your job is to write the story the way they want it. Don't go into business for yourself. **Don't make any changes in the story without consulting with your contact person**. If you think you have a great idea but it changes the story even a little bit, call your contact person and pitch your idea to them before you put it in your outline.

Turn in your outline on the day they want it. If they give you a week, take the whole week. If they give you two weeks, and you get your outline done in ten days, put the outline aside for a day or two, then take one final pass at it when your mind is fresh. You may have some new ideas. Once you turn your outline in, the producers may not read it for a week, but they'll appreciate that you were prompt.

Never turn work in late! Never! If you are a procrastinator by nature, now is the time to get over it. Television is about making deadlines. The beast must be fed. You don't want to get a reputation as someone who isn't dependable. No one will want to hire you. Always get your work in on time!

After you turn in your outline, you will sit home and sweat waiting to hear from them. There's no way around this. Don't panic if a few days go by, and you hear nothing. All kinds of unexpected problems break out on a sitcom every day. Stars have meltdowns. This week's show may be a disaster. Everything that can go wrong does go wrong. The producers may not read your outline for a week or more.

NOTES ON YOUR OUTLINE

Eventually, they will call you in and give you notes on your outline. If you have put everything in your outline that was pitched in your story meeting, I would expect the notes meeting for your outline to go very smoothly. There'll be a few tweaks, and they'll send you to script.

It's always possible that the Show Runner will have some sort of epiphany after he reads your outline, and there will be major changes in your story. Again, don't panic. This is not unusual. You did nothing wrong. One of the reasons we write outlines is to make sure that we are in love with the story the way it stands. If an outline gives the producers an insight into the story and inspires some major improvements, all the better!

THE BAD STORY

This usually doesn't happen, but every once in a while a freelance writer will be given a real dog of a story. It has happened to me. In fact, it happened on one of my first freelance assignments. The producers of the series pitched me a real turd. It wasn't my fault. It wasn't even their fault. Producers have "off" days. And every series does at least one or two clunkers every season.

My "bad story" meeting was confusing. The producers seemed preoccupied with other matters. They didn't fill in all the details. They left big holes in the story. They were phoning it in. It happens. I went home, organized my notes, and wrote the best outline I could. But I knew in my gut that the story stunk.

I was a good soldier. When I went back for notes on my outline, I took them. I gently voiced what concerns I had, but I deferred to the producers because it was their show. Who was I to tell them how to write it? I wrote the best script I could. They ended up rewriting my script heavily because they finally realized that the story didn't work. But they also ended up liking me, and offered me another assignment. Being a good soldier paid off.

YOUR FIRST DRAFT

Once you've turned in an outline and gotten notes on that outline, writing your First Draft should not be any more mysterious than writing the scenes for your spec scripts. The story is all worked out now. All you have to do is write it real, stay consistent with the premise and formula of the series, and base your dialogue on the established personalities of the regular characters. Follow these rules and you will do a good job.

After you get notes on your outline, **ask for a few sample scripts to take with you**. As with the outline, studying the sample scripts will help you to write a First Draft that sounds like the series. Hopefully, you will have already bought some sample scripts for this series from Planet MegaMall. But reading a few very recent scripts from this series will also help you. You'll be up to the minute on the development of the characters and on any recurring stories or themes that are running through the series that season.

If you are writing a script for a new series, you'll absolutely need copies of the scripts they have written so far. The formula of the series will still be evolving. You'll want to know what the staff writers are doing so your script can sound like their scripts.

Take all the time they give you to write your First Draft. If they give you two weeks, take the whole two weeks. Write a "rough" draft without worrying about jokes. Just be sure the scenes make sense and sound real. Then go back and find the jokes naturally and organically from the established personalities of the regular characters. If you get stuck or lost or confused, please call your contact person. Better to suffer a little embarrassment on the telephone and get your questions answered than to guess wrong and turn in a script with flaws.

If you can finish a draft in six or seven days, I recommend putting the pages aside for a while. Rest your head. Get some distance from the material. Go to Santa Monica and sit on the beach for a day. Then go back and do your very best to sharpen all the jokes. Make the script as tight and polished as possible.

THE SECOND DRAFT

No matter how good a job you do with your First Draft, when the staff writers read your script it is the first time that your voice is being heard. Because you're an outsider, your script is going to sound to them like a foreign tongue. This isn't your fault. You aren't on staff. You haven't had the advantage of sitting in the Writers' Room every day and listening to the Show Runner.

The Show Runner is the voice of the series. If you sat with him or her every day, you'd know how that voice sounds. All of the staff writers have had weeks, months or even years to learn that voice. But as a freelance writer turning in your First Draft, you've had maybe two meetings with the Show Runner. You've done the best you can to learn the nuances of the series, but it's like meeting your girlfriend's family. You can't possibly understand their shorthand the first few times that you go over there for dinner.

Every series develops its own unique language. No matter how many episodes you watch or how many sample scripts you read, you cannot fluently speak that language if you don't work every day on that show.

For these reasons, after you turn in your First Draft, and *if* you get called in for a Second Draft, expect a lot of notes. Expect to do a big rewrite. This absolutely doesn't mean that you have failed with your First Draft. In fact, if you are called in to do a Second Draft, you have scored a huge victory! If they're letting you do a Second Draft, then they liked at least some of what you did. But try not to be thrown if, as you endure a notes meeting after the First Draft, the staff writers start tearing your carefully crafted script apart and cramming in a million new ideas. This is very likely to happen.

I have seen perfectly wonderful First Drafts by outside writers torn to pieces by the writing staff. Sometimes there's a legitimate reason. After they read the First Draft, the producers may discover a flaw in the story, and now they're going to fix it. If they've discovered a flaw in your story or found a way to improve the story, be glad. Now your Second Draft is going to be much better.

It is just as likely, however, that they are going to tear your First Draft to pieces just because they can. It isn't out of malice or a dislike for you, so try not to take it personally. (I mean, you *will* take it personally, of course. It couldn't be *more* personal. This is your work and now somebody is crapping all over it! But try not to take it *too* personally.) They are tearing your script to pieces because they are all neurotic, insecure competitors, and if they leave your script the way you wrote it, then they won't seem as indispensable to the series. See what I mean? They are tearing your script apart in order to hang on to their own jobs. Most staff writers are heavily rewritten by the producers. Every time a staff writer turns in a script, and the Show Runner rewrites the whole thing for no apparent reason, it drives the staff writers crazy. "What was wrong with that joke or with that scene? Why did he change it?" Nothing was wrong. He changed it because he likes his own stuff better than he likes anyone else's.

So now you come in, the freelance writer from the outside. The alien. Here's a chance for the staff writers to tear your stuff apart just the way the Show Runner tears their stuff apart. It's like the middle child who is beaten up every day by the oldest child, and then beats up on the youngest child when no one is around.

If you get called in for notes on your First Draft, expect a lot of them. Expect a lot of perfectly good jokes to get tossed. Expect a lot of seemingly arbitrary changes in what you have written. Smile through it as best you can. Look, a lot of their notes are going to be legit. But some of them are going to be B.S. Smile through it all, then go home and write the best Second Draft that you possibly can. Leave them liking you.

CUT OFF

Many, many freelance writers are cut off after turning in their First Draft. "Cut off" means that the producers are not going to ask you for a Second Draft. The writing staff is going to write the Second Draft. Often the reason given for cutting a writer off is time constraints. "We love the script, and we're actually moving it up in the rotation, and that means we have to get it to the table fast, so we're having one of our guys do the Second Draft." That is perhaps a lie, but you'll never know.

Getting cut off is horrible. You're going to feel very bad if it happens to you. Take solace in the fact that everybody gets cut off at least once. You may not have done anything wrong. Some producers cut off everyone at First Draft, even their own staff. The only advice I can offer if you do get cut off is to suck it up and move on. Don't press your agent to find out why they cut you off. You have no guarantee that the reasons given will be the truth.

If you get cut off, it may very well be that they simply want to start rewriting the script themselves. They're going to rewrite it anyway, so why eat up a few more weeks waiting for your Second Draft? If they cut you off, it doesn't mean that you have no chance at a second assignment. The nicer you are about everything — the more you are perceived as a good sport and a team player — the more likely you are to get a second assignment.

You will probably drive yourself nuts trying to figure out what you did wrong. I understand. But try to keep the self-flagellation to a minimum. Getting cut off is just one of those "Welcome to Show Business" moments.

THEY REWROTE ME!!

Here's an Insider's tip: Even if you write two wonderful drafts of your script, and the producers call you or call your agent and rave about what a wonderful job you have done; even if you got barely any notes on your First Draft and sailed through your Second Draft with only a few little tweaks; no matter how sure you are that all or most of your words are going to find their way into the actors' mouths; *you are going to be rewritten*. You are going to be rewritten heavily. No matter how good a job you do on any freelance assignment, be it your first script or your twentieth, the staff writers are going to heavily rewrite your script. They are going to change most of your jokes and may even alter the story. The script that they end up shooting may not even be recognizable to you.

Try not to take this too personally! It happens to *everyone*!

Sitcom scripts go through a million changes from the initial story idea to the pages that actually get shot. Changes are part of the process. Changes occur to improve the story or improve the dialogue. Changes are also made to satisfy some concern from the studio or the network or to placate an actor. Freelance writers are heavily rewritten by the writing staff, and the staff writers are heavily rewritten by the producers. Everyone but the Show Runner sees their words tossed out for all kinds of reasons every single day. Even the Show Runner has to bow down and make changes when he or she confronts "The Star."

When your first assignment finally makes it to the air, you may not recognize much of your own work.

On the evening that your first script is to be shown on TV, someone who loves you will likely want to have a party to celebrate. Someone will want to invite all your friends or family over so you can all watch your show together. That someone probably won't be you.

If the producers had the decency to send you a shooting script, then you've already read it long before the episode airs. You know what's coming. You've gagged over all the changes that they made and all the great jokes of yours that they discarded. If you were invited to come by and watch your episode being shot, you have already squirmed through those changes in person. I went to the taping of my first freelance assignment. I was introduced from the studio audience by the Show Runner, who was being extremely gracious to publicly acknowledge my contribution. Then the show started. There wasn't a comma left from what I had written. I mean, my relationship to that episode was about as real as my relationship to *The Great Gatsby*. I had nothing to do with what the actors were saying. I was devastated. "Welcome to Show Business."

When this happens to you, my advice is:

GO AHEAD AND HAVE THE PARTY!

Let your friends and family make a fuss over you. When your name appears on the TV screen under the words "Written By," it is a seminal moment in your life. You are now a professional writer. You have accomplished something that few people ever get to enjoy. This moment will never come again. Please try to savor it. Think of all the times that you spent watching other people's names appear on that same screen, and wishing that someday it could be you. Now it *is* you! This is huge! Allow yourself the joy that you richly deserve for all the work that you did and for the enormous risk that you took to follow this dream. Very few people have the courage to go out on a limb the way you did. So let the folks who love you make a little fuss.

Who ever died from a little fuss?

GETTING THAT SECOND ASSIGNMENT

The key to getting a second writing assignment is doing a good job on the first assignment. The key to doing a good job in the first assignment is writing the episode that the producers want. The best way to insure that you will write the script that the producers want is to take extensive notes in your story meeting. Write down everything they suggest and incorporate their ideas into your outline and into your script. Organize your outline and your script as you organized your spec scripts, following the guidelines in the previous chapters.

As you incorporate the ideas of the producers and staff writers into your outline and later into your script, you may not feel that you are doing much actual "writing." You may feel more like a secretary than an artist. This is part of paying your dues. Your chance at artistic expression comes later, when you have a staff job or when you end up running your own series. But on your first assignment, and indeed on the first dozen scripts that you write professionally, your main job is to organize and execute the ideas of the people running the show. That's the best way to get a second assignment and to keep working.

I once sat on a panel at the Writers Guild of America, West, in Los Angeles. The subject of the evening was, "Getting That Second Assignment." Several veteran writers and producers were invited to speak about how to keep your career going after your first Lucky Break. We all offered good advice.

What I remember most about the evening was the frustration of some of the writers in the audience. Most of them had landed a job or two in Hollywood, but a number of them were having trouble keeping their fledgling careers alive. I guess the WGA recognized a problem. Writers who had landed a Lucky Break were having trouble getting a second assignment. Thus, the seminar.

As audience members got up and asked questions or voiced their frustrations, I began to see what the problem was. These struggling writers didn't understand their job. Their job was to write what the producers wanted. That's how you get a second assignment, and a third assignment and a fourth one. These writers hadn't yet realized that fact. They were hung up on hearing their own voices and expressing their own ideas. I thought, "If that's your concern, then write a novel. This is television, for Heaven's sake!" In the world of the television series, whether a writer agrees with a producer or not, **it's the writer's job to write what the producer wants**.

The best way to get a second assignment in Hollywood, and to build an entire career, is to **do what the people above you ask you to do**.

It's not your job as a freelance writer to fix a bad story. That's the producer's job! If you have questions about your story, don't hesitate to gently and respectfully voice your concerns. Hopefully, your questions will wake everyone up, and your story will be improved. If you have ideas, offer them. But don't insist. If your concerns are ignored, you've done your job by merely voicing them. The rest of your job is to do the best you can with what you've been given.

Sometimes producers are preoccupied with other issues on their series and a bad story slips by. Sometimes producers don't see story problems until the script is finished. Sometimes they don't see problems until the table reading.

Whether you get a good story or a flawed one, you want the producers to remember you as someone who was pleasant to work with. You want to be remembered as cooperative and supportive and respectful. You want to be remembered as someone who delivered what was pitched.

I wrote two freelance episodes of M*A*S*H. The first story was my idea, and I believe that episode came off better than my second episode, when I was given a story by the writing staff. I did the best I could with both scripts. Both of my scripts were heavily rewritten, but some of my stuff made it into both episodes. What I have cherished most over the years from the opportunity of writing for a classic series like M*A*S*H was the honor of being included in the pantheon of truly great sitcom writers who had also written for that show. My best stuff wasn't half as good as the worst script that Larry Gelbart ever wrote on M*A*S*H. I will never be as talented as Jim Fritzell and Everett Greenbaum. Dozens of other wonderful writers wrote much better scripts than I did for that series. They won awards for those scripts. My two little episodes came and went without much notice. But I am more proud than I can say to have just been a tiny part of *M*A*S*H*. Those shows still get re-run in syndication. People still see my name on the screen almost thirty years after I wrote those episodes.

Your first assignment will be an experience you never forget. It may be a little challenging in places, but it will surely be exciting. I wish I could be there with you when it happens. But when it does happen, I am certain that you will feel that all the effort you put into getting there was worth it.

CHAPTER RECAP — THE ELEPHANT REMEMBERS

If your first assignment as a sitcom writer comes as the result of you pitching a good story to the producers of a series, congratulate yourself on how well you prepared for this opportunity. But don't be surprised if your story idea is drastically changed by the producers and writers. Remember, it's their series. They know it better than you do.

Your job as a sitcom writer is to write the script that the producers want.

Listen to their suggestions. Put all of their ideas into your outline and into your script.

Expect a lot of notes on your outline and on your first draft. Take the notes graciously and incorporate them into your script.

Expect to be rewritten. It's just part of the process.

Enjoy the enormous accomplishment of landing your first professional assignment. If this book plays a small role in helping you to land that first assignment, please write to me and let me know. Nothing would make me happier.

YOUR "TO DO" LIST

1) It's probably too soon to begin preparing for a real story meeting. I imagine you're still working on spec scripts. Well, why not try a story meeting for your spec script? Do you have a few friends or some classmates who would be willing to sit with you for an hour or two and participate in a pitch session on one of your spec script stories? You be the Show Runner. Pitch out the story idea you have, even if it isn't fully developed. Use a whiteboard if you have access to one. Write the Seven Plot Elements on the whiteboard. Write down whatever ideas you have for the plot elements. Now get everyone pitching. You may come up with some great ideas together. You may also discover some of the problem areas in your story and get some help in solving them. Be like Tom Sawyer. Get your friends to help you whitewash that fence!

2) Writing the outlines and the drafts of your spec scripts will be excellent practice for your first paid assignment. As you write your spec outlines and scripts, try not to cling to unworkable story ideas, or to particular scenes, or jokes if they don't move the story forward. Writers are bull-headed, as my friend, Blake Snyder, loves to say. We fall in love with an idea for a scene or with a joke, and we cling to it desperately, even when it begins to work against us. Hold tight to the Seven Plot Elements. If you have a scene or a section of dialogue that you absolutely love, but that doesn't specifically serve one of the Seven Plot Elements, let it go. You'll easily find a stronger scene to replace it. Letting go of what doesn't move the story forward will make you a better writer, and it will train you to let go when you're working professionally. Writers must learn to let go of jokes or scenes that they love when they don't move the story forward.

Chapter 10

WORKING
ON STAFF

I have never gotten over the thrill of actually working with people whose faces and names I have seen on the TV screen. And not just stars. I've been an even bigger fan of TV's top sitcom writers and producers. I worked hard to get my work noticed. Finally, my Lucky Break arrived. Now I was sitting in offices with some of the biggest names in television, and they were listening to my ideas, and putting my ideas into scripts! Wow!

My first sitcom job was a staff job. I was making less money than the secretaries, but, hey, I was on staff!

Since then, I've worked on the writing staffs of eleven prime time network situation comedies. That's a lot of experience with every kind of sitcom staff. I've worked mostly on series that were shot in front of a studio audience, like *Newhart* and *Coach*, but *Sabrina, the Teenage Witch*, where I worked over the course of four TV seasons, was shot without an audience. I've worked for male and female Show Runners. I've worked for Show Runners who were writers and for non-writing Show Runners as well. I've been an executive producer several times, and a Show Runner twice.

I think I've pretty much seen it all.

Even if your Lucky Break comes as a freelance assignment, you will eventually work on staff at a sitcom. It will probably happen sooner rather than later. Very few sitcom writers earn a living with freelance assignments anymore. In fact, at this point there may not be any full-time freelance writers left. The freelance market pretty much disappeared in the 1970s.

Since a staff job is inevitable for all sitcom writers, I thought I'd spend a few pages describing the experience.

As I keep saying, preparation is everything. I've prepared you for your Lucky Break and prepared you for your first assignment. Now it's time to prepare you for your first staff job.

When I got my first staff job on a sitcom I had no idea how a writing staff operated. I had no clue what a production week was like. I didn't know how to handle myself around actors, directors, executives or even around my fellow writers. I was a babe in the woods. I didn't even know how to order take-out food.

Let me describe the experience of working on a sitcom staff, share some of my experience, and impart a little hard-won wisdom that I wish someone had shared with me when I was first starting out.

THE SITCOM WRITING STAFF

A sitcom writing staff can be small or quite large. When Barry Kemp and I started *Newhart*, we had a staff of only three writers: Barry, Emily Marshall and me. Bob Ellison came in on Tuesday nights to help us with jokes. But for the rest of the week the show operated smoothly with just three of us.

Some series are packed like an Egyptian ferry with throngs of producers, story editors and consultants. I'm told by people who worked on *Roseanne* that at one point there were so many writers that they couldn't even fit them all into a single conference room.

Most staffs are larger than the one we had on *Newhart*, but not as unwieldy as that staff on *Roseanne*. Figure your first sitcom writing staff will have between five and ten people.

The Show Runner

At the top of the writing staff will be the Show Runner, who will undoubtedly have the title of Executive Producer. The Show Runner is the person in charge of getting the series produced every week. The Show Runner on a sitcom is almost always a writer. He or she will likely be the person who created the series.

Being Show Runner is a beast of a job. I've done it a couple of times. The Show Runner is under constant pressure all day every day to make everything work right. He has to turn out a funny episode every week, stay on budget, and stay on schedule with the production of this week's show, postproduction on last week's show, and preproduction for next week's show. He has to worry about the ratings. He has to cast the guest actors, approve the sets, edit the episodes that are already shot, and keep the writing staff moving ahead on the upcoming scripts. He has to please the actors — particularly "the star." And he has to please "the suits" — the network and studio executives who supervise his show.

The Other Producers

There will be other Executive Producers, Co-Executive Producers, Supervising Producers or even Consulting Producers on any sitcom payroll. These "producers" may not all be part of the writing staff. One or two of them may be Line Producers. Line Producers are people who handle budgets, scheduling, and postproduction — the nuts and bolts of getting the show done — but they have nothing to do with writing the scripts.

These days it seems that every sitcom star insists on having a "Producer" credit. Sometimes it's just vanity, and the star does nothing to earn their "Producer" title, but occasionally the star makes an actual contribution to the writing. I take it on faith that Jerry Seinfeld and Ray Romano did real writing on their series.

Sometimes the star's husband or wife or mother or boyfriend or personal trainer or manager is given a "Producer" credit. Those people contribute nothing and just have to be endured. But they usually spend very little time around the writers' offices.

Under the Show Runner will be some number of experienced writers with "Producer" credits. The Producers are the *A* group, the heavyweights of any sitcom writing staff. You'll want to get in their good graces and stay there.

Story Editors

Under the Producers are the "Story Editors." Story Editor is one of the dumbest titles in the history of show business. I've been a Story Editor and an Executive Story Editor and an Executive Story Consultant. These terms are meaningless. I didn't "edit" any "stories." I was a staff writer. They should have just called me that. But instead, your agent negotiates these fancy sounding titles in lieu of more money. "Story Editors" and "Story Consultants" are staff writers. Story Editors are the second tier, or the *B* group.

When you start out, you'll be a "Story Editor." You'll be at the bottom of the *B* group. Your prestige on staff will be slightly above that of the guy who delivers the lunch order.

My advice is to relax and enjoy your lowly status. My earliest jobs were some of my happiest. I didn't have much responsibility. I never got yelled at by the star or by the network. Every contribution I made was appreciated. I was "The Kid," and everyone was rooting for me. Savor your first job. Hollywood loves a virgin. You've arrived, but you haven't made any mistakes yet. Your first job may end up being one of the most enjoyable jobs you ever have.

THE PRODUCTION SEASON

Every established situation comedy produces between twenty-two and twenty-six new episodes per season. A new series will start out with an order for only thirteen episodes. A mid-season series may start out with an order for only six. If the series earns good ratings, they get an order for more episodes.

The preproduction season starts in May or June, right after the networks announce their fall schedules. These are the easiest weeks of the year. The writing staff is assembled and the stories for the first ten or fifteen episodes are plotted out. Writers start cranking out the first scripts. Production has not begun. Writers come in at ten in the morning and go home at six. Everyone is usually loose and happy. Preproduction is like a paid vacation. Then the actors show up in July or early August. Now the real work begins. You start producing episodes.

THE PRODUCTION WEEK

A situation comedy produces a new episode in a week — five working days. Most series will produce about three episodes per month. Then they take a one-week "hiatus." During the hiatus, the actors and the director go home for a week of rest. The writing staff works furiously to try to get caught up on scripts or maybe even get a little bit ahead.

Most sitcom producers prefer a Monday-Friday production schedule. If you're working on a multi-camera show, you start the production week on Monday morning with a brand new script. The actors rehearse and the writers rewrite that script all week and then shoot the episode in front of a studio audience on Friday night. If you're working on a single-camera series or a multi-camera hybrid series (*Sabrina, the Teenage Witch* was a multi-camera hybrid; we shot without an audience but with three cameras), you rehearse a little during the first half of the week and then shoot the episode without an audience in the second half of the week. But you're done by Friday night.

Some multi-camera series work a Wednesday-Tuesday production week. You start with a new script on Wednesday morning and shoot it on Tuesday night. The Wednesday-Tuesday schedule is utilized when a series is sharing a crew (camera operators, grips, electricians, etc.) with another sitcom that shoots on Friday. The crew works Monday and Tuesday on one series and Thursday and Friday on the other. Sharing a crew with another sitcom is cost-effective and it allows you to hang on to your best people. The crew doesn't go looking for other jobs if they've got a full week of work on two sitcoms. As a writer, I hated the Wednesday-Tuesday schedule because when the weekend comes you are only half way through your production week. You inevitably end up rewriting on Saturday and often on Sunday, too.

Here's how the production week of a situation comedy unfolds on the Monday-Friday schedule:

Monday

10:00 a.m. — Production Meeting. The Producers, Director, and the heads of the various production departments meet to discuss the production issues of this week's episode. The Art Director (sets), Property Master (props), Wardrobe Department, Director of Photography (cameras and lighting), Hair and Makeup, Special Effects, Script Supervisor and everyone else responsible for making the production successful use this opportunity to ask questions or raise concerns about this week's script. The production meeting is a very effective way of anticipating problems before they crop up. As a fledgling staff writer, you probably won't attend the production meeting.

11:00 a.m. — Table Reading. The Producers, Director, Actors, Writers, Studio and Network Executives and Script Supervisor gather around a large table. There are usually a lot of bagels and Danish and a lot of schmoozing and joking before the reading gets underway. Everyone is nervous before the Table Reading, hoping the week is going to go smoothly. The Actors have undoubtedly read the script already. Hopefully, they liked what they read. Still, everyone is anxiously waiting to hear how the script is going to sound as the Actors read their dialogue out loud for the first time. Everyone opens their clean, white script, and the Table Reading begins. The Director usually reads the stage directions. The first few minutes of a Table Reading can be pretty tense. Everyone is waiting for the laughs to begin. If the script is funny, the laughs will start right away. You can see everyone relax, sip their coffee, take a bite of Danish, and exchange looks of relief. But if the laughs are few and far between then the sweat starts pouring into your shoes, the coffee grows cold, the bagel tastes stale, nobody looks at anybody, and everyone knows immediately that they've got a long week ahead. Most of the time, Table Readings go pretty well. It's fun to hear your words out loud for the first time.

The Script Supervisor times the reading so that the Producers will have their first indication of whether the script is too long and thus will require immediate cuts. The Producers and Writers make notes in the margins of their scripts of scenes or jokes that need improvement.

Noon — After the Table Reading
After the reading, the actors can raise any concerns that they have. The Director will meet with the Producers to discuss any issues affecting that day's rehearsal. The Producers will also meet with Studio and Network Executives to hear their concerns.

When the post-Table Reading discussions have been completed, the Director and Actors will move to the stage to begin rehearsal of the episode.

"Blue Pages"

After the Table Reading, the Producers and Writers (including you) convene back at the production offices and go through the script page by page, discussing their concerns and the concerns of the Director, the Actors, and the Executives.

The Show Runner presides over this meeting and decides which parts of the script need to be rewritten or cut. The writing staff will make these changes as a group. This rewrite session is sometimes called "Blue Pages" because the changes made to the script will be issued at the end of the day printed on blue paper. With each set of revisions, the color of the paper changes so that the Director, Actors and all members of the production team can easily identify the new material, incorporate these new pages into their scripts, and make any adjustments necessary based on the changes.

During the "Blue Pages" rewrite session, all the writers are expected to offer ideas on how the script can be improved. If the Table Reading went well, "Blue Pages" may only take a few hours. If there are bigger problems with the script, the "Blue Pages" session may last late into the night. It is not unusual for the writing staff to eat both lunch and dinner at the conference table as they work together on "Blue Pages."

Your Job as a Staff Writer on Monday

Get plenty of sleep on Sunday night. Even if you're the lowliest writer on the staff, it's important for you to be alert, rested and confident on Monday morning.

Monday is the most important day of the sitcom production week. If Monday goes well, it sets a positive tone for the week ahead. The Actors and Director will feel much more confident if most of the script problems are solved on Monday. You'll want to be ready to help.

During the Table Reading, make a mark in your script next to any jokes that seem to fall flat. If you have an idea for a better joke, jot it down. When you get back to the office after the Table Reading, you'll likely join the Producers and other Writers for the "Blue Pages" rewrite session. If you have ideas for better jokes, don't hesitate to pitch them.

If this is your first staff job, no one expects you to fix the big problems in the script. The Show Runner will probably offer most of the ideas and will be the final arbiter of how the script is changed. Let the Producers tackle the big problems. Listen and learn. How the Producers solve the script problems will be an education for you. You'll learn how to effectively fix a script by listening to the more experienced writers. You'll also learn the Show Runner's likes and dislikes. The more you understand the mind of the Show Runner, the more effectively you can pitch ideas that he or she will like and use.

As a fledgling staff writer, you can contribute most by having a few good jokes to pitch on Monday.

Tuesday

Daylight

The writing staff will usually spend the daylight hours of Tuesday working on future scripts. You may be involved in story meetings or rewrite sessions for upcoming scripts, or you may spend the day writing a script of your own.

The Tuesday Run-Through

The most important event on Tuesday is the "Run-Through" on Tuesday afternoon. A "Run-Through" is an informal performance of the entire episode by the actors using the actual sets. The actors rehearse on Monday and Tuesday under the guidance of the Director. They show the Producers and Writers what they have accomplished during the Tuesday Run-Through at around 3:00 or 4:00 in the afternoon.

The Tuesday Run-Through is usually the first chance that the Producers and Writers have to see this week's episode "on its feet" (i.e. to see a rehearsal of the entire script with the actors moving about as they will when the episode is shot).

The actors are usually still "on book" during the Tuesday Run-Through, meaning they are holding their scripts and reading from them as they act out each scene. Actors on sitcoms seldom memorize their lines until the last minute since many changes to the script are likely during the week. It is a waste of the actors' time to commit dialogue to memory that is going to be changed or cut.

Like the Table Reading on Monday, the Tuesday Run-Through is one of the critical events of the production week. The Producers evaluate the entire episode to see if it is working. Even the best writing staff on the biggest hit series will encounter script problems at the Tuesday Run-Through. Some jokes that worked on Monday won't work on Tuesday. Some of the jokes from "Blue Pages" will fall flat. It's just the nature of comedy. Don't be alarmed to discover unforeseen problems at the Tuesday Run-Through. That's why the Tuesday Run-Through is scheduled — to discover these unforeseen problems and fix them.

Sometimes the Show Runner will give notes after each scene to both the Actors and to the Director. The Show Runner may ask questions of the Director or suggest different staging. Some Show Runners prefer to wait until they have seen the entire Run-Through, and then meet privately with the Director. Other Show Runners will walk right onto the set and begin making suggestions or addressing problems on the spot. There is no perfect way for a Show Runner to manage the Tuesday Run-Through. He or she has to find an approach that is useful for the series. Whatever approach the Show Runner takes, he or she wants to send the Actors and the Director home on Tuesday night feeling confident that all of the script problems will be solved by the time they come back to work on Wednesday morning.

All of the problems that are identified during the Tuesday Run-Through will have to be fixed by the writing staff on Tuesday evening. There's no time in a production week to leave script problems until tomorrow. Script problems have to be addressed immediately so that the actors can learn their lines and set their performances. If the scenes are funny and the actors are comfortable, the writing staff will have a lot less work to do on Tuesday night. If some scenes aren't funny or the actors have issues with the script, then the writing staff will have to rewrite those scenes.

Your Job at the Run Through

Your job at the Tuesday Run-Through is the same as your job at the Table Reading. Note the jokes that fall flat. Jot down any ideas you have for improving the script. Listen to what the Show Runner, the Actors and the Director are saying to each other if they let you in on the conversation. This will tell you where the problems are in the script and will give you a head start toward thinking about how these problems can be solved. Again, it isn't up to you to solve the big problems. The Show Runner will likely have his or her own ideas about how to improve the script. But if you have ideas or a new joke to offer, jot them down and be prepared to pitch later if the need arises.

The Walk Back to the Office

It is normal for the writing staff to experience some anxiety after the Tuesday Run-Through. Often you have a long night of work ahead of you, and you don't know yet how you are going to solve all the problems. But a competent Show Runner with a loyal and motivated staff will be able to solve those problems.

After the Run-Through, the Actors and the Director usually go home. You walk back with the other writers across the studio lot from the sound stage to the production offices. It may be 5:00 or 6:00 at night. You may be tired already, and maybe even annoyed at the actors for the lousy job they did with the Run-Through. Try to relax. Everything is going to be okay.

Rewrite Night

The Writers return to the production offices to begin what is famously known as "Rewrite Night."

Every sitcom writer knows better than to make plans after work on a Tuesday evening. During the many production weeks that I have worked in Hollywood, I have never been home on a Tuesday night. Tuesday is "Rewrite Night." As soon as you get back to the office, everyone makes quick personal calls before the rewrite gets started, usually offering an overly optimistic prediction to wives or husbands about just how long a night lies ahead.

Rewrite Dinner

Dinner is ordered, and is usually one of the take-out staples — deli, Chinese food or pizza. Sitcom writers learn to order food that travels well. Always remember when ordering take-out that it may be half an hour before the food gets from the restaurant to you. Avoid ordering food that is going to be a soggy mess by the time you eat it. Chinese food stays warm and together in the little paper boxes. Dry sandwiches hold their integrity. Pizza stays reasonably hot. Never order a meatball sandwich on Rewrite Night. It's going to be a cold mess by the time you bite into it. Along with everyone else, sitcom writers have learned to live a little healthier in recent years, and with more women on sitcom staffs, I have seen many more salads and vegetables at Rewrite Night dinners. That's been good for all of us.

Some writing staffs make a big production out of Rewrite Night dinner: "As long as we have to work late anyway, we might as well enjoy ourselves." Elaborate meals are sometimes ordered from top-notch restaurants. Everyone takes a break from working and relaxes for half an hour over a sumptuous meal. But most staffs just order something simple and get to work.

I have many very fond memories of wonderful Rewrite Night dinners. A room full of comedy writers and a warm plate of food can make for a delightful respite in the middle of a long evening of work.

The Work

As with the "Blue Pages" session on Monday, the Show Runner presides over Rewrite Night. The entire writing staff will go through the script page by page, fixing jokes and restructuring scenes that need improvement. It is critical for the writing staff to make a strong effort on Rewrite Night. You want to solve most of the remaining script problems on Tuesday evening so that the actors can start learning their lines and setting their performances, the director can set the blocking of the scenes and work out where he is going to position the cameras, and all the other production departments can make their final decisions.

If the script was in good shape on Monday, Rewrite Night may last only a few hours. If there are serious problems, Rewrite Night can drag on until the wee hours of the morning.

Fatigue

As a new staff writer, you may find Rewrite Night exhausting. It's hard to be funny or clever at midnight. My first few Rewrite Nights were very challenging for me. I was only twenty-four years old, but by 11:00 at night I got tired. I couldn't understand how writers and producers who were twice my age could keep pitching and arguing so late into the evening. You'll get used to it. Over time I built up my comedy muscles. A lot of exhaustion comes from fear. When you learn from experience that even the most vexing script problems are going to be solved, you use up less energy worrying. Sitcom writing staffs are amazing engines when it comes to fixing a troubled script. I have been stunned again and again at how much great work can be done in a short time by people who are tired. When I was producing and running shows I got to the point where I could stay alert and focused and funny until 2:00 in the morning. When you absolutely have to do something, somehow you find the resources to do it. Oh, and there's also caffeine and sugar to keep you going.

The Light at the End of the Evening

Eventually, the writing staff gets through the entire script. Most of the remaining problems are solved. New jokes are added. You walk across an empty studio lot to your car, exhausted and drained, but pleased with a job well done.

Wednesday

No matter how late Tuesday Rewrite Night goes, you're back at work on Wednesday morning. I've driven home from Tuesday Rewrite Night, taken a shower, had something to eat, then gotten in my car and driven back to work without ever visiting my bed. Fortunately, I only had to do that a few times.

Wednesday Morning

The Show Runner will likely get an early heads-up from the Director about how the changes from Tuesday night are going over on the stage. Hopefully, the actors are happy with their new jokes and the day can proceed smoothly.

Morning through Afternoon

Wednesday of the production week should be a slightly easier version of Tuesday. You'll spend the day working on upcoming scripts. You'll see another Run-Through on Wednesday afternoon.

The Network Run-Through

The Wednesday Run-Through is called the "Network Run-Through." The Suits show up for this one. They watch the Run-Through with the writing staff. They always have notes. The Show Runner does his best to wrangle the executives.

(These days it isn't uncommon for The Suits to show up on Tuesday. As ratings have slumped at all the broadcast networks, management has decided that instead of nurturing more creative freedom, they are more comfortable with increasing their own level of participation. Is this a good idea? Look at the state of sitcoms today. Sitcoms used to top the ratings and be the flagship series on every network. "Must See TV" was built on *The Cosby Show*, *Cheers*, *Seinfeld* and *Friends*, not on forensic police shows and reality nonsense. Have sitcoms faced a challenge lately in the Neilsen Ratings because there are no more good ideas? Certainly not! There are wonderful premises and concepts for sitcoms still to be discovered. But the networks and studios, operating from panic, have ramped up their involvement in production and stifled creativity. But don't worry. Sitcoms are charging back!)

Wednesday Evening

After the Wednesday "Network Run-Through," the writing staff will return once again to the Writers' Room to address any last minute script issues and to grapple with the network notes. For a hit series, network interference is usually minimal to non-existent. Networks have so many series that are failing during any given season that there's no need to mess with the few shows that are succeeding. Freedom is another perq of success. But if you are working on a series that is new or struggling to find an audience, your Show Runner will have to contend with a substantial amount of "help" from the network and studio. (These days, the network and studio will probably be the same company.)

If you're a staff writer on a series that is a hit, it is usually pretty easy to address the network concerns. The Show Runner will handle it. Stand ready with a few new joke ideas after the Wednesday Run-Through.

If your series is struggling, you may be in for another long night on Wednesday. But guess what? Just as you learn more from your mistakes than from your triumphs, you will learn more on a struggling series than on a hit. Hit series usually run like clock-work. You don't face the weekly catastrophes that plague a struggling series. I found my chance to shine on struggling shows. They needed me. My ideas were gratefully accepted. I learned how to solve script problems on the fly. I learned that you can take a bad script and turn it into a pretty good one, sometimes in a single night. When you're a young writer starting out, you really want to learn how to navigate the heavy seas. You'll get that chance on a struggling series. If you land a job on a hit series, no one will be happier for you than I will. You will get to work with the best writers in the business, and you will learn a lot. But most writers start out working on struggling shows. This is always a blessing in disguise. Even if you have to put in long hours and face an unhappy cast and a discouraged writing staff every day, you will learn how to pilot a ship through a storm. Just to take the nautical analogy one step further before we all get sea sick, anyone can sail a boat on calm waters. The strong captain is the one who can guide her through the rough swells. Watch how your Show Runner handles the challenge of a struggling series. Learn from his mistakes and remember what he does right. That'll be you at the helm some day!

Thursday

Thursday has traditionally been "camera blocking day." This is a day of largely technical rehearsal on the stage. The director is positioning his cameras and the Director of Photography is setting the lights. It's a tedious day for the actors, but it gives them the chance to learn their lines and get ready for "Show Night" on Friday. On a multi-camera sitcom like *Two and a Half Men*, Thursday should be the lightest day of the week. You'll be in the office working on upcoming scripts. You should be able to go home at a decent hour.

Friday

On *Newhart* and *Coach*, Friday was the most enjoyable day of the week. I guess Friday is a great day in an escrow office, too, but it's particularly fun on a multi-camera sitcom because it's "Show Day." We'd do some work during the day, usually go out for a nice lunch, and then walk over to the stage in the afternoon for Dress Rehearsal. The actors would do a Run-Through in costume. The Writers might make some final tweaks to the script.

I always hated making changes to the script on Friday because I felt it harmed the confidence of the actors. How much better of a joke can you come up with on Friday that you couldn't have thought of earlier in the week? I avoided changes on Friday. I felt the actors should be free to work on their performance.

You may work for a Show Runner who keeps rewriting even as the episode is being shot. If the actors are accustomed to last-minute changes, handing them a new joke just as they go on stage can energize them. Every series finds its own

The Dining Room set from *Newhart*.

approach. It will be enlightening for you to work for different Show Runners with different styles. You'll learn that every Show Runner's style can work.

On some series, they bring in an audience for Dress Rehearsal and roll the cameras. On other series they don't.

After Dress Rehearsal, a meal is usually served for the cast and crew. If the actors show up for the meal, hang out with them. There can be a huge chasm of distrust between actors and writers. Any chance to bridge that gap ought to be taken. The Friday meal is also a great chance for the writers to mingle with the crew. Some writers think it's uncool to attend the meal on Friday afternoon. I suggest you go. Meet the crew. Get to know them. These guys and gals are seasoned veterans. You'll learn a lot from them.

Show Time!

On a multi-camera series, a studio audience will be brought in for the "Air Show" at around 6:30.

The first time you stand on the floor on Show Night is intoxicating. This is one of those magical moments in show business when you feel all of your hard work pay off. You realize that you really do have the talent to be a comedy writer. Professional actors are reciting your words. An audience is laughing at your jokes. It's great!

I loved Show Night. As I've said earlier, I always had to pinch myself. I couldn't believe I was actually there, part of a sitcom staff, watching "my" show get shot on a sound stage in Hollywood with real actors and real cameras. It was enormously exhilarating. I've loved every Show Night that I've had the privilege to be a part of.

Sore Butts

On *Coach* and *Newhart* we seldom kept the audience in their seats for more than two hours. If you've ever sat in the studio audience of a multi-camera sitcom, the seats are often pretty uncomfortable. Many audience members come in thinking that since it's a half-hour show, it'll only take thirty minutes to shoot. But of course capturing a sitcom episode on film or videotape is more complicated than that. Actors often have to change wardrobe between scenes. Hair and makeup have to be touched up. The lights and cameras have to be repositioned when the story moves to a new set. Actors may flub a line while a scene is being shot. We've all seen those "blooper" and "outtake" reels.

It usually takes at least two hours to shoot a sitcom episode in front of an audience. When I was producing multi-camera sitcoms, we used to send the audience home as soon as possible, usually just as soon as we'd gotten through one pass at the entire show. That way, the audience got to see all the scenes, and they left happy. We were rarely finished shooting when we sent the audience home, but any show-biz veteran knows that you always want to leave them laughing. When audiences get bored or tired, they stop laughing. So it's silly to keep them in their seats past the limits of their patience and support.

Pick-Ups

After the audience goes home, the cast and crew will usually keep working for another hour or more shooting "pick-ups." Pick-ups are re-shoots of specific parts of each scene. Pick-ups are often necessary to get complete coverage of a scene. Sometimes you do a pick-up to get a close-up shot of a particular speech or a reaction shot of a particular actor that you couldn't get earlier. Sometimes pick-ups are shot to correct a mistake.

Pick-ups are vitally important for the editing process, but they are boring to watch, so we'd send the audience home.

The End

Show Night usually ends around 11:00 p.m. Each series has its own schedule. Some multi-camera sitcoms are done shooting as early as 9:00 p.m. Others go late into the night.

I went home exhausted most Friday nights. Writing staffs often put in a sixty-hour week. Some staffs work weekends no matter what their production schedule. It all depends on the personality of the Show Runner and the needs of that particular series.

SINGLE-CAMERA SERIES

A series like *My Name Is Earl* or *The Office* are "single-camera series" and are shot more like a movie. A staff job on a single-camera series can be like working on a one-hour drama. There is often much less rewriting because there's no audience to worry about. The big rewrite is done after the Table Reading on Monday. The writing staff will spend most of the week working on upcoming shows. You won't even see the episode until it is shot. Sometimes you won't see it until it's on the air. Writing staffs on single-camera series often have much shorter hours because there are no Run-Throughs. A series like *Earl* that shoots on location can't do Run-Throughs.

You may do less pitching in the room and more writing by yourself on a single-camera series. But you'll learn a lot, and you may get to go home earlier.

Working on staff at a well-run single-camera series can be as close as you'll get to leading a normal life. It isn't always as exciting as a multi-camera series because there's no Show Night, but you'll more than compensate for the loss of excitement with the gain of a personal life after work. Writers on single-camera series get to go to restaurants and movies and live like normal people.

YOUR PRIMARY JOB AS A STAFF WRITER

Your primary job as a staff writer on a TV sitcom is to support the Show Runner.

Here are some tips on how to support the Show Runner:

#1: *Write your scripts the way the Show Runner wants them written.*
You may not always agree with the Show Runner's ideas. But guess what? The Show Runner is the one who gets to decide what goes in the scripts. He or she has worked a long time to get this job. The Show Runner wants his or her ideas in the scripts and has earned the right to insist on that. Your job as a staff writer on any TV series is to execute the vision of the Show Runner. A sitcom will not succeed unless it is consistent from week to week. The characters have to remain the same people. The stories have to be compatible with the series formula. The show has to develop and maintain its own special tone and style. The Show Runner is in charge of setting and monitoring all of that. The Show Runner will have his or her hands full

wrangling the cast and the network while trying to keep the vision of the series alive. A Show Runner has to be able to depend on the writing staff for creative support. You can help the Show Runner and yourself by learning what the Show Runner is trying to achieve and then writing in his or her style.

#2: *Treat your ego like an overcoat and check it at the door.*
The Show Runner has a lot of jobs to do, but making you happy isn't one of them. Your job is to make the Show Runner happy, not the other way around. Show Runners often test the patience of their writing staffs with long hours, indecision, disorganization, ego, selfishness, lack of praise and inflexibility. Hey, we're all creative people in this business, not accountants or bank managers. Don't expect a Show Runner to be anything other than an eccentric artist. It's that art and eccentricity that got him where he is! Don't expect the Show Runner to be a parent or a cheerleader. When you are feeling frustrated or unappreciated (and you most certainly will feel that way sometimes), try to keep in mind that the Show Runner is the person who was charitable enough to hire you. Your job is to support his or her ideas. To do that, you may have to put your own ideas and your own feelings on hold.

THE OTHER WRITERS

You'll make friends on any writing staff, and some of those friendships will endure beyond the length of the job. I was extremely lucky on my first job to work with an extraordinarily generous group of professional writers. They made me feel at home, gave me invaluable advice, and were a source a comfort and support when I was confused.

But remember that the writing staff of a TV sitcom is made up of talented, emotional and ambitious people. Everyone is looking to advance his or her career. There's nothing wrong with that. You'll be trying to do the same thing.

Just as with your first assignment, when you land your first staff job — and upon landing every staff job thereafter — you'll want to cultivate good relationships with the other writers. Jealousy and competition are going to be a part of the dynamic in any office.

The smartest writers are the ones who keep a smile on their face even when everything around them is falling apart. If they need to vent their frustrations, they wait until they get home.

If you treat everyone with the respect that they are due you will avoid making unnecessary enemies. Be deferential to the writers who are more experienced than you. You can learn a lot from them. They may also be in a position to give you a job someday. Once your career gets going, be helpful to the writers who are less experienced. Remember to be nice to everyone on your way up the ladder because you may meet them again on the way down.

Most of the writers that you work with will to be a joy to know. A writing staff becomes a second family. You suffer and triumph together. And you're often in a room with these people for eight or ten hours at a stretch. If you have to be in a room with any group of people for ten hours, it might as well be comedy writers. At least they're funny. If you've felt like an outsider all of your life, chances are you'll feel right at home on a sitcom writing staff — maybe more at home than you feel in your actual home.

ACTORS

There's an old Spanish proverb (which I picked up from the movie *The Philadelphia Story* with Katharine Hepburn, Cary Grant and James Stewart) that goes, "With the rich and mighty, always a little patience."

I can honestly say that most of the actors I have worked with have been delightful people. But when you're working on the writing staff of a sitcom, you may find that some of the actors are a challenge to deal with.

Some actors are confrontational. I once worked with an actress who made a point of insulting me every time I saw her.

Some actors cry. One time I found myself kneeling on the pavement next to a tough-guy male actor who was sobbing like a three-year-old into the steering wheel of his Porsche.

Some actors ignore you. You can work with them for two years, and they still won't remember your name.

On your earliest jobs, you won't have to worry about any of this. The

Producers will deal with the cast. Frustrated actors may keep you working late sometimes, but it won't be up to you to fathom their issues or exorcise their demons. That's the Show Runner's happy job.

I was well into my career before I finally learned that the best way to deal with unhappy actors is to just let them talk. This is true for almost anyone, but it really works with actors. If an actor is upset with a joke, or with his or her character, or with the director, or with his or her dressing room, the best course for you is to just stand there and let them get it off their chest. It's called "diffusing the situation." Most of the time people just want to know that someone is listening to them.

The right cast is a sitcom's greatest asset. Larry David and his staff did some great writing on *Seinfeld*, but it was the magical combination of Jerry, Julia Louis Dreyfus, Jason Alexander and Michael Richards that made that show such a gigantic hit. Without the actors the greatest script ever written is just words on a page.

"With the rich and mighty, always a little patience."

THE PRODUCER'S CHAIR

Once you establish yourself as a successful sitcom writer and have worked on staff for a few years, I'm sure you'll eventually want to become a producer. I want you to be a producer, too. That's why I called this book *Elephant Bucks*. I want you to make Elephant Bucks. I want you to live Elephant Bucks. But on your journey from coach to First Class, from Taco Bell to The Grill, from being "The Kid" to having your name printed on the back of a chair, don't be in too big a hurry to make the leap.

If things go well for you, and I hope they will, you may find yourself in a position to acquire a "producer" title in a couple of years. You may even feel ready. You may even *be* ready. Your agent may be very eager to get you that title, and you may covet the title.

Don't let your agent or your friends push you into a producing job before you are ready. Give yourself time to gain the confidence and experience that you'll need. Too many so-called "producers" on sitcoms are just glorified staff writers. They don't have any real "producer" responsibilities. Show Runners often take on most of the "producer" responsibilities themselves. They do all the budgeting, casting, postproduction, approval of sets and negotiations with actors and executives. The other "producers" are really just writers.

If you have the title of producer, but all you are really doing is writing and rewriting scripts, you aren't acting in the capacity of a producer. If this is the case, you aren't acquiring the experience you need to function effectively as a producer. You aren't getting the opportunity to make creative decisions that will affect the series. Working as a producer in name only can be problematic when you move to another series where suddenly you are required to perform "producer" duties. If you haven't made these decisions before on another series, you're going to be unprepared.

Remember, *preparation is everything*. So don't take a "producer" title just for the sake of the title.

If you're lucky, at some point during your tenure as a staff writer, you'll work for a Show Runner who offers you some "producer" responsibilities. He or she may invite you to sit in on casting sessions, or will take you along to postproduction, or will include you in dealing with the actors or executives. You'll be able to get a sense of what it's like to be a real producer.

If the opportunity to learn "producer" skills isn't offered to you while you are a staff writer, I suggest asking one of the producers to include you. It's premature to ask for inclusion on your first staff job, unless that job lasts for more than one season.

By your second or third season as a staff writer, though, I think it is prudent and appropriate for you to ask one of your producers to take you with him or her to an editing session or to casting or to a budget meeting. Don't make this request during a particularly difficult production week. At those times you'll want to demonstrate your support for the Show Runner by keeping your mind on writing. But at the beginning of the production season, before everything gets crazy, most producers will be happy to let you tag along and observe. They'll be flattered that you see them as a teacher and mentor. Make sure you have some producer skills before you take the job.

Being a producer is a management job. A big part of the job is handling people. You'll need to deal skillfully with upset actors and nervous executives as well as with the production team on your own show, many of whom will also be temperamental, creative people. You'll want everyone on your side, liking you and respecting you.

Some writers are natural managers. They have great people skills. But not all writers are born extroverts. Lots of writers are very creative and talented as writers, but understandably insecure as psychiatrists, politicians or salesmen.

If you're like me and many other writers, you won't feel naturally entitled to produce a TV series. "This is a job for grown-ups! How did I end up here?!" At first you'll feel undeserving of the job, and perhaps overwhelmed by the responsibility. "My God, they built that whole set for forty thousand dollars just because I said so??!! Help!!"

When you're standing on a Hollywood sound stage surrounded by cameras and microphones and actors and a hundred-person crew, and everyone is looking to you for guidance, it is quite natural to suddenly feel like a fraud. "Speilberg belongs here! Not me!" Relax. Most of us feel that way. That's why you want to be as prepared as possible when the day finally comes.

Ask the producers with whom you work to show you how they handle the responsibility. Make friends with some of the directors who work on your series. At the end of the season, find out which directors that you know are shooting pilots. Ask if you can spend a week observing a director as he or she directs a pilot. You'll learn a lot and further prepare yourself for your first job as a producer.

I worked as a staff writer for six years before I got the opportunity to be a producer. I'm glad it wasn't sooner. I wasn't ready.

Give yourself at least a few years to learn how to write professionally. Over time you will develop an innate sense of how to construct a story and write a script. When writing scripts has become second nature to you, then you will be ready to make the leap to producer. By then, you will have logged enough time on staff to develop an appreciation for the second set of skills that you will need as a producer.

CREATING YOUR OWN SERIES

You'll want several years of producing experience before you tackle your first pilot. Again, don't let your agent push you into a job that you aren't ready for. When you get your first pilot opportunity, you want to be fully prepared. You don't want to crumble in front of the studio and the network.

Writing pilots is a subject large enough for an entire book, and maybe I'll get to that someday.

For the purposes of this book, however, my advice to you is to wait before trying to create your own show. Take a few years to thoroughly learn how to write a script. Take a few more years to learn how to be a producer. Then you'll be ready for pilots.

Right now, it's a big enough task for you simply to learn how to write a solid spec script.

YOUR PERSONAL LIFE

Don't expect a big social life if you're working on staff at a multi-camera sitcom. You won't have the free time to go out during the week, and you'll often be too tired on the weekends. It's a great job for unmarried workaholics.

Spouses sometimes have a hard time understanding the crazy, endless hours of a sitcom writing staff. You're coming home every night at midnight. You're always tired. Personal relationships can suffer because the writer seems married to his job.

The best advice I can give to help you preserve your personal life while working on a sitcom staff is to remember that actual production only takes up about seven months. The other five months you'll have lots of free time. Sitcom staffs usually start their work in May or June and wrap in February or March. If you're lucky enough to land a staff job on a recurring series, and you're invited back next year, you'll have a long wonderful vacation between March and June. Spend as much time as possible with your significant other and/or with friends. Pull the kids out of school if you have to and take a family vacation. If those closest to you see that you love what you do, but you're also making a real effort to be with them, your personal life will thrive.

Throughout my long career, I've noticed that for many comedy writers, myself included, succeeding on staff is often much easier than surviving at home. At work, no one needs anything from you emotionally. All a sitcom requires is your sense of humor and your laser-beam focus. For many comedy writers, these are the easiest things to give. We got to be professional sitcom writers because we are funny and because we can force ourselves to work. We're self-motivated, driven, and ambitious.

Even the most chaotic sitcom writing staff has some kind of structure and a common goal. You have to get that script written. You have to get that episode shot. Everyone works together toward that end.

Home can be an emotional free-fire zone. Spouses, lovers, kids have all kinds of emotional demands to make on us. A crazy star, a megalomaniacal Show Runner, a panic-stricken network executive can seem much easier to deal with than a neglected child or spouse. A lot of TV producers put in very long hours every week because they don't *want* to go home. Work is the one thing they can handle. Going home is too scary. Either they're single and the loneliness is intimidating, or they're married and the family is too needy.

My wish for you is a long and very successful career writing and pro-ducing sitcoms. I wish you high ratings, a shelf full of Emmy Awards and Humanitas Prizes, and AGR back-end points.

But don't hide at work. The real living that you are going to do on this planet will happen away from your job.

Remember why people watch sitcoms in the first place. They watch them for a sense of family. Whether the family is Jerry, Elaine, George and Kramer or Monica, Rachel, Phoebe, Chandler, Ross and Joey, or the Barones, the Bradys, the Bunkers, the Keatons, the Cunninghams, the Clampetts, the Huxtables or the Ricardos, almost everyone longs to be a valued member of a loving family. That's why they watch sitcoms.

Make sure you set aside the time to make a real family of your own, however you define it.

CHAPTER RECAP — THE ELEPHANT REMEMBERS

Working on a sitcom writing staff is great fun. Jokes all day long and Elephant Bucks! Pinch me. Am I dreaming?

When you land your first staff job, you'll be thrilled and probably a little nervous. You'll want to make a big contribution, and I'm sure you will, especially if you've taken the time to compile that portfolio of solid spec scripts and gained confidence and competence from the experience. When you go to work on your first staff, enjoy the excitement and glamour of production. Keep in mind that supporting the Show Runner is your primary task. It's quite a challenge to get out a new episode of a network sitcom every week. It always amazed me that scripts got written and sets got built and rehearsals were completed in such a short time. Five days to turn out such a professional and funny half-hour of entertainment. That's remarkable!

The more that the Show Runner can depend on his or her staff, the easier it is to turn out good episodes.

One of the most professional staffs I ever worked with was our group on *Sabrina, the Teenage Witch*. *Sabrina* never won any awards, but we sure had a wonderful cast, staff and crew of hard-working people. We made the most of every day. *Sabrina* was often a production nightmare. I worked there for four seasons as a producer and writer. I even directed a few episodes. Let me tell you, with all the special effects every week, the green screen stuff we had to shoot, and scripts that sometimes had forty-five scenes, it was a miracle that the show was completed on time and on budget week after week. But it all works like clockwork when you have a good staff and everyone works together.

YOUR "TO DO" LIST

1) Are you taking a writing class? Are you in a writers support group? Ask the teacher or group leader to run at least one meeting of the class or group as if it were a sitcom staff. Build a hierarchy. Assign two or three people to be "producers." Make one person the "Show Runner." Everyone else will be "story editors." Then pitch out a story for a sitcom that everyone knows. Let the "producers" have the final say over how the story develops, but get everyone pitching. What you'll see are the individual quirks of different people. You'll see people cling to ideas that don't work or offer ideas that don't fit the story or pitch jokes that aren't funny or don't match the characters. You'll also hear a lot of great ideas! After you're finished, talk about how it all went. Ask yourself if you are clinging to unworkable ideas in your scripts. It's a good way to discover how bull-headed you may be about your own work.

2) Take an acting class. Even if you have no aspirations to be an actor, an acting class can be invaluable to a writer. Even if you just audit the class and never do any acting yourself, it's great to see how actors work and what their problems and challenges are. Observe how the acting teacher coaches the actors. That's how a director on a sitcom works. You'll see how the acting teacher gives notes. This will prepare you for the day when you may have to give notes to an actor. Learn how to give notes that improve the actor's performance and build his confidence. As a sitcom writer, you are writing words that are intended to be spoken by actors. The more you understand the acting process, the better your writing will be.

3) Audition for a play or offer to direct a play. If you're at school or there's a community theater nearby, get involved in a theatrical production. Learn first hand about all the hard work and emotions that go into any theatrical production, whether it's for the stage or the screen. Working on staff is largely about being a team player. But creative people can be quite temperamental. Get used to working and cooperating with sensitive artists. You may be a Show Runner some day!

Chapter 11

AGENTS & EXECUTIVES

A fellow sitcom writer told a story about going to the network with his agent to get notes on a pilot that he was writing. The network notes were extensive. As the writer and his agent emerged from the meeting, one of the executives gave the writer a beach towel with the network logo on it. The writer barely noticed, concerned about addressing the network notes on his script. As they drove away from the network, the agent looked at his writer client, shook his head in dismay, and said, "Well, I don't get it." The writer thought, great! My agent agrees with me that the network notes were brutal. Now he's going to give me the pep talk that I sorely need. He's going to tell me that my script was great, that I'm going to do a wonderful rewrite, that the pilot is going to be picked up, and that the series is going to be a big hit. "I really don't get it," the agent said again. "They gave you a beach towel, and I didn't get anything!"

AGENTS

Nearly every time I speak with aspiring writers they ask me the same question: "How do I get an agent?" In fact, I wouldn't be surprised if a few of the people who buy my book read this chapter first.

Okay, how do you get an agent?

The answer to that question is very, very simple: *You get an agent by getting a job!*

Too many people mistakenly think it's the other way around. They think that the way to get a job in Hollywood is to get an agent first. Those are the people who skipped over the previous ten chapters of the book and flipped right to this one.

Remember earlier when I mentioned the movie *Tootsie*? Of course, if you skipped all the other chapters to get to this one, you won't know that reference, so let me make it again:

If you want to understand what agents do, rent *Tootsie* with Dustin Hoffman. Sydney Pollack is the director of that movie, but he also plays Hoffman's agent. Watch the scene in the First Act of the movie that takes place in Sydney Pollack's office. That scene explains everything that you need to know about what agents do. Agents field offers. They don't get you your first job.

I couldn't get an agent before I had a job. No agent would take me. Why should they? The agents I met already had plenty of clients who didn't have jobs. They didn't need another one. Agents want clients who are in demand. Agents want clients who are already working. They don't need clients who *want* to be working. *Everyone* wants to be working!

Your first job as a sitcom writer will come after you write a stack of wonderful spec sitcom scripts, and then use the connections you make on your own in Los Angeles to get some of those spec scripts read by people who can hire you. (If you skipped ahead to this chapter, I wrote a number of chapters earlier in this book that explain how to write the scripts and how to make the connections.)

Once you have written the spec scripts, made the connections and landed your first job as a professional TV sitcom writer, *THEN* you will get an agent. Prior to landing that first job you won't need an agent. Once you have a job, an agent will appear. You won't even have to look for one. One will materialize magically on your door step. I guarantee it.

My first agent showed up unsolicited at my office at NBC. That's how I signed with a big Hollywood agency. I got the office (and the job that went with it) first, using my portfolio of spec scripts, and with the help of connections I made on my own. Once I had that job, I didn't have to put any effort at all into getting an agent. He appeared out of the ether.

PICKING AN AGENT

Once you have a job as a writer, you may find that several agencies are interested in representing you. If that's the case, some of your colleagues on staff may give you advice about which agency to go with. Listen to their advice. You may hear debate about whether you'll be better off at a large agency like CAA or ICM or at a small boutique agency. I've been at both places. Both types of agencies have their pluses and minuses. You may enjoy more opportunities at a big agency but get more personal attention at a boutique. If you strike up a good relationship right away with another writer or with one of the producers on your first series, they may set you up with their own agent. That's what happened to me. I signed with an agent who represented one of my fellow writers. It worked out fine. I was with the agent for fourteen years.

If you have the opportunity to meet with several agents, do so. All of them will give you a big story about how rich and famous they are going to make you. Enjoy the flattery but don't take it too seriously. The person who is going to make you rich and famous is not the agent. It's YOU! You're the one who worked hard and launched your career. You're the one who is going to get you the Elephant Bucks and make your dreams come true.

Which agent you eventually pick isn't really going to matter that much. Truly, it isn't that big a decision early in your career. I'd pick an agent the same way you picked which series to spec. Go with the one you like.

A BUSINESS RELATIONSHIP

You and your agent are going to have a very important relationship. You want your agent on your side. The best way to keep your agent in your corner and working for you is to work hard yourself. Get to work on time. Turn your scripts in on time. Get along with the other writers and producers on staff. Give the Show Runner your full support. Get along with the actors and with the studio and network executives. (More advice about executives later in this chapter.)

Show business is like school, and your agent is like your mother. If you mess up in school, the principal is going to call your mom. If you mess up in show business, the producer is going to call your agent. Your agent is also going to check up on you. Like your mother calling the teacher to see if you're turning in your homework, your agent is going to call the producer of your series and see how you're doing. You want your agent to hear good reports about you from your employer. You want your agent to hear that you work and play well with others.

A colleague of mine was writing a pilot when his agent called. Writing this pilot was a big career move for the colleague, so it was extremely important that he nail the script. Pilots are always a challenge to write, and the colleague was feeling the pressure. No one was more aware of what was riding on this than his agent, who had brokered the deal and was calling to see how the writing was coming along. The colleague confessed to the agent that he was struggling. The characters weren't yet coming to life, and he was wrestling with the Second Act. The agent flew into a panic. What were they going to do if he couldn't finish on time?! What were they going to do if the network was unhappy with the script?! The colleague was already agitated. Now his agent was having a meltdown. He had to stop writing, pull himself together and calm down his hysterical agent.

Your agent wants to know that everything is fine. Your agent wants to know that you are writing the best script of your life, or that you are having a grand time on the new series. No matter how much you like your agent, never let him see you sweat. It causes him to lose confidence in you. It makes him reluctant to pitch you for the big jobs because he doesn't want to be blamed if you screw up.

Relationships between artists and agents can get very personal. You've seen actors at award shows clutching their golden statue and gushing about their beloved agent. It's okay to have a personal relationship with your agent. If you two want to have dinner together sometimes or go to a ball game, that's a great idea. But remember that first and foremost this is a business arrangement. Don't tell your agent too much about your personal life. Don't discuss breakups with boyfriends or girlfriends. Don't reveal your insecurities. Never, ever have sex with your agent! You want your agent to think that you are the most stable, calm, rational person in the history of the world.

NEVER THE BIGGEST FISH

Every artist wants to believe that he or she is the most important client that the agent represents. Agents want you to believe that, too.

Early in your career, there is no way that you are going to be your agent's most important client. Early in your career, you don't even want to be your agent's most important client! If you are a lowly story editor and the most important client that your agent represents, then your agent isn't doing his or her job very well!

A successful agent is going to represent ten or twenty or thirty other writers, producers, and directors. At the beginning of your career, most of those other clients will be making much more money than you are and will demand more of the agent's time and attention. Let them have it. If you're lucky, you may get the inside track toward working for one of your agent's hotter clients.

Even when you become a producer, you will probably never be your agent's most important client. There will always be some Super Show Runner who gets more attention than you do.

Wanting or needing to be more important than you are is a good way to mess up what could be a very useful relationship with your agent. There will be times when your agent doesn't read your latest script or doesn't return your phone call as quickly as you would like her to. This can cause resentment, especially if you're going through an insecure time. Try to remember that there will always be bigger fish than you swimming around in the Hollywood pond. It's okay to ask your agent who her other clients are. You should ask that during the first interview. The more you know about who else your agent represents, the more realistic you can be about what your agent has to offer. But don't kid yourself into thinking that you're the big shot.

Keep your mind on your work, not on your competition. A writer who does good work and gets along with everyone is easy for an agent to sell. The harder you work, the more offers will come in. When offers are coming in, an agent will delight in representing you. Keep your relationship with your agent about business, and business will come your way.

GROW AT YOUR OWN PACE

You and your agent should have a flexible career plan that allows you to grow at your own pace. If you land on a hit series early in your career, you may get very hot very fast. There may be a temptation on your part or on your agent's part to rush your career forward. Even with all the good advice in this book, you will have a lot to learn before you are a seasoned professional. I think you should allow yourself two or three seasons to fully learn how to write a solid script and to solve script problems.

Don't rush ahead toward the producer's chair. When you get there you will have one chance to prove yourself. If you aren't ready, you will falter and everyone will know it. Hollywood is a small town. News of failure travels faster than a stolen Maserati. Your agent will not know when you are ready to be a producer. Your agent will only know when the opportunity arrives. If the opportunity arrives before you are ready, your agent may want to push you forward. Take your time. If you have the courage to wait until you are ready, another opportunity will arise. I guarantee it.

You may see colleagues leaping ahead of you. I stopped subscribing to *Variety* years ago simply because it was too painful to read articles about writers who were less experienced than I was landing huge deals. When one of those articles appears, agents can count on receiving many phone calls from unhappy clients wondering why they didn't score a similar deal. Every career moves at a different pace. If you are a lowly story editor, set your sites on becoming an Executive Story Editor. Log some time in edit bays and casting sessions and budget meetings and some hours on the stage observing directors before you demand to lurch forward to Producer. Nagging your agent to push you faster may strain the relationship. Your agent cannot make an opportunity happen for you. She can only recognize one when it arrives.

NOT A PARENT

Dennis Palumbo wrote a very wise column in the Writers Guild magazine a few years ago about how an agent is not a substitute for an unloving parent.

This was poignant advice because too many of us unconsciously look to our agents to fill the hole in our soul left over from an unhappy childhood, an unsatisfying personal life, lost loves, insecurities or a lack of recognition. Agents have enough trouble being parents to their own kids. They don't need to add you to the list.

Your agent is not a priest, a rabbi or a therapist. Your agent is not a friend or a fellow writer who understands what you are going through. Your agent is a business associate with his own set of worries. If you are stuck on a tough script or are suffering a crisis of confidence, the last person you want to confess this to is your agent.

All writers go through tough times, and there will be plenty of people to help you through those times. Call a friend. Call a shrink. *But don't confess your problems to your agent.*

I always wanted my agents to "get" me. I wanted my agents to see how special my writing was and to champion my work to the world. To a reasonable extent they all have done that. But an agent's job is *not* to appreciate your uniqueness as an artist. This takes me right back to *Tootsie* because that's exactly what Dustin Hoffman's character wants his agent — and everyone else — to do. He wants everyone to appreciate his uniqueness. He wants his agent to love him as a parent would.

Don't expect that. An agent's job is to field offers.

AGAIN, TRUST YOUR OWN INSTINCTS

Your agent's most strongly held views are too often based on the last conversation he or she had. Agents don't know what they believe. They believe in making money. They believe in becoming more important at the agency. They believe in getting invited to the right parties. But they seldom know a good script from a bad one. And they are too easily influenced by the latest rumor circulating around town. "The networks want family comedies!" "They're looking for anything with a female lead!" "It's urban sitcoms this season! That's all they're buying!"

Hollywood is all about the current hot thing. Your agent will bring you the current hot thing. He'll tell you to write a pilot about a ghost, or he'll advise you to put more slang in your scripts because the executives want dialogue that sounds more "street." If you don't like the current hot thing, don't fall for it. Don't turn yourself into someone you aren't because of something your agent told you. Whatever is hot today is going to be cold tomorrow. And your agent will never remember any of the bad advice that he gave you. Go with your own instincts. Don't ever let your agent sway you creatively.

CHINATOWN

Have you ever seen the movie *Chinatown* with Jack Nicholson? It's a classic now, but you may have caught it on TCM. The signature line from that movie is, "Forget it, Jake. It's Chinatown." The reference means that much of life is a mystery. You can't always know what's going on.

You'll never really know what's going on in Hollywood. You'll never really know what's going on at the agency that represents you. You'll never really know if your agent is telling you the truth. It's all Chinatown.

Don't expect your agent to unravel Hollywood for you. Write the best scripts you can. Support the Show Runner. Don't rush ahead to a job you aren't ready for.

I want you to have a productive working relationship with your agent. The best way to do that is to expect only what an agent can reasonably deliver and nothing more.

You retain an agent so he or she can field offers for you, so he or she can make you aware of opportunities to advance your career, and so he or she can make and close deals for you with production companies. That's all you should expect any agent to do for you.

EXECUTIVES

Executives who go to Table Readings and Run-Throughs for sitcoms have a pretty thankless job. They're supposed to give notes to the producers. They're supposed to tell the producers what's wrong with this week's show. They're supposed to represent the interests of the network or the studio, which, these days, is often the same company. They're supposed to make sure that the producers don't shoot a show that isn't funny. They're supposed to make sure that the producers don't shoot an episode that is offensive to the viewers or to any of the sponsors. They're supposed to make sure that the episode isn't too esoteric or difficult to understand. The job has all the glamour and prestige of being a hall monitor. Yet most executives are pretty nice about it.

No one enjoys criticism. Producers want the network or the studio executives to love their show, not poke holes in it. So very few producers welcome notes from The Suits.

Executives aren't writers. As a result, they often have a hard time garnering respect for their observations because they don't have a background in writing or producing. The surgeon doesn't take notes from the hospital administrator, so why is an executive with an MBA telling me how to write my show?

Executives don't speak the language of writers. Sometimes an executive has an observation to offer or a criticism to make, but he or she struggles to find just the right language with which to express his or her concerns. The producer stands there with a blank look on his face because he has no idea what the executive is trying to tell him. This is where the "kernel of truth" rule from Chapter Seven comes in especially handy.

Executives' concerns often sound trivial to writers. When you are trying to keep the actors happy and the audience laughing and still get home before three in the morning, the concerns of executives about a specific joke or line of dialogue can often feel like nit-picking. There are one or two moments in every episode of every sitcom that don't play as well as we'd like them to. But if the episode basically works, do we have to catch every little flaw?

Executives can be overly concerned with offending the audience. In fairness to executive fears, we know how much people like to write angry letters, and how interest groups love to initiate boycotts. Someone is out there waiting to be offended no matter what you do. Networks want funny, provocative, promotable shows, but they also want to avoid offending their audience because an offended viewer will tune in to another network and/or complain to the sponsors or hold a news conference. Trying to write a funny, sexy episode that offends no one is like trying to make Indian food without spices. Writers often feel that executives are trying to homogenize all the life out of every script in a silly effort to avoid bothering anyone.

Executives sometimes underestimate the intelligence of the audience. That seems impossible to do given how dumb the public can be, but audiences usually get all the jokes on a sitcom. Comedy dies when you over-explain it. Occasionally a writer will feel that an executive is pushing him more toward explaining than entertaining.

These conflicting agendas can strain the relationship between writers and executives.

My concern is you and your career. You're going to have to work with the executives. You're going to be encountering them early on in your career. If you can get along with them, and earn their respect, you're going to enjoy a great deal more success.

Now more than ever it is extremely important for writers to work successfully and harmoniously with executives. As the broadcast networks have lost audience to cable, pay-per-view, video rental, computer games and the Internet, the aspirations of both writers and executives have become more difficult to achieve. We both want and need an audience, but it's more difficult than ever to attract one. Viewers have so many options every night that it is a huge challenge to get and keep their attention.

Writers and executives all want hit shows. We have to be able to work together to produce hit shows.

BE NICE

Even at the earliest stages of your career, you will do yourself an enormous favor if you present yourself to executives as open-minded, friendly and willing to listen. On your first few jobs as a staff writer, it probably won't be your responsibility to take the executives' notes. Executives usually expect to talk with the producers. But you'll want to present a smiling face to executives even on your first job. When your time comes to take your first notes from executives, treat those notes as you would the notes you receive from your producers. Listen calmly. Even if you think the notes are from the moon, try not to give too much away on your face.

EVERYTHING CAN BE FIXED

Sometimes you get hit with a note from a studio or network executive and you think, "My God, that tears the whole Second Act apart!" Don't panic. It has been my experience that many notes which sound huge on the stage are small on the page. In other words, you come back to the office thinking you've got this enormous problem to confront because some executive has a note, and then when you open the script, you find that you can solve the problem with one line of dialogue.

I've been in rewrite sessions on over three hundred sitcom episodes. I've never found a problem that couldn't be fixed or a note that couldn't somehow be addressed (or skillfully ignored.) Sitcom writers are really smart and really resourceful. When we put our heads together, we can fix anything.

Early in your career, you may hear some executive's notes on your script and start to panic. You'll feel that if you follow those notes, the whole show will be ruined. Look at the Show Runner. If he's calm, you shouldn't worry. Go back to the office. Relax. Look for the kernel of truth in the note. Someone on staff will understand what the executive is trying to communicate. Someone will have an idea about how to address the executive's concern.

When I was producing series, we'd always try to address all of the notes from the network or the studio. Usually, we could deal with them pretty easily. If there were one or two notes that were just stupid (and you get those all the time), we'd just ignore them. Most of the time, the executives wouldn't even remember all of their notes, so if we skipped one or two, they'd never catch it. On those occasions when we did get caught ignoring a note, it was easy to be truthful and say, "You know, we talked about that note, and we tried a few things, but it seemed to create other problems because…" The executives usually only wanted to know that we had thought about what they said. If we had a pretty good reason for not incorporating one of their suggestions, they seldom made a stink about it.

These days, executives are much more aggressive than they used to be. Notes used to be "suggestions." In the last few years, they've turned into "edicts." You'll learn from the producers which notes must be addressed, and which can be sloughed off. Experience will teach you that everything can be fixed, and often with far less trouble than you feared.

THE KERNEL OF TRUTH

Threshing out the kernel of truth from the chaff of their inarticulate concerns can be the hardest part of addressing a note from executives. Often, you won't know what they're talking about. They will point to one part of the script when really their problem is somewhere else. Because executives aren't trained as writers, they don't always know what is bothering them, or they can't find the right words to express their concerns. But when they are bothered it becomes the writer's job to figure out what is bothering them and then fix it.

That kernel of truth can be buried inside a lot of confused language. But the kernel of truth is always worth looking for.

As I've said before, writers usually know where the weak moments are in our scripts. Occasionally, we try to slip those weak moments by, not because we're lazy, but because we really don't know yet how to fix them. But someone almost always catches us. Sometimes, it's The Suits. "The kernel of truth" that you sift out of an executive's awkwardly worded note is often that pesky weak spot that you knew was there all along. This is just the universe reminding you that you still have one more problem to solve in your script. Consider this an opportunity. Wouldn't you rather catch that problem now and make the script better?

"WE HAVE A HUGE PROBLEM IN ACT TWO"

This is a common preamble to executive notes, and it can throw writers for a loop.

"A *huge* problem?! In Act Two?! Really?!"

If you don't already see a huge problem in Act Two, where the heck is this note coming from? If there is a huge problem in Act Two, and you missed it, you could be stuck in the office all night trying to fix it!

Relax.

Because executives are not writers, they seldom know how to solve a writing problem when they see one. Too often they present a problem as bigger than it really is. Most of the "huge problems" that executives have brought to my attention could be solved in five minutes. Executives can't always tell the big problems from the little ones. It's like when you hear a noise while driving your car, and you panic and think, "Oh, God, what's this problem going to cost me?" Usually, it's a small issue that can be fixed easily by the mechanic.

Don't let the executives throw you with inflammatory comments like "We have a huge problem," even if there is panic in their eyes. Again, watch the Show Runner. If he isn't sweating, you shouldn't worry. Chances are you'll get back to the office and fix the problem without too much effort.

"WE JUST HAVE ONE TINY LITTLE NOTE"

These can be deceptively dangerous words from an executive, and they are the reverse of "We have a huge problem in Act Two." When they think they're bringing you an innocuous tweak, they are often tossing a clanking monkey wrench into your well-oiled machine. "We just have one tiny little note." Translation: "Call your wife. It's going to be a long night."

Sometimes a note that they think you can address with one line actually *will* tear apart the whole Second Act. But not necessarily. Again, you look for the kernel of truth. A script that is properly structured and well-written is not going to be torn apart by one note from executives. Often the solution is to talk to the executives until you fully understand what is really bothering them. When you understand the problem you are confronting, it is always possible to find a reasonable solution without tearing a script to pieces.

Remember this when you get feedback on your spec scripts. If a note alarms you, relax and look for the kernel of truth.

Here's a "tiny little note" from executives that could have destroyed an entire script — but it didn't. It's a true story:

A friend of mine was writing a one-hour TV pilot about a hard-boiled detective. The network read the pilot and loved it. They had "just one tiny little note." And here's what the note was: They asked if the writer could put a dolphin in the show. The writer shook his head in disbelief. "A dolphin?" This was a police drama set in Chicago. How the heck was the writer supposed to shoehorn a dolphin into it? There are no dolphins in Chicago! Were the executives smoking something? How could they possibly give this note?! The writer asked the network executives to please explain why they felt he needed a dolphin in his crime drama. Their answer? "Our research shows that people like dolphins." That was their rationale for the note.

I share this anecdote as still another reminder that executives are not writers. So don't expect them to be. They will seldom understand all the potential ramifications of every suggestion that they make. The writer's job is to take the note, give it careful consideration, try to find the "kernel of truth," and then address the note as best he can.

Your good script will not be torn asunder by a bad suggestion from The Suits. An experienced and skillful producer will find a respectful and diplomatic way to dissuade executives from silly ideas. Watch how your Show Runner handles the really stupid notes, whether the notes come from executives, actors or even someone on the writing staff. If he handles the bad ideas deftly, you'll want to copy his approach and use it yourself when you're in the producer's chair.

By the way, my writer friend didn't have to rethink and rewrite his detective drama in order to give the Main Character a dolphin friend. The network executives eventually dropped the note.

WHY MAKE ENEMIES WHEN YOU DON'T HAVE TO?

It's in your interest to always treat executives with respect. Why make enemies when you don't have to?

I confess that I haven't always done a good job in this area. A few years into my career I got kind of high and mighty. I was producing hit series and making big money. I decided that I was smarter than my agents and smarter than the executives. I used every lie told to me by agents and every silly note given to me by executives as reasons to be inflexible. Dumb.

We're all in the same business: agents and executives, writers and producers, actors and directors. We're all trying to put on a show and get paid to do it. The more you can turn your co-workers and colleagues into allies instead of competitors, the happier you're going to be, the more friends you're going to make, and the longer you'll be able to hang around in Hollywood.

Right now, as you read this book and decide if you're actually going to go for it as a sitcom writer, whether you're a twenty-year-old film major or a forty-three-year-old tax attorney, you're an Outsider trying to crash the gate in Hollywood. For you to get inside, an Insider like me has to step aside or be forced aside so you can find a space. Hollywood is like a parking lot. There are only so many spots available at any given time. If the lot is full, and it *always* is, you have to wait for someone to leave before you can park there. One really great way to lose your spot inside the gate is to be a jerk. So don't be.

We all have our jerky moments. We all get full of ourselves. We all get panicky. Being a jerk for ten minutes or even for a whole day is no big deal. Everyone will forgive you and give you a fresh start tomorrow. But falling into the habit of being a jerk all the time is a guaranteed ticket out of town. It catches up with everyone. Believe me. The highest and the mightiest eventually fall. So better to avoid acting too high or mighty.

As an aspiring writer, you're going to use your spec scripts to try to prove that you're better than the guys who are already there. That's how to make a space for yourself. Even as you wait outside to get your Lucky Break, you're going to meet other writers who are a lot like you, with whom you will feel an immediate affinity, and you'll meet people like The Suits, who seem to be from a different planet.

I've found that the more I could put myself in the other person's shoes and try to understand where they were coming from, the easier it was for me to keep my cool and treat everyone with respect. I can't say I've succeeded at this as much as I would have liked to, but I keep trying to do better.

Everyone has a different role to play in putting on the show. But every player does have a role. Knowing what those roles are, being realistic about them, and treating everyone with respect is just common sense. Why make enemies when you don't have to?

CHAPTER RECAP — THE ELEPHANT REMEMBERS

The difference between writers and agents (or executives) is that we're the show and they're the business.

Together, we're show business. But show business is two words. It is part show but it is absolutely a business. The more that artists and "suits" can remember that and work together, the happier we'll all be.

Now is *not* the time for you to be worrying about getting an agent!

Now *is* the time for you to be writing spec scripts!

When you compile a portfolio of solid spec scripts, and use those spec scripts to get your first job as a sitcom writer, an agent will magically appear. I absolutely guarantee it!

Chris Rock says that during the first six months of a relationship "your representative is dating my representative." He means that nobody reveals their true nature right up front. Well, your agent is your representative in Hollywood. Keep it that way. Treat your entire relationship with your agent as if it were the first six months of dating. Be that cool unflappable person that you show to potential lovers. Put on the "dating act" for your agent the entire time you're with him or her. You'll never be spending a weekend in Vegas with your agent (I mean, I sure hope you won't!), so keeping up the front won't be too difficult to accomplish.

Don't expect to be the biggest fish in your agent's pond and don't let your agent push you too fast.

Executives have a thankless job most of the time, and the more sensitive you can be to that, the better relationships you'll have with them.

Look for the kernel of truth in all of their notes and suggestions.

Even regarding your spec scripts, remember that everything can be fixed. If you structure your story properly and follow the rules, your script will never be too far off the mark. So don't let someone's notes throw you now or later.

Big notes on your spec scripts or on a professional script are often easily solved.

Little notes can turn into large problems, but often when you find the kernel of truth you are halfway home to fixing those problems.

YOUR "TO DO" LIST

1) Rent *Tootsie*. Truly, if you haven't seen this movie you should. Not only will it explain agents to you, but it's a good way to take an honest look at what we artists are sometimes like. We can be temperamental and difficult and self-absorbed. It's only when we walk in someone else's shoes that we gain some perspective on ourselves.

2) UCLA and other places around Los Angeles offer seminars and events where you can hear from the business people in Hollywood: the agents, lawyers, and studio and network executives who run the town. Go to one or two of these. And not just to make a connection, although you might. But also to hear about the "business" side of show business. The less starry-eyed you are about Hollywood, the better you'll navigate your career.

CHAPTER 12

LEARN FROM
THE BEST

For me the journey to becoming a comedy writer began
a long, long time ago in front of a black-and-white TV with
a situation comedy called *The George Burns and Gracie Allen Show*. I watched
reruns of this series at lunch time when I was a child. I got the bug to be in
show business at an early age. When I was nine, I discovered a new series
called *The Dick Van Dyke Show*. The main character was a TV comedy writer
named Rob Petrie. From the moment I first saw that series, I wanted more
than anything else to become Rob Petrie. And guess what? I did! Years later,
I was a television sitcom producer sitting in a Hollywood restaurant having
lunch with Dick Van Dyke. How did the dream come true? Well, I watched
a lot of sitcoms. Some of them were classics. Many of them are now forgotten.
But I learned from every one of them. I learned how to twist a simple
phrase and turn it into a joke. I learned how to tell a story. I learned to write
from my heart. I grew up at a time when there were dozens of wonderful
series on the air each season. I was exposed every night to the best comedy
writers in the world. I was very lucky, because from the time I was a little
kid, I got to learn from the best!

As I said in the very first chapter, I don't care which series you decide to
spec. I stand by my conviction that you should go with the series that you
love. You are going to write the best spec scripts for series that you know
well and to which you feel a connection.

But as part of your education and training to become a sitcom writer, I
do suggest that you sample as many of the classic sitcoms as you can to see
how the best writers did it. I believe in setting the bar as high as possible and
then always trying to reach it.

Fortunately, most of the classic sitcoms are readily available on broadcast and cable TV, on tape, and on DVD.

WHERE TO LOOK

I know I don't really need to tell you this, but your local video rental store may have boxed sets of many of the classic sitcoms. I know they'll have *Friends* and *Seinfeld*. If that's all they have, that's good enough to start. These are two of the best sitcoms of all time. If you studied only those two series you'd get a heck of a good education on the right way to write for situation comedy.

You can also rent most classic TV series on DVD from NetFlix or from other by-mail video rental services.

Before you pay to rent anything, though, check websites and surf your TV dial to see what's available for free. Most of the classic sitcoms are running in syndication somewhere. It may take a little searching, but I'll bet if you look long enough you'll find nearly every show you're searching for somewhere on TV, and it won't cost you a dime..

Classic sitcoms are broadcast daily on many local TV stations and on cable. "Nick at Night" and "TV Land" are probably the surest bets for finding classic sitcoms every day. You can also check TBS for more recent hits such as *Sex and the City* and *Everybody Loves Raymond*. Classic sitcoms can also be found on WGN, USA and the Hallmark Channel.

I used *Frasier* as an example in this book. Reruns of *Frasier* are, at the time of this writing, shown daily on Lifetime.

WEBSITES

There are dozens of good websites for researching classic sitcoms and finding out where to buy or view episodes. Here's a short list:

www.tv.com
www.imbd.com
www.sitcomsonline.com
www.museum.tv.com
www.tvland.com

These websites will also provide pages about specific series and links to websites dedicated to those series. I was amazed at how much is out there on the web. I found information and entire sites dedicated to obscure and short-lived comedies that I thought were only available in museums.

SPEAKING OF MUSEUMS

The Museum of Television & Radio in New York City and in Beverly Hills, California, has a huge library of hard-to-find classic TV series. You can stop by the museum, pay a small entrance fee and screen episodes on demand. I've done this several times. It's great fun.

The museum also has special programs and seminars all the time. If you live in the New York City area or in Los Angeles, this is another great resource for making connections.

Find the museum on the web at *www.mtr.org.*

WHAT TO WATCH

I'm not picky. I believe you will learn from any sitcom that you watch. Even the worst shows have valuable lessons on what *not* to do.

But since this chapter is titled "Learn from the Best," let me give you a short list of what I believe are the most notable and best-written situation comedies. My list is personal and subjective, and I know I'm going to leave out a number of important series. But here goes anyway:

I Love Lucy
The classic sitcom of all time. If you study no other show, study this one. *Lucy* invented TV sitcom. This is the series against which all others are measured. Active Main Character. Simple premise. The best formula ever. It endures generation after generation because it really was that good. Brilliantly written and flawlessly performed. Note how you root for Lucy even in the most preposterous situations because you understand her motives and you believe that her character would behave this way!

(*Easy to find on free TV. Reruns of* I Love Lucy *are showing somewhere in the world every hour of every day. Classic episodes available for rent from NetFlix and for sale from Amazon.com.*)

The Honeymooners

Besides *Lucy* this is the *other* classic of classics from TV's Golden Age. The model for *The Flintstones, All in the Family* and the whole "married to a fat guy" sub-genre of the last few seasons including *The King of Queens, According to Jim* and *Still Standing*. I'd even argue that *The Sopranos* is a version of *The Honeymooners*. Jackie Gleason's Ralph Cramden was the male Lucy. Ralph, the egocentric, boorish, dim-witted New York City bus driver, was the quintessential Active Main Character, the underdog schmoo who was always scheming, always trying to beat the system and get rich quick, and always falling on his face in the process. Audrey Meadows' Alice was the sharpest TV wife of all time, and Art Carney's Ed Norton was the best next-door neighbor character ever. You want to learn how the premise of the series and the personality of the Main Character combine to create stories? Here is the best example possible.

(*Classic episodes available for rent from NetFlix, for purchase from Amazon.com, and may be running in various places on free TV.*)

The George Burns and Gracie Allen Show

What is most notable about this classic '50 s sitcom is how they broke the fourth wall. George Burns was not only a character "within" the series, he was also a narrator and guide "outside" the series. George talked directly to the camera, explaining the stories as they unfolded and purposely interfering in the plots. He even had a magic television set on which he would watch his own show, as it was happening, so he could keep up with Gracie's latest schemes. When daffy Active Main Character Gracie ran into an obstacle that she couldn't overcome, George would dash downstairs and move the obstacle out of her way. This was an extremely sophisticated sitcom formula that no one has ever been able to replicate.

(*Available for rent from NetFlix. Collections for sale from Amazon.*)

The Adventures of Ozzie and Harriet

"America's favorite family." That's how we all knew Ozzie and Harriet Nelson and their two boys, David and Ricky. I've said for years that every sitcom is essentially about a family. The characters on a sitcom may not be related, but they always *function* as a family: there's always a Dad character, a Mom and the kids. This is true of *every* sitcom. Well, the Nelsons were not only a family on their show, they actually were a family in real life. Ozzie and Harriet were really married, and their two real-life sons appeared in this series with them. Ricky Nelson went on to be a hugely successful recording star. Years before *Seinfeld, Ozzie and Harriet* was the original "show about nothing." The premise was almost non-existent: It was about the Nelson family. Ozzie seemed to have no job. (He was, in fact, a retired band leader on the series and in real life.) The stories were infinitesimally small, often revolving around a minor insult from a neighbor, a tiny misunderstanding or a quart of ice cream. What made this single-camera series work was the genius of Ozzie Nelson. The stories were driven by his on-screen personality, a classic Reactive Main Character. Ozzie was hypersensitive and a worrier, the polar opposite of his unflappable wife, Harriet. It was Ozzie's overreactions to minor problems that created the formula for this classic sitcom.

(*For rent from NetFlix. Collections for sale from Amazon.*)

Leave It to Beaver

Remembered for its almost antiseptic view of domestic life — June Cleaver vacuuming the rug wearing pearls and high heels — this is one of the best-written family comedies of all time. There is a deceptive sophistication to *Leave it to Beaver* that a lot of people miss. Wally Cleaver's buddy, Eddie Haskell, was one of the most unique and complex characters ever created for a sitcom. The series also had a quiet dignity rarely seen on TV today, with a strong emphasis on integrity and compassion. Ward and June Cleaver may have been unrealistically calm and competent parents, but their willingness to talk to their children and solve problems with understanding and maturity made them about the best role models that TV ever conjured. This series was written and produced by one of the best sitcom writing teams of all time, Joe Connelly and Bob Mosher. Connelly and Mosher came from radio's *Amos and Andy* and would go on to write and produce *The Munsters.*

(Always running somewhere on broadcast or cable TV. Collections available from rent from NetFlix and for sale from Amazon.)

The Andy Griffith Show
Any list of the Top Ten Sitcoms of All Time would have to include *The Andy Griffith Show*. This warm and gentle single-camera series about a small-town sheriff presented an idyllic view of life that was typical of sitcoms in the 1950s and '60s. Imagine a rural Southern town with no African-Americans and a police chief who refuses to carry a firearm. But populated with some of the most memorable supporting characters in sitcom history — Deputy Barney Fife, Gomer Pyle and Floyd, the barber — *The Andy Griffith Show* was brilliantly written, putting forth a sense of dignity and honor that today may seem quaint and anachronistic. The "family values" championed in this series were not about condemning others for their weaknesses, but rather were about accepting and tolerating the flaws in all of us. This series was produced by Danny Thomas (star of *Make Room for Daddy*, and father of Marlo Thomas of *That Girl*) and Sheldon Leonard (Nick, the bartender, in *It's a Wonderful Life* among dozens of movie tough-guy roles.) Thomas and Leonard collaborated to produce three of the best TV series ever, this one, the aforementioned *Make Room for Daddy*, and the groundbreaking *I Spy*.

(Always running somewhere on broadcast or cable TV. For rent from NetFlix. Collections for sale from Amazon.)

The Flintstones
Even though *The Flintstones* was a cartoon, it was also a half-hour situation comedy, as *The Simpsons* is today. *The Flintstones* was truly a groundbreaking sitcom not only because it was the first animated series in prime time, and the first adult-oriented cartoon on television, but also because it was perhaps the best "high-concept" sitcom ever. The flaw in high-concept series is that they typically burn through their premise too fast. Audiences quickly grow weary of talking horses or Martians or robots. But no high-concept series ever got more mileage out of their premise than *The*

Flintstones. A shameless knock-off of *The Honeymooners,* this series has become an enduring part of American culture, and very few TV shows can make that claim. Watch how an episode of *The Flintstones* follows all of my guidelines for constructing a story. Fred Flintstone was another perfect Active Main Character — Ralph Cramden in bare feet — an underdog working stiff always scheming to outwit his wife, Wilma, or his boss.

(*Still running in syndication on broadcast TV and on cable. For rent from NetFlix and collections for sale from Amazon.*)

The Dick Van Dyke Show

My all-time favorite comedy series and the reason I became a sitcom writer. With due respect to *Lucy* and *The Honeymooners, The Dick Van Dyke Show* was the gold standard for TV sitcom writing. It may be neck-and-neck with *All in the Family* and *M*A*S*H,* but nobody ever wrote situation comedy with more sophistication than Carl Reiner did on *The Dick Van Dyke Show.* Look at the shelf of Emmys that this series won during its six-season run. If you want to know where the bar is set for sitcom writing, this series is where. When I say, "Learn from the best," look no further. If you aren't familiar with this series, get familiar.

(*Still running in syndication. For rent from NetFlix. Collections for sale at Amazon.*)

The Beverly Hillbillies

This single-camera sitcom from the 1960s is an excellent example of the "high-concept" genre. "High Concept" generally means a sitcom with an unusual premise. In this case, a family of "hillbillies" strikes it rich and moves to Beverly Hills where they become permanent "fish out of water." The Clampetts never adapt to their new surroundings, preferring to maintain their simple, country folk ways as they live in a Beverly Hills mansion. Only Cousin Jethro "goes Hollywood." As stated earlier, most high-concept series burn through their gimmicky premise in a short time. This series was another notable exception. It was a hit for many years, owing largely to the expert writing and interesting characters. Unlike the shallow, self-centered characters on many of today's sitcoms, the irony of this series was that the naïve, bumpkin Clampetts had more honor and integrity than any of their allegedly more sophisticated Beverly Hills neighbors. Like *The Andy Griffith Show*, this series promoted the idea that "the simple folk know best," a concept that seems quaint today.

(*Undoubtedly in syndication somewhere. For rent from NetFlix. Collections available from Amazon.*)

All in the Family

One of the classic sitcoms of all time, this award-winning series from the 1970s was truly a television landmark. Like *The Honeymooners*, this series featured a boorish, Active Main Character, the perennially insensitive Archie Bunker. Like Ralph Cramden, Archie suffered again and again from his human weaknesses. Watch how this series would often play out an entire episode in close to real time. The First and Second Acts were often one continuous scene, yet you'll still find all of the Seven Plot Elements in every episode. Using only one set, the Bunker living room, this series demonstrates as well as any how a simple premise (a middle-aged couple share a small home with their grown daughter and her husband) combines with the personality of the Main Character (a blue-collar bigot) to create memorable stories.

All in the Family was also one of the only sitcoms ever to successfully tackle social issues and politics. It ushered in the "Norman Lear style" of situation comedy which was often as much issue-driven as character-driven. Created amid the Vietnam War, the Watergate scandal, and the emerging women's movement, *All in the Family* and spin-off series such as *Maude*, *The Jeffersons*, and *Good Times*, all from producer Norman Lear, were hard-edged comedies that yanked sitcom out of the softly-lit America of *Andy Griffith* and *Leave It to Beaver* and into the harsh light of videotape and contemporary problems.

(*Available in syndication on free TV. For rent from NetFlix. Collections for sale from Amazon.*)

The Mary Tyler Moore Show

If you had any trouble understanding the Six-Scene Template from my earlier chapter, watch an episode of this series, and all will become clear. One of the best Reactive Main Characters ever, Mary Richards was America's sweetheart long before Julia Roberts or Jennifer Aniston. When I think of *The Mary Tyler Moore Show*, one word comes to mind: *Classy.* This was a series that wrote "up" to its audience, never down. The writers took it for granted that its viewers were smart. This is another of those gold-standard series that demonstrates the best of what situation comedy can be.

The Mary Tyler Moore Show was the flagship series of what would become a whole style of situation comedy, "the MTM style," which included both of Bob Newhart's hit series, *Rhoda, Phyllis,* and *WKRP in Cincinnati.* MTM, the independent studio which produced all these series, would be home to many of the best sitcom writers of the 1970s and '80s, including James L. Brooks, Alan Burns, Ed. Weinberger, David Lloyd, Bob Ellison, Treva Silverman, Charlotte Brown, Pat Nardo and Gloria Banta, Tom Patchett and Jay Tarses, Earl Pomerantz, Glen and Les Charles, Gary David Goldberg, Hugh Wilson, and Barry Kemp. (Recent examples of "the MTM style" would be *Frasier* and the short-lived *Out of Practice.*) The MTM Era was a mini-Golden Age all by itself. I am privileged to have hung around at MTM a couple of times during that magic period and worked with and for some of the aforementioned writing stars.

(*Still running in syndication. For rent from NetFlix. Collections available from Amazon.*)

*M*A*S*H*

I'm running out of superlatives, and now I have to write about *M*A*S*H*. Reading a *M*A*S*H* script was like listening to music. It was lyrical. It was melodic. It just flowed. What situation comedies used to have that they don't have any more is "heart." A good sitcom made you laugh, but it also moved you. "Heart" doesn't happen much these days. *Seinfeld, Will and Grace* and other cynical series tore the heart out of sitcom. It's too bad. Maybe that's why there are so few memorable sitcoms on the air right now.

There was heart in every single episode of *M*A*S*H* over eleven award-winning, glorious seasons. If it is in you, I would like you to try to write with heart. I don't see any point to writing if you don't try to move people at least some of the time. I've also harped at you about writing real. Here is an example of how best to do it. *M*A*S*H* was a series that strove for dignity and honor. In a time when too much of television seems to be about humiliating people — perhaps because we feel humiliated already — *M*A*S*H* was a series that treated viewers with respect. Learn from the best. Here's "the best."

(*Still in syndication on free TV. To this day I get residuals. For rent from NetFlix. Collections for sale at Amazon.*)

Barney Miller
When the producers discovered that the domestic side of this series about a New York City police captain wasn't working, *Barney Miller* quickly evolved into one of the best ensemble or "gang" comedies ever. It's hard to think of a smarter, more low-key series than this one. The humor was unusually hip and dry for a half-hour comedy. A largely one-set workplace sitcom, *Barney Miller* is invaluable for learning how to write multiple story lines, which are all the rage on sitcoms these days.

(*Still running on TV Land. For rent from NetFlix. Collections available from Amazon.*)

Taxi
One of the most honored sitcoms of the 1970s, *Taxi* was more popular in syndication than when it was in production. Perhaps it took audiences a while to learn to appreciate it. An ensemble or "gang" comedy, *Taxi* evolved thematically into a struggle between good and evil. Reactive Main Character Alex Reiger played by Judd Hirsch did battle weekly with the venal and scheming "Louie De Palma" played by Danny De Vito.

(*Still in syndication. For rent from NetFlix. Collections for sale from Amazon.*)

Happy Days (and *Laverne & Shirley*)

Happy Days and *Laverne & Shirley* exemplified "the Garry Marshall style" of family-friendly, big scene sitcoms. Garry Marshall has been one of the most prolific television producers of his time, turning out a string of successful sitcoms in the '70s and '80s that included these two mega-hits as well as *Mork & Mindy* with Robin Williams. The Garry Marshall comedies were the antithesis of the controversial Norman Lear shows, turning back the clock to a simpler and more innocent time. Like *I Love Lucy*, the "big scene" approach builds the entire episode toward one hilarious block comedy scene in the second act. These are two series which provide a wonderful example of the "big scene" approach to sitcom. (Recent examples of "the big scene" or "Garry Marshall style" of sitcom would be *Third Rock from the Sun* and *That '70s Show*.)

(*On TV Land. For rent from NetFlix. Collections for sale from Amazon.*)

Cheers

One of the two best sitcoms of the 1980s, *Cheers* is another classic example of the character-driven situation comedy. With little premise or built-in conflict to go on — a bar in Boston — *Cheers* survived on the writers' ability to mine the depths of the superb and complex characters they had created: numbskull ladies' man Sam Malone, the even dumber Coach and Woody, neurotic intellectual Diane Chambers, the skanky Carla, pompous Fraiser Crane, and bar buddies Norm and Cliff. *Cheers* is also a superb example of one of the mainstay elements of a successful television series: unrequited love. Two people who can't quite get together will create a rooting interest among viewers that can energize a TV series seemingly forever. One can go back all the way to the 1950s Western *Gunsmoke*, where U.S. Marshal Matt Dillon and saloon-keeper Miss Kitty kept an itch unscratched for over two decades. Fast forward to the on-again, off-again romance between Ross and Rachel on *Friends* or the recent NBC sitcom *The Office* where the unacknowledged infatuation between receptionist, Pam, and salesman, Jim, is the emotional link that ties the episodes together and gives the entire series an arc. So was the mismatched romance between Sam Malone and Diane Chambers on *Cheers*.

(*Still in syndication. For rent from NetFlix. Collections for sale at Amazon.*)

The Cosby Show

The other best sitcom of the 1980s, *The Cosby Show* was a landmark of dignity. If the Cleavers or the Nelsons were the model families of the 1950s, the Huxtables were America's First Family of the 1980s. The fact that they were also African-American was as irrelevant to the premise — about a successful physician and his attorney wife raising their four complicated children — as it was immeasurably important to this classic series' place in the sitcom pantheon. Arguably the best family comedy ever on television, I think it is fair to say that *The Cosby Show* lifted up an entire nation. This is that truly exceptional television series that asked us as viewers to reach for the best in ourselves. *The Cosby Show* was positive and inspirational, a series where two very human parents did a superb job of raising their family. At the same time, it was a series that kept its audience laughing, interested and never feeling inferior. *The Cosby Show* would have been just as meaningful if the characters had been white. The fact that they were African-American gave the series a transcendence that television can only rarely hope to achieve.

(*Still in syndication. For rent from NetFlix. Collections for sale at Amazon.*)

Frasier

Arguably the most successful spin-off sitcom ever. (The only other spin-off I can think of that comes close to being as successful as *Frasier* was *Gomer Pyle, U.S.M.C.*) I will always be impressed with how skillfully the producers took this supporting character from *Cheers* and developed him into one of the most interesting Active Main Characters in sitcom history. The stroke of genius in developing the *Frasier* series was the introduction of Frasier's brother, Niles. Niles was even more pompous than Frasier, which made

Frasier more likeable and relatable than he might have been without the Niles character in support. I used it as a prime example in this book because of its use of the Six-Scene Template, its extremely well-developed characters, the intelligent writing, and the simple premise.

(*In syndication and on* Lifetime. *For rent from* NetFlix. *Collections for sale from* Amazon.)

Seinfeld

No series ever celebrated immaturity, shallowness and selfishness with more aplomb than *Seinfeld*. The fact that the characters were locked in a prison of eternal adolescence is what made their self-important suffering possible to endure, and delightfully entertaining to watch. Here's another example of unrequited love and my theory that every sitcom is about a family, because weren't Jerry and Elaine really a married couple who just didn't actually live together? And weren't Kramer and George really their children? "Significantly evolutionary" is the term I'd used to describe *Seinfeld*, which followed the rules, drew on what had gone before it, and moved all of situation comedy an inch further along the developmental trail. On *Seinfeld* we went from the Six-Scene Template to the Fourteen-Scene Template, but the Seven Plot Elements remain in place. *Seinfeld* at its best focused multiple story lines toward a single climax, as when Kramer's golf ball landed in the blow hole of a whale that George had to rescue.

(*If you can't find* Seinfeld *then there's no hope for you.*)

Friends

Friends will go down as a classic sitcom because of its huge popularity, longevity, and the consistent quality that the series maintained throughout its run. *Friends* was perhaps the purest ensemble or "gang" comedy ever. There was no Main Character, which is highly unusual. *Friends* is of special interest to you because of how skillfully the writers blended multiple story lines in every episode. Make note of the fact that in a *Friends* episode, there are usually two story lines that contain the Seven Plot Elements. Look for the First Goal or First Problem, Obstacle, First Action, Act Break, Second Goal, Second Action and Resolution of the main story lines in each episode. In addition to the main story lines, a *Friends* episode would usually contain one or two "runners," small stories with only two or three beats that serviced the characters not involved in the main story lines. (This is also how *Seinfeld* worked.) *Friends* will provide you with an excellent education in developing multiple story lines and keeping all the regular characters alive in an episode.

(*As ubiquitous in syndication as* Seinfeld. *Collections available for rent and for sale everywhere.*)

Everybody Loves Raymond

Raymond is an excellent recent example of the Reactive Main Character. Ray was not really a schemer like Frasier Crane or Ralph Cramden, though he often tried to manipulate the other characters to get himself out of trouble. Ray often found himself unwittingly caught up in a problem that he had to solve, which is the plight of the Reactive Main Character. What is most significant to me about *Everybody Loves Raymond* was that at a time when networks were screaming for "edgier," "hipper," "urban" sitcoms — almost all of which failed — *Raymond* was as traditional a sitcom as you could find. It was about a family. It had dignity and charm. It never tried to be hip or trendy. And it anchored Monday night for CBS for many years. *Raymond* was a series that followed all the rules, and did so with real skill.

(*Ubiquitous in syndication and available for rent and for sale on DVD.*)

Sex and the City

Here's a quasi-ensemble sitcom — a rare "girl gang" comedy — that also had a strong Main Character in Carrie Bradshaw, played by Sarah Jessica Parker. Carrie was both active and reactive, a female Hamlet who couldn't decide what she wanted beyond new shoes. Her rudderless search for meaning in her life — through romance and through her work — gave the series its premise. *Sex and the City* is significant for its skillful use of multiple story lines. *Sex and the City* was also one of the more thematically strong sitcoms. Each episode was tied to Carrie's newspaper column. There was a definite "theme" stated for each episode — literally spelled out on Carrie's laptop. The multiple story lines explored that theme in different ways based on the established personalities of the Main Characters.

(*In syndication locally and on TBS. DVDs available for rent from NetFlix and for sale everywhere.*)

THE CURRENT HITS

By the time you read this book I have no idea which situation comedies will be on the air. It's pointless for me to list which currently running sitcoms I think you should watch because every one that I list could get cancelled before the book is published. Just since I started writing this book two entire networks were combined into one, and who knows if that will work? A much ballyhooed new situation comedy on CBS, *Courting Alex* starring Jenna Elfman, premiered and was pulled off the air all while I was working on the last chapters.

You can see, I'm sure, how pointless it is for me to try to advise you on what to watch right now, much less what to spec. Go back to the first pages of this book. Watch what you like to watch. Spec the series that you know and love.

As I write this chapter, the top two sitcoms on TV are *Two and a Half Men* and its current time-slot partner, *The New Adventures of Old Christine* starring Julia Louis-Dreyfus. *Men* is in its second season and looks as though it's going to make it to a hundred episodes. It's a genuine hit. As of this writing, the jury is still out on *Christine*. Renewed for a second season, this vehicle seems more workable than Dreyfus' previous and ill-conceived *Watching Ellie*. But the weak supporting characters and unwieldy premise may sink this series if adjustments aren't made.

For all that you may have heard or read about "hipper" or "edgier" sitcoms like *Arrested Development*, which garnered lots of critical acclaim but never found an audience, or about "hybrid" sitcoms like *Entourage*, where some of the dialogue is scripted and some is allegedly ad-libbed, it's not surprising to me that *Two and a Half Men* has been the top half-hour on

TV for all of the 2005-2006 season, and that the previous top sitcom was *Everybody Loves Raymond*. Neither of these very successful series was or is "hip" or "edgy" or a "hybrid." Both of these hit series were or are fully scripted and about as traditional as you can get.

Yeah, there are a million sex jokes each week on *Men*. It has some "edge" and it is "hip" to an extent. But it's a very by-the-book sitcom, just as *Raymond* was.

Two and a Half Men usually has about six or eight scenes per episode, and is clearly structured from the Six-Scene Template. It always has a strong Act Break. It has one Active Main Character (Alan) and one Reactive Main Character (Charlie). Alan is the character most likely to have a clearly defined goal in each week's episode: Alan wants to improve his son's grades or outwit his ex-wife. Alan is easily upset, desperate, a bigger-than-life character who is always grasping for control. Alan is therefore very "active." Charlie is "reactive." Charlie is a laid-back guy who finds himself unwittingly and unwillingly embroiled in Alan's problems or in Alan's schemes, just as Ethel Mertz was often caught up in Lucy's schemes. Because Charlie is irresponsible and immature, he gets into trouble occasionally and/or gets Alan into trouble, but it is usually the hyper-kinetic Alan who is racing around in search of an answer.

Two and a Half Men is "*The Odd Couple* with a kid." And it works. It's funny. The characters are likeable. We enjoy watching uptight Alan — the "Felix" character — in weekly conflict with his hedonistic brother, Charlie — the "Oscar" character. The series is very well-written. It is real. It has a strong formula based on the premise (two very different men try to live together) and on the personalities of the two Main Characters (an anal-retentive nerd and his freewheeling playboy brother.)

As you watch *Two and a Half Men*, check out reruns of *The Odd Couple* on TV Land. During the main titles of *The Odd Couple*, you'll hear a narrator ask this rhetorical question: "Can two men share an apartment without driving each other crazy?" That question stated the premise of *The Odd Couple*. Isn't that also the premise of *Two and a Half Men*?

Two and a Half Men follows the guidelines I laid out for your spec scripts. Each episode is about the Main Characters. Each episode follows the series formula: The stories evolve from the premise and from the personalities of the Main Characters. Each episode has a First Goal or First Problem, an Obstacle, a First Action, Act Break, Second Goal, Second Action and Resolution.

I suggest you watch *Two and a Half Men* every week and see how well this series follows all of the guidelines I laid out for you in the earlier chapters. *Two and a Half Men* is a hit because it uses an inspired premise, because it was very well cast, because it is very well-written, and because it follows all the rules!

CONCLUSIONS

When I started this book, I wasn't sure how I was going to explain sitcom writing. I'd been doing it my entire adult life, but I'd never tried to lay out the rules or define a method for writing sitcoms. I have spoken to college writing classes and even taught a couple of graduate level courses on sitcom writing. I knew what I wanted to say about picking the right series to spec and finding the right story, but I was still working on how to explain structure. My graduate students and I would pitch out story ideas together. As I spoke with them in person, I was able to show them how to solve their story problems. This book was my first one-sided conversation on the subject, so it was almost as much of an education for me as I hope it was for you.

I was certainly going to mention the Two-Act Framework and Six-Scene Template, but I had to discover the Seven Plot Elements because I'd never really thought them out before. It's funny how you can spend your entire career writing on instinct without ever thoroughly identifying what you're doing.

Very few writers want to think of their work as formulaic. But "formulaic" isn't always a bad word. Don't let TV critics get you upset about formulas. All movies are formulaic, except a few incomprehensible foreign films. Novels are formulaic. You think *The Da Vinci Code* doesn't follow the "bestseller formula"?

"Formulaic" can mean unimaginative, but that's a choice. You can also choose to follow the formula and be ingenious in the process. There are rules for composing music and for hitting a baseball. So why shouldn't there be rules for writing TV sitcoms? There are rules. I've explained those rules to you as best I can.

Don't be turned off by the rules. Use them. Let them become second nature to you. Once you understand the rules on a visceral level, then you can start bending them in your own unique and creative way!

Maybe you'll be the next sitcom writer to cleverly "break" the rules, as Larry David did with *Seinfeld*. But you have to *learn* the rules *before* you can alter them!

The TV situation comedy has too often been equated with bad writing. Sitcom writing doesn't have to be bad. In fact, it usually *isn't* bad! It's usually pretty good! And good comedy is hard to write. Go to any movie comedy these days and tell me that the writing — the story, the dialogue, the character development — is superior to the writing on a good TV sitcom. It won't be. Movies can give Jim Carrey the power of a god or hand Adam Sandler a magical remote control and get big laughs. But that isn't necessarily better writing. That's just a bigger budget.

It's much easier to write well if you know how to organize your thoughts. The best writing is *always* built on a solid structure. An architect can design the most original and revolutionary new building that anyone has ever seen, but if he doesn't give it a secure foundation, strong walls and a sealed roof, there's going to be a big collapse in his future.

If you know how to find the right story and structure it properly, then you will have the *freedom* to show us how talented and clever you are by writing fresh, funny, quirky, original, insightful, surprising scenes within that structure!

I've laid out my set of guidelines so that you could start writing solid spec sitcom scripts yourself. I showed you how to write scripts that will sound professional. Once you have a few scripts under your belt, I expect you to start experimenting. I did the same thing when I was specing scripts. But without the rules — the formula — to light the way, you'd be experimenting in the dark.

I've tried to pass along what I've learned about writing for situation comedy over a career that has now spanned four decades. I know that as soon as this book goes to the printer, I'll remember something else that I wanted to mention. But I'm confident that I got most of the major stuff in.

As I said earlier, ask ten veteran sitcom writers what you should know about writing spec scripts or how you can break into the business, and you'll get ten different answers. If you can find ten veteran sitcom writers willing to talk to you, I'd make a point to ask them. I'm confident that from each of them you'll get at least one gem of wisdom that I didn't think about or a fresh insight that I don't have. Talking to other veteran sitcom writers, or reading interviews in newspapers or magazines — such as *Written By*, the magazine published each month by the Writers Guild of America — is another great way to *learn from the best*.

I WISH ALL OF THIS FOR YOU

It's a daunting task to try to make a successful career as an artist in Hollywood. Thousands of eager and talented actors, directors, writers, designers and others come to Los Angeles every year. Few of them end up starring in a movie or directing a video or running a hit sitcom. But *it is possible to make it*, even if you arrive here without knowing a soul and without a single Hollywood connection. I didn't know anybody, and I made it!

You'll need Talent, Determination and a Lucky Break. If you've been blessed with talent, if you can marshal the determination to work very hard by yourself with no one to force you, learn and follow the rules, knock on doors for favors, and endure rejection and frustration, then you *will* move yourself toward that Lucky Break.

No one is more on your side than I am. I want you to succeed. I know that the advice in these chapters can help to move you toward success.

I'm deeply grateful for the career that I have enjoyed. I've had more fun than I can ever describe to you.

Yeah, it's exciting to meet stars, to earn Elephant Bucks, to have your own parking space on a studio lot or go to the Emmy's.

But here's my final piece of Inside Information:

The best part of being a sitcom writer is working with other sitcom writers. Sitcom writers are funny and brilliant and eccentric and a kick in the head to be around. The absolute best moments of my career were sitting in a room late on a Tuesday night with six other tired writers and cold Chinese food, fixing a script problem that we thought was unfixable. Or standing together on a sound stage on a Friday evening and listening to an audience of strangers laugh out loud at our jokes.

I wish all of this for you!

CHAPTER RECAP — THE ELEPHANT REMEMBERS

Study as many of these classic series as you can. Sit with a note pad. Watch an old episode of *I Love Lucy* or *The Dick Van Dyke Show* or *The Cosby Show*. Look for the First Goal or First Problem, Obstacle, First Action, Act Break, Second Goal, Second Action and Resolution. Check out my rules and see if they hold up. I'm confident they will. I didn't make any of this up. This was all taught to me by more experienced writers.

Every classic sitcom has one thing in common: They were all well-written. Even silly stuff like *Gilligan's Island* was well-written. That's why these sitcoms have survived so many years in syndication. The series that are still around in reruns have continued to please audiences and attract new viewers because they had good scripts. The writers followed the rules. Studying these classic series is a great way to *learn from the best*.

Watching the classic series will help you train yourself to think in the sitcom formula. Then it will be easier for you to construct your own stories.

YOUR "TO DO" LIST

1) Compile your portfolio of solid spec scripts.

2) Go to the Sitcom Universe and make a connection.

3) Get your first job in Hollywood.

4) Sign with a trendy agency.

5) Start making Elephant Bucks.

6) Buy a big house and a fancy car. (Oh, and something nice for Mom.)

7) Get married to someone who loves to laugh. (And is *extremely* good-looking.)

8) Go to the Emmy's and win! (Everyone you went to high school or college with will be watching and dying of envy!)

9) Collect the back-end points on your hit series and retire to Kauai.

ABOUT THE AUTHOR

Sheldon Bull has earned Elephant Bucks as a highly successful TV writer and producer for thirty years.

He has held positions from Story Editor to Executive Producer on eleven different prime time network situation comedies, working with and writing for stars like Bill Cosby, Alan Alda, Danny DeVito, Bob Newhart, Henry Winkler, Craig T. Nelson, Loni Anderson, Betty White, and Melissa Joan Hart.

Sheldon has produced a string of hit series including *Newhart*, *A Different World*, *Coach*, and *Sabrina, the Teenage Witch*.

He lives in the Los Angeles area.

Click on *www.elephantbucks.com*
for up-to-the-minute information
and updates about
the current television writing market,
articles, appearances, and workshops.

If you'd like to contact
Sheldon Bull
he can be reached at
sheldon@elephantbucks.com

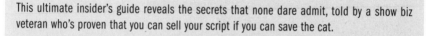

WRITING THE COMEDY FILM
MAKE 'EM LAUGH

STUART VOYTILLA AND SCOTT PETRI

This book takes you into the world of comedy and helps you discover what makes us laugh. Using concise examples from Preston Sturges to the Farrelly Brothers – in comedy masterpieces from *Duck Soup* to *Shrek*, Voytilla and Petri show you how to apply the "tenets of laughter" to your comedy writing. With easy-to-use guidelines, you'll learn the successful mechanics and characteristics of various comic story forms, including farce, the gender-bender, fish-out-of-water, parody, ensemble comedy, military comedy, sports comedy and more.

"Anyone looking for help honing their ability to write humor will find Writing the Comedy Film *a useful reference. The various comic genres are all here... definitely worth a look."*
> – *Video Maker* Magazine

STUART VOYTILLA is the author of *Myth and the Movies*.
SCOTT PETRI is an award-winning humorist and veteran screenwriter.

$14.95 · 180 PAGES · ORDER NUMBER 106RLS · ISBN: 0941188418

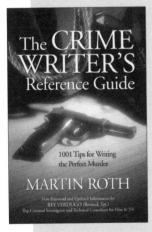

THE CRIME WRITER'S REFERENCE GUIDE
1001 TIPS FOR WRITING THE PERFECT MURDER

MARTIN ROTH

NEW FOREWORD AND UPDATED INFORMATION BY SGT. REY VERDUGO, TOP CRIMINAL INVESTIGATOR AND TECHNICAL CONSULTANT FOR FILM AND TV

Here's the book no writer of murder mysteries, thrillers, action-adventure, true crime, police procedurals, romantic suspense, and psychological mysteries – whether scripts or novels – can do without. Martin Roth provides all the particulars to make your crime story accurate.

"Now you don't need a friend on the force, a buddy in forensics, a contact in the D.A.'s office, or a pal in the morgue – all you need is this book."
> – Lee Goldberg, Two-time Edgar Nominee

MARTIN ROTH wrote over 100 TV scripts and several best-selling books, including *The Writer's Partner*.

$20.95 · 300 PAGES · ORDER NUMBER 105RLS · ISBN: 0941188493

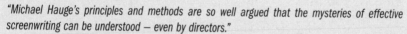

WRITING THE TV DRAMA SERIES
2ND EDITION

HOW TO SUCCEED AS A PROFESSIONAL WRITER IN TV

PAMELA DOUGLAS

What's the hottest job in Hollywood? No, it's not acting as a referee for the feud between Rosie and The Donald, it's a top writing job working on a TV drama series. This 2nd edition of Douglas's hit book gives the latest inside scoop on obtaining success in this highly competitive industry.

Television is changing with new shows, new ways of storytelling, and opportunities which didn't exist when *Writing the TV Drama Series* was first published in 2005. The second edition takes readers inside *Lost*, *Grey's Anatomy*, *Battlestar Gallactica*, and *CSI: Miami*, as well as the great shows covered in the first edition. Today pilots are in play as never before, so advice on pilot writing and tips from the experts on creating original series are added, as are cutting-edge venues. To understand the tactics behind the most dynamic television screenwriting of our time, this book — acknowledged as the top book on television drama writing — offers you more than ever.

"This is a must read for any screenwriter that wants to get in - and stay in - the television series loop."
  – Catherine Clinch, *Hunter, Jake & The Fatman;* Contributing Editor,
    Creative Screenwriting Magazine

"Right now is the golden age of TV drama, and Pamela Douglas's Writing the TV Drama Series *is far and away the best resource I know of for any writer wishing to work in this tremendously challenging and rewarding field."*
      – Daniel Petrie, Jr., President, Writers Guild of America, west,
        Oscar®Nomination for writing *The Big Easy*, Writer, *Beverly Hills Cop*

"Remarkably comprehensive and up-to-date, Writing the TV Drama Series *is a candid, enthusiastic introduction to the craft and culture of dramatic television."*
      – Jeff Melvoin, Executive Producer, *Alias*, *Northern Exposure*

PAMELA DOUGLAS has won the Humanitias Prize, been nominated for an Emmy,® and has received many other screenwriting awards including those from the Writers Guild of America and American Women in Radio and Television.

$26.95 · 300 PAGES · ORDER NUMBER 74RLS · ISBN 10: 1932907343

24 HOURS | **1.800.833.5738** | **WWW.MWP.COM**

MICHAEL WIESE PRODUCTIONS

Since 1981, Michael Wiese Productions has been dedicated to providing both novice and seasoned filmmakers with vital information on all aspects of filmmaking. We have published nearly 100 books, used in over 600 film schools and countless universities, and by hundreds of thousands of filmmakers worldwide.

Our authors are successful industry professionals who spend innumerable hours writing about the hard stuff: budgeting, financing, directing, marketing, and distribution. They believe that if they share their knowledge and experience with others, more high quality films will be produced.

And that has been our mission, now complemented through our new web-based resources. We invite all readers to visit www.mwp.com to receive free tipsheets and sample chapters, participate in forum discussions, obtain product discounts — and even get the opportunity to receive free books, project consulting, and other services offered by our company.

Our goal is, quite simply, to help you reach your goals. That's why we give our readers the most complete portal for filmmaking knowledge available — in the most convenient manner.

We truly hope that our books and web-based resources will empower you to create enduring films that will last for generations to come.

Let us hear from you at anytime.

Sincerely,

Michael Wiese
Publisher, Filmmaker

www.mwp.com

Cinematic Storytelling: *The 100 Most Powerful Film Conventions Every Filmmaker Must Know* / Jennifer Van Sijll / $24.95

Complete DVD Book, The: *Designing, Producing, and Marketing Your Independent Film on DVD* / Chris Gore and Paul J. Salamoff / $26.95

Complete Independent Movie Marketing Handbook, The: *Promote, Distribute & Sell Your Film or Video* / Mark Steven Bosko / $39.95

Could It Be a Movie?: *How to Get Your Ideas Out of Your Head and Up on the Screen* / Christina Hamlett / $26.95

Creating Characters: *Let Them Whisper Their Secrets* Marisa D'Vari / $26.95

Crime Writer's Reference Guide, The: *1001 Tips for Writing the Perfect Crime* Martin Roth / $20.95

Cut by Cut: *Editing Your Film or Video* Gael Chandler / $35.95

Digital Filmmaking 101, 2nd Edition: *An Essential Guide to Producing Low-Budget Movies* / Dale Newton and John Gaspard / $26.95

Digital Moviemaking, 2nd Edition: *All the Skills, Techniques, and Moxie You'll Need to Turn Your Passion into a Career* / Scott Billups / $26.95

Directing Actors: *Creating Memorable Performances for Film and Television* Judith Weston / $26.95

Directing Feature Films: *The Creative Collaboration Between Directors, Writers, and Actors* / Mark Travis / $26.95

Eye is Quicker, The: *Film Editing; Making a Good Film Better* Richard D. Pepperman / $27.95

Fast, Cheap & Under Control: *Lessons Learned from the Greatest Low-Budget Movies of All Time* / John Gaspard / $26.95

Film & Video Budgets, 4th Updated Edition Deke Simon and Michael Wiese / $26.95

Film Directing: Cinematic Motion, 2nd Edition Steven D. Katz / $27.95

Film Directing: Shot by Shot, *Visualizing from Concept to Screen* Steven D. Katz / $27.95

Film Director's Intuition, The: *Script Analysis and Rehearsal Techniques* Judith Weston / $26.95

Film Production Management 101: *The Ultimate Guide for Film and Television Production Management and Coordination* / Deborah S. Patz / $39.95

Filmmaking for Teens: *Pulling Off Your Shorts* Troy Lanier and Clay Nichols / $18.95

First Time Director: *How to Make Your Breakthrough Movie* Gil Bettman / $27.95

From Word to Image: *Storyboarding and the Filmmaking Process* Marcie Begleiter / $26.95

Hitting Your Mark, 2nd Edition: *Making a Life – and a Living – as a Film Director* Steve Carlson / $22.95

Hollywood Standard, The: *The Complete and Authoritative Guide to Script Format and Style* / Christopher Riley / $18.95

I Could've Written a Better Movie Than That!: *How to Make Six Figures as a Script Consultant even if You're not a Screenwriter* / Derek Rydall / $26.95

Independent Film Distribution: *How to Make a Successful End Run Around the Big Guys* / Phil Hall / $26.95

Independent Film and Videomakers Guide – 2nd Edition, The: *Expanded and Updated* / Michael Wiese / $29.95

Inner Drives: *How to Write and Create Characters Using the Eight Classic Centers of Motivation* / Pamela Jaye Smith / $26.95

I'll Be in My Trailer!: *The Creative Wars Between Directors & Actors* John Badham and Craig Modderno / $26.95

Moral Premise, The: *Harnessing Virtue & Vice for Box Office Success* Stanley D. Williams, Ph.D. / $24.95

Myth and the Movies: *Discovering the Mythic Structure of 50 Unforgettable Films* / Stuart Voytilla / $26.95

On the Edge of a Dream: *Magic and Madness in Bali* Michael Wiese / $16.95

Perfect Pitch, The: *How to Sell Yourself and Your Movie Idea to Hollywood* Ken Rotcop / $16.95

Power of Film, The Howard Suber / $27.95

Psychology for Screenwriters: *Building Conflict in your Script* William Indick, Ph.D. / $26.95

Save the Cat!: *The Last Book on Screenwriting You'll Ever Need* Blake Snyder / $19.95

Screenwriting 101: *The Essential Craft of Feature Film Writing* Neill D. Hicks / $16.95

Screenwriting for Teens: *The 100 Principles of Screenwriting Every Budding Writer Must Know* / Christina Hamlett / $18.95

Script-Selling Game, The: *A Hollywood Insider's Look at Getting Your Script Sold and Produced* / Kathie Fong Yoneda / $16.95

Selling Your Story in 60 Seconds: *The Guaranteed Way to get Your Screenplay or Novel Read* / Michael Hauge / $12.95

Setting Up Your Scenes: *The Inner Workings of Great Films* Richard D. Pepperman / $24.95

Setting Up Your Shots: *Great Camera Moves Every Filmmaker Should Know* Jeremy Vineyard / $19.95

Shaking the Money Tree, 2nd Edition: *The Art of Getting Grants and Donations for Film and Video Projects* / Morrie Warshawski / $26.95

Sound Design: *The Expressive Power of Music, Voice, and Sound Effects in Cinema* / David Sonnenschein / $19.95

Stealing Fire From the Gods, 2nd Edition: *The Complete Guide to Story for Writers & Filmmakers* / James Bonnet / $26.95

Storyboarding 101: *A Crash Course in Professional Storyboarding* James Fraioli / $19.95

Ultimate Filmmaker's Guide to Short Films, The: *Making It Big in Shorts* Kim Adelman / $16.95

Working Director, The: *How to Arrive, Thrive & Survive in the Director's Chair* Charles Wilkinson / $22.95

Writer's Journey, – 2nd Edition, The: *Mythic Structure for Writers* Christopher Vogler / $24.95

Writer's Partner, The: *1001 Breakthrough Ideas to Stimulate Your Imagination* Martin Roth / $24.95

Writing the Action Adventure: *The Moment of Truth* Neill D. Hicks / $14.95

Writing the Comedy Film: *Make 'Em Laugh* Stuart Voytilla and Scott Petri / $14.95

Writing the Killer Treatment: *Selling Your Story Without a Script* Michael Halperin / $14.95

Writing the Second Act: *Building Conflict and Tension in Your Film Script* Michael Halperin / $19.95

Writing the Thriller Film: *The Terror Within* Neill D. Hicks / $14.95

Writing the TV Drama Series: *How to Succeed as a Professional Writer in TV* Pamela Douglas / $24.95

DVD & VIDEOS

Field of Fish: *VHS Video* Directed by Steve Tanner and Michael Wiese, Written by Annamaria Murphy / $9.95

Hardware Wars: *DVD* / Written and Directed by Ernie Fosselius / $14.95

Sacred Sites of the Dalai Lamas – DVD, The : *A Pilgrimage to Oracle Lake* A Documentary by Michael Wiese / $22.95